# Dream Aircraft

## The Most Fascinating Airplanes I've Ever Flown

## Also by Barry Schiff

*Flight 902 is Down!**

*The Vatican Target**

*Golden Science Guide to Flying*

*The Boeing 707*

*All About Flying*

*Basic Meteorology*

*The Pilot's Digest*

*The Proficient Pilot, Volume 1*

*The Proficient Pilot, Volume 2*

*Flying Wisdom: The Proficient
Pilot Volume 3*

*Test Pilot: 1,001 Things You Thought You
Knew About Aviation*

*in collaboration

# Dream Aircraft

## The Most Fascinating Airplanes I've Ever Flown

## Barry Schiff

**Aviation Supplies & Academics, Inc.**

Newcastle, Washington

*Dream Aircraft: The most fascinating airplanes I've ever flown*
by Barry Schiff

Aviation Supplies & Academics, Inc.
7005 132nd Place SE • Newcastle, WA 98059
(425) 235-1500
Email: asa@asa2fly.com
Internet: www.asa2fly.com

Published 2007 by Aviation Supplies & Academics, Inc.

Most of the material in this book was first published in periodical format in *AOPA Pilot*.

Photography by and © Mike Fizer, except where otherwise noted. Photos from the author's collection are found on pages vii, xi, 23, 37–43, 56, 59, 63, 65, 68, 76, 81, 83, 90, 93–94, 97, 127, 129, 132, 137, 138, 146, 148, 151, 193–199, 211, 215, 286, 289, 292, 297–301, 304–305. Other photography credits are as follows: p. ix © Jorge Moro–Fotolia.com; p. 27 courtesy Jawed Karim; pp. 49 and 52, courtesy Austin John Brown; p. 87 © Patick McCabe–Fotolia.com; pp. 101, 106 courtesy Ron Dupas at "1000aircraftphotos.com"; p. 109 courtesy Adrian Pingstone; pp. 153, 158 courtesy Beech Aircraft Co.; p. 269 courtesy Jim Thompson.

Design by Dorian Kensok

Printed in the United States of America
2010  2009  2008  2007      9 8 7 6 5 4 3 2 1

**ASA-DREAM**
ISBN 1-56027-680-0
    978-1-56027-680-7

Library of Congress Cataloging-in-Publication Data:
Schiff, Barry J.
  The most fascinating airplanes I've ever flown / Barry Schiff.
    p. cm.
  ISBN-13: 978-1-56027-680-7 (pbk.)
  ISBN-10: 1-56027-680-0 (pbk.)
  1. Airplanes. 2. Airplanes--Piloting. 3. Schiff, Barry J. 4. Air pilots--United States--Biography. I. Title.
  TL670.S3523 2007
  629.133'34--dc22
                          2007042709

# Contents

## Aircraft

CULVER CADET . . . . . . . . . . . . . . . . . . . . . . . . . . . . . . . . . . . 2
FAIRCHILD 22 . . . . . . . . . . . . . . . . . . . . . . . . . . . . . . . . . . . 10
SPIRIT OF ST.LOUIS . . . . . . . . . . . . . . . . . . . . . . . . . . . . . . . 18
LINCOLN PT-K . . . . . . . . . . . . . . . . . . . . . . . . . . . . . . . . . . . 28
AERONCA 7AC CHAMPION . . . . . . . . . . . . . . . . . . . . . . . . . . 36
HELIO COURIER MARK II . . . . . . . . . . . . . . . . . . . . . . . . . . . . 46
INTERSTATE S-1B2 ARCTIC TERN . . . . . . . . . . . . . . . . . . . . . 54
GOODYEAR BLIMP . . . . . . . . . . . . . . . . . . . . . . . . . . . . . . . . 62
MCCULLOCH J-2 GYROCOPTER . . . . . . . . . . . . . . . . . . . . . . 70
THE ORBITER (SPACE SHUTTLE) . . . . . . . . . . . . . . . . . . . . . 82
TRANSAVIA PL-12U AIRTRUK . . . . . . . . . . . . . . . . . . . . . . . 92
CHAMPION 402 LANCER . . . . . . . . . . . . . . . . . . . . . . . . . . 100
ANTONOV AN-2 . . . . . . . . . . . . . . . . . . . . . . . . . . . . . . . . 108
SIAI MARCHETTI SF.260 . . . . . . . . . . . . . . . . . . . . . . . . . . . 116
IAI ARAVA 201 . . . . . . . . . . . . . . . . . . . . . . . . . . . . . . . . . 126
SAAB SAFARI . . . . . . . . . . . . . . . . . . . . . . . . . . . . . . . . . . 134
LOCKHEED U-2 "DRAGON LADY" . . . . . . . . . . . . . . . . . . . 142
BEECH T-34 MENTOR . . . . . . . . . . . . . . . . . . . . . . . . . . . . 152
DeHAVILLAND CHIPMUNK . . . . . . . . . . . . . . . . . . . . . . . 160
DOUGLAS DC-3 . . . . . . . . . . . . . . . . . . . . . . . . . . . . . . . . 168
MARTIN 404 . . . . . . . . . . . . . . . . . . . . . . . . . . . . . . . . . . 176
GRUMMAN G-44 WIDGEON . . . . . . . . . . . . . . . . . . . . . . . 184
LAKE LA-4 AMPHIBIAN . . . . . . . . . . . . . . . . . . . . . . . . . . 192
SIKORSKY AMPHIBION S-38 . . . . . . . . . . . . . . . . . . . . . . . 200
PIPER COMANCHE 600 . . . . . . . . . . . . . . . . . . . . . . . . . . . 208
ANDERSON GREENWOOD AG-14 . . . . . . . . . . . . . . . . . . . 216
BERIEV BE-103 . . . . . . . . . . . . . . . . . . . . . . . . . . . . . . . . . 224
CURTISS WRIGHT CW-1 JUNIOR . . . . . . . . . . . . . . . . . . . . 232
AEROMOT SUPER XIMANGO MOTORGLIDER . . . . . . . . . . . 240
SIPA MINIJET . . . . . . . . . . . . . . . . . . . . . . . . . . . . . . . . . . 248
LOCKHEED 12A ELECTRA JUNIOR . . . . . . . . . . . . . . . . . . . 254
P-51 MUSTANG . . . . . . . . . . . . . . . . . . . . . . . . . . . . . . . . 262
RYAN PT-22 RECRUIT . . . . . . . . . . . . . . . . . . . . . . . . . . . . 270

## Special Treats

AROUND THE WORLD IN A BOEING 707 . . . . . . . . . . . . . . . 280
SENTIMENTAL JOURNEY . . . . . . . . . . . . . . . . . . . . . . . . . 296

For my wife, Dorie,
and our "son," Boychik
(a Havanese puppy).

# *Introduction*

When I was a flight instructor working my way through college in 1956, a P-51 taxied onto our ramp. Its pilot was Vance Breese, the Mustang's original test pilot. During a brief and fascinating conversation with him, I learned that he had flown more than 100 types of aircraft.

Wow, I thought, that's a lot of airplanes, and it prompted me to check my logbook to see how many different types I had flown. At the time, July 24, 1956, I had checked out in 18 types. The first, the airplane in which I learned to fly, was an Aeronca 7AC Champion, colloquially known as the "Champ" and the "Airknocker." One hundred types seemed an impossible goal, but for reasons I could not immediately explain, I felt challenged and made it a point to fly as many different types of aircraft as opportunity would allow.

I ultimately flew my 100th type on June 13, 1968. The aircraft was a Piper Comanche 600, a Comanche 400 whose 400-hp piston engine had been replaced with a Garrett turboprop engine. It is one of the aircraft described in this book. I flew my 200th type, a French Robin 2160 Sport, on November 10. 1983. And on December 18, 2005 I flew my 300th, a Lockheed 12A Electra Junior, another aircraft featured in this book.

I am still an avid "collector" and my current goal is to fly 400 types, although I doubt if I have enough years left to do that. Even that, by the way, would not be a record. Royal Navy Captain Eric "Winkle" Brown apparently does hold the record for his reportedly having flown 487 different types of aircraft. (Brown commanded Enemy Aircraft Flight, an elite group of British pilots who test-flew captured World War II German aircraft. He personally flew 53 of them. On December 3, 1945 Brown made the first landing of a jet, a deHavilland Sea Vampire, on an aircraft carrier.)

As the years rolled by and my list grew, I began to realize that I had flown some aircraft that I probably would not recognize even if I saw them clustered on a ramp. These include such scarce aircraft as the Lombardi FL-3, the Morelli M-100S, the Warwick Bantam, and the Scheibe Bergfalke III.

Being somewhat obsessive-compulsive, I decided to put together an album containing a representative photo of each type that I had flown just to remind myself of what each of these aircraft look like. The drawing below is a copy of the cover that album.

Some may wonder why I would want to fly such a large variety of aircraft. For me, every flight in a new airplane is an adventure, an opportunity to sample a designer's talent and ingenuity of which some obviously have more than others. While we applaud some designs, such as the Siai-Marchetti SF.260 and the Lockheed U-2, one can only wonder what inspired the manufacturers of others to risk the embarrassment of bringing their creations to market. A few are so underpowered or fly so poorly that a prayer should be included on their before-takeoff checklists.

Sampling a wide variety of aircraft provides an opportunity to compare handling qualities, performance, and systems. It helps me to know what is possible in an aircraft design and to distinguish between the good, the bad, and the ugly.

Reflecting on my first flights in some aircraft returns memories of where I flew them. For example, I once recall renting a deHavilland Chipmunk in Bristol, England, and flying it over the white cliffs of Dover and low over the English Channel while imagining that my wing-mounted twin-50s were armed and at the ready. Ghostly images of the Normandy beaches emerged from the morning mist as the Chipmunk and I dashed to assist in freeing France from the grip of the Hun.

The book you hold in your hand describes 33 of the wonderful aircraft I have been lucky enough to have flown. I also have added two chapters that describe two of the more memorable flights that I have made. I hope you enjoy the ride.

Barry Schiff

Los Angeles, California

# Chronological Sequence of Types Flown (305)

(as of October 12, 2007)

| | | |
|---|---|---|
| 1. | 11-07-53 | Aeronca 7AC/DC Champion |
| 2. | 04-03-54 | Cessna 120, 140 |
| 3. | 04-10-55 | Cessna 170 |
| 4. | 05-05-55 | Cessna 180, 185 |
| 5. | 07-03-55 | Beech 35 (through V-35B) Bonanza |
| 6. | 07-11-55 | Piper J-5 Cruiser |
| 7. | 07-18-55 | Stinson 108 Voyager/ Station Wagon |
| 8. | 07-22-55 | Met-Co-Aire Tri-Cessna 170 |
| 9. | 07-26-55 | Cessna 310 |
| 10. | 11-27-55 | Piper PA-22 Tri-Pacer |
| 11. | 11-30-55 | Luscombe 8E, F Silvaire |
| 12. | 01-06-56 | Ercoupe 415 |
| 13. | 02-18-56 | Ryan STA |
| 14. | 03-12-56 | Culver LFA Cadet |
| 15. | 06-26-56 | Cessna 165 Airmaster |
| 16. | 06-29-56 | Mooney M-18 Mite |
| 17. | 07-03-56 | Aero Commander 600 Series |
| 18. | 07-23-56 | Globe/Temco GC-1B Swift |
| 19. | 07-25-56 | Fairchild 24 |
| 20. | 08-15-56 | North American Navion |
| 21. | 09-16-56 | Riley D-16 Twin Navion |
| 22. | 10-06-56 | Beech 18 Twin Beech |
| 23. | 10-21-56 | Cessna 182 Skylane |
| 24. | 11-11-56 | Piper J-4 Cub Coupe |
| 25. | 11-12-56 | Piper PA-12 Super Cruiser |
| 26. | 11-18-56 | Aeronca 11AC Chief |
| 27. | 01-07-57 | Fairchild PT-26 Cornell |
| 28. | 03-20-57 | Ryan PT-22 |
| 29. | 05-30-57 | Pratt-Reed PR-G-1 |
| 30. | 05-30-57 | Cessna 172 Skyhawk |
| 31. | 06-01-57 | Piper PA-16 Clipper |
| 32. | 06-14-57 | Taylorcraft BC-12 |
| 33. | 07-27-57 | Mooney Mark 20/21 |
| 34. | 08-24-57 | Piper PA-18 Super Cub |
| 35. | 10-20-57 | Bellanca 14-19 Cruisemaster |
| 36. | 12-28-57 | Stinson SR-5 Reliant |
| 37. | 01-11-58 | Stits FA-3B Playboy |
| 38. | 03-21-58 | Piper PA-23 Apache |
| 39. | 04-06-58 | Waco UPF-7 |
| 40. | 06-29-58 | Piper PA-24 Comanche |
| 41. | 09-23-58 | Cessna 175 Skylark |
| 42. | 12-20-58 | Piper J-3 Cub |
| 43. | 12-26-58 | Morrisey/Shinn 2150 |
| 44. | 12-26-58 | North American AT-6, SN-J Texan |
| 45. | 06-04-59 | Cessna 150 |
| 46. | 07-01-59 | Champion 7FC Tri-Traveler |
| 47. | 09-26-59 | Beechcraft Model 18 Super Twin Beech |
| 48. | 10-15-59 | Cessna T-50, UC-78 Bobcat, Bamboo Bomber |
| 49. | 10-31-59 | Luscombe 8E Floatplane |
| 50. | 01-24-60 | Cessna 210 Centurion |
| 51. | 04-19-61 | Beech 33 Debonair |
| 52. | 06-25-61 | Schweizer TG-3 |
| 53. | 08-12-61 | Fairchild PT-23 |
| 54. | 09-07-61 | Convair 240 |
| 55. | 11-21-61 | Cessna 190, 195 |
| 56. | 01-31-62 | Piper PA-23 Aztec |
| 57. | 02-21-62 | Beech 50 Twin Bonanza |
| 58. | 06-23-62 | Piper PA-28 140, 150, 160, 180 Cherokee |
| 59. | 11-07-62 | Cessna 205 |
| 60. | 12-28-62 | Schweizer 2-22 |
| 61. | 01-17-63 | Schweizer 1-26 |
| 62. | 05-24-63 | Bell 47D, G1 |
| 63. | 06-29-63 | Hughes 269A, 300 |
| 64. | 06-30-63 | Hiller UH-12 |
| 65. | 07-13-63 | Commonwealth Ranger 185 |
| 66. | 07-22-63 | Meyers OTW |
| 67. | 07-26-63 | Beech 23 Musketeer |
| 68. | 11-14-63 | Schweizer 1-23 |
| 69. | 08-02-64 | Lockheed 1049G Super Constellation |
| 70. | 08-10-64 | Lockheed 749, 749A Constellation |
| 71. | 10-09-64 | Piper Colt |
| 72. | 12-21-64 | Boeing 707-331 Intercontinental (pure jet) |

| 73. | 01-07-65 | Boeing 707-131 (pure jet, water wagon) |
|---|---|---|
| 74. | 01-08-65 | Boeing 707-131B (fan jet) |
| 75. | 01-24-65 | Boeing 707-331 Inter-continental series (fan jets) |
| 76. | 02-20-65 | Piper PA-28 Cherokee 235 |
| 77. | 06-13-65 | Piper PA-30 Twin Comanche |
| 78. | 08-28-65 | Alon A-2 Ercoupe |
| 79. | 10-30-65 | Cessna 170 floatplane |
| 80. | 04-30-66 | Lake LA-4, Buccaneer |
| 81. | 07-24-66 | Aero Commander 500 series |
| 82. | 01-31-67 | Siai-Marchetti SF.260 (Waco Meteor) |
| 83. | 02-04-67 | Partenavia P-64 Oscar |
| 84. | 04-28-67 | Aero Commander 200 |
| 85. | 05-26-67 | Roberston Cessna 182, 210 STOL |
| 86. | 08-22-67 | Bellanca 7EC Citabria |
| 87. | 09-19-67 | Helio Courier H-250 Mark II |
| 88. | 10-19-67 | Beech T-34 Mentor |
| 89. | 12-03-67 | Schweizer 2-33 |
| 90. | 12-29-67 | Siai-Marchetti 220 Sirius |
| 91. | 01-12-68 | Piper PA-32 Cherokee Six |
| 92. | 02-03-68 | Wren 460 Beta STOL |
| 93. | 02-11-68 | Cessna 177 Cardinal |
| 94. | 03-16-68 | Boeing 727-100, 100QC |
| 95. | 05-05-68 | Reims F-172 Rocket |
| 96. | 05-11-68 | Scheibe Bergfalke III |
| 97. | 05-17-68 | Boeing 727-200 |
| 98. | 05-26-68 | Hughes 500 |
| 99. | 05-31-68 | Fornier RF-4D |
| 100. | 06-13-68 | Piper Comanche 600 (turboprop) |
| 101. | 08-06-68 | Cessna 206 Super Skylane |
| 102. | 09-27-68 | Aero Commander 100 Darter |
| 103. | 11-08-68 | Temco T-610 Super Pinto |
| 104. | 12-02-68 | Beech F33C Aerobatic Bonanza |
| 105. | 12-24-68 | Cessna 320 Skyknight |
| 106. | 01-17-69 | NASA 808 (PA-30) Test Vehicle |
| 107. | 02-14-69 | Sud Rallye MS-894A Minerva |
| 108. | 02-26-69 | Stinson L-5E Sentinel |
| 109. | 03-08-69 | Conroy STOLifter |
| 110. | 05-05-69 | Piper PA-28 Arrow |
| 111. | 05-11-69 | DeHavilland DHC-1 Chipmunk |
| 112. | 07-26-69 | Schweizer 2-32 |
| 113. | 08-29-69 | Learjet 24 |
| 114. | 10-04-69 | Cessna 150 Aerobat |
| 115. | 01-24-70 | Britten-Norman BN-2A Islander |
| 116. | 02-08-70 | Morovan-Otrokovice Zlin 526 Trener Master |
| 117. | 03-28-70 | Piper PA-39 Twin Comanche C/R |
| 118. | 04-03-70 | Mooney M-10 Cadet |
| 119. | 04-28-70 | Siai-Marchetti A.S. 202 Bravo |
| 120. | 06-20-70 | North American Rockwell 1121 Jet Commander |
| 121. | 07-20-70 | Bücker BU-133 Jungmeister |
| 122. | 08-30-70 | DeHavilland Gypsy Moth |
| 123. | 01-24-71 | Schweizer 1-34 |
| 124. | 01-26-71 | American Jet Industries 402 TurboStar |
| 125. | 04-12-71 | McCulloch J-2 Gyroplane |
| 126. | 10-15-71 | Enstrom F-28A |
| 127. | 11-02-71 | American Yankee AA-1A Trainer |
| 128. | 11-18-71 | Champion 402 Lancer |
| 129. | 01-20-72 | Francis Lombardi FL-3 |
| 130. | 02-19-72 | Bellanca 17-31A Super Viking |
| 131. | 03-01-72 | Cessna 337 Super Skymaster |
| 132. | 03-05-72 | Cessna 177 Cardinal RG |
| 133. | 04-08-72 | Bell 47H-1 |
| 134. | 05-01-72 | Beech E-90 KingAir |
| 135. | 06-11-72 | Thurston TSC-1A1 Teal |
| 136. | 06-11-72 | Schempp-Hirth Cirrus |
| 137. | 06-14-72 | Lockheed L-1011 TriStar |
| 138. | 06-22-72 | Piper PA-18 Floatplane |
| 139. | 06-24-72 | Interstate S-1B2 Arctic Tern |
| 140. | 08-06-72 | Warwick Bantam |
| 141. | 10-31-72 | Sud Aviation Gardan Horizon GY-80 |
| 142. | 11-30-72 | Israel Aircraft Industries 1123 Westwind |
| 143. | 02-12-73 | Cessna 150/150 with Owl STOL Conversion |
| 144. | 03-04-73 | Jodel D117 |
| 145. | 03-15-73 | Beech 95 Travel Air |
| 146. | 05-14-73 | Citabria 7GCBC-S Floatplane |
| 147. | 05-23-73 | Grumman American AA-5 Traveler |
| 148. | 09-01-73 | Navion G-1 Rangemaster |

| 149. | 10-20-73 | Bellanca Champ 7ACA |
| 150. | 02-05-74 | Transavia Airtruk PL-12U |
| 151. | 03-11-74 | Cessna 414, 414A Chancellor |
| 152. | 06-12-74 | Blanik L-13 Sailplane |
| 153. | 06-12-74 | Cessna L-19 Birddog |
| 154. | 07-12-74 | Maule M-5 Lunar Rocket |
| 155. | 08-19-74 | Piper Warrior, Archer, Dakota |
| 156. | 10-28-74 | Aerostar 601P |
| 157. | 11-09-74 | Beech 55 Baron |
| 158. | 04-10-75 | AES Ltd. Airtourer T3A |
| 159. | 04-10-75 | DeHavilland Tiger Moth |
| 160. | 04-13-75 | Beech B24R Sierra |
| 161. | 04-21-75 | N.Z. Aerospace CT/4 Airtrainer |
| 162. | 04-21-75 | N.Z. Aerospace FU-24-950 Fletcher |
| 163. | 01-09-76 | Beech 200 Super King Air |
| 164. | 03-12-76 | Israel Aircraft Industries 201 Arava |
| 165. | 04-17-76 | Messerschmitt BO-209 Monsun |
| 166. | 05-27-76 | Beech Model 76 Test Bed |
| 167. | 06-17-76 | Beech A-36, B-36TC Bonanza |
| 168. | 11-19-76 | Piper Lance |
| 169. | 05-09-77 | SAAB MFI-15 Safari |
| 170. | 05-18-77 | Piper Seneca II |
| 171. | 05-18-77 | Robertson Cessna 310 II w/ Fowler-flap conversion |
| 172. | 05-18-77 | Robertson Bonanza w/ full-span flap/spoiler (roll) conversion |
| 173. | 09-25-77 | Malmo Flygindustri MFI-9 Floatplane |
| 174. | 03-24-78 | Rockwell Commander 112, 114 |
| 175. | 05-09-78 | Polish PZL-104 Wilga |
| 176. | 05-22-78 | Piper PA-38 Tomahawk |
| 177. | 09-15-78 | Sportavia RF-5B Sperber |
| 178. | 10-14-78 | Piper PA-44 Seminole |
| 179. | 11-25-78 | Polish PZL SZD-4 Ogar |
| 180. | 02-15-79 | Douglas DC-4 Carvair |
| 181. | 04-09-79 | Pitts S-2A |
| 182. | 04-15-79 | Scheibe-Flugzeugbau SF-25E Super Falke |
| 183. | 09-28-79 | Robertson Cessna P210 w/ spoilerons |
| 184. | 10-20-79 | Funk Model C |
| 185. | 02-25-80 | Robertson Cessna 402C w/ Fowler flap conversion |
| 186. | 02-27-80 | Rutan Defiant |
| 187. | 02-27-80 | Rutan Long-EZ |
| 188. | 03-12-80 | Cessna 172RG Cutlass |
| 189. | 04-07-80 | Great Lakes 2T-1A-2 |
| 190. | 05-18-80 | Morelli M-100S |
| 191. | 06-26-80 | Goodyear GZ-20 Blimp |
| 192. | 12-14-80 | Piper Pawnee Brave |
| 193. | 07-06-81 | Cessna 441 Conquest |
| 194. | 07-11-81 | Piper PA-31T Cheyenne II |
| 195. | 11-12-81 | Beech 77 Skipper |
| 196. | 01-23-82 | Partenavia P-68 |
| 197. | 07-08-82 | Cessna T210 w/ Glide Path Control Spoilers/Speed Brakes |
| 198. | 11-11-82 | Boeing 747 |
| 199. | 01-13-83 | Boeing 747SP |
| 200. | 11-10-83 | Robin 2160 Sport |
| 201. | 02-08-84 | Boeing 767-200 |
| 202. | 10-05-84 | Cessna Citation I -501SP |
| 203 | 02-21-85 | Aerospatiale TB-9 Tampico |
| 204. | 03-01-85 | Bücker C-104 Jungmann |
| 205. | 08-20-85 | Piper PA-31-350 Navajo Chieftain |
| 206. | 09-14-85 | Grob 109 Motorglider |
| 207. | 09-11-86 | Cessna 425 Corsair, Conquest I |
| 208. | 09-29-86 | Cessna 335, 340 |
| 209. | 02-28-87 | Aerospatiale TB-20 Trinidad |
| 210. | 04-09-87 | Beech 80 Queenair |
| 211. | 04-19-87 | Piper J-3 Floatplane |
| 212. | 06-18-87 | Varga Kachina 2180 TG |
| 213. | 06-20-87 | Allison Propjet Bonanza |
| 214 | 08-18-87 | Bushmaster 2000 |
| 215. | 08-25-87 | Learjet 35A |
| 216. | 04-02-88 | Aerospatiale SA-314G Gazelle |
| 217. | 05-11-88 | Bellanca 8KCAB Decathlon |
| 218. | 05-16-88 | Mooney M-20L PFM Porsche Flugmotor |
| 219. | 07-04-88 | Glassair I, SH-2R |
| 220. | 07-23-88 | Porterfield PF-65 Collegiate |
| 221. | 09-10-88 | Cessna 208 Caravan (amphibious floats) |
| 222. | 09-14-88 | Beech 76 Duchess |
| 223. | 09-17-88 | Cessna 140 Floatplane |
| 224. | 09-24-88 | Glassair III |

| | | |
|---|---|---|
| 225. | 01-31-89 | Questaire Venture |
| 226. | 06-24-89 | Piper PA-46-310RT Malibu |
| 227. | 10-08-89 | Grob G-103A Twin II Acro |
| 228. | 03-12-90 | Rutan Model 143 Triumph |
| 229. | 08-25-90 | Grumman American GA-7 Cougar |
| 230. | 10-11-90 | Beech 2000 Starship I |
| 231. | 10-30-90 | LoPresti Swiftfury II |
| 232. | 10-25-91 | American General Tiger |
| 233. | 01-21-92 | Kitfox IV Speedster |
| 234. | 08-13-92 | Cessna 150/150 Floatplane |
| 235. | 09-24-92 | Schleicher ASK-21 |
| 236. | 11-11-92 | Robinson R-22 Beta |
| 237. | 12-22-92 | Berkut |
| 238. | 02-08-94 | Douglas DC-3 |
| 239. | 02-11-94 | Cessna 172 Floatplane |
| 240. | 05-31-91 | Augusta A-109 |
| 241. | 10-24-94 | Aerospatiale TBM 700 |
| 242. | 11-05-94 | Diamond Katana |
| 243. | 05-05-96 | American Champion 8GCBC Scout |
| 244. | 06-26-96 | Meyers 145 |
| 245. | 07-20-96 | Siai-Marchetti SF.260TP |
| 246. | 03-07-97 | Cessna 208 Caravan |
| 247. | 10-19-97 | Boeing 757 |
| 248. | 01-25-98 | Aerospatiale TB-10 Tobago |
| 249. | 01-30-98 | Norman NDN-1T Firecracker |
| 250. | 03-08-98 | Cresco Turboprop Agplane |
| 251. | 03-13-98 | Schleicher ASH-25 |
| 252. | 03-15-98 | Beagle B-121 Pup |
| 253. | 10-30-98 | Nicco SP-20 |
| 254. | 11-13-98 | Ximango AMT-200 |
| 255. | 11-17-98 | Martin 404 |
| 256. | 12-08-98 | Space Shuttle Orbiter Simulator |
| 257. | 06-14-99 | Grumman G-44 Widgeon |
| 258. | 11-27-99 | Boeing 737-200 |
| 259. | 03-08-00 | Piper Saratoga SPII |
| 260. | 07-21-00 | Aviat A-1B Husky |
| 261. | 07-29-00 | Fairchild 22 |
| 262. | 07-30-00 | Holste MH.1521 Broussard |
| 263. | 09-28-00 | Lockheed U-2 |
| 264. | 10-23-00 | Lancair Columbia 400 |
| 265. | 12-06-00 | Beech 60 Duke |
| 266. | 04-02-01 | Antonov AN-2 Colt |
| 267. | 04-28-01 | Pilatus PC-12 |
| 268. | 05-08-01 | Lincoln-Page PTK |
| 269. | 10-16-01 | Ryan NYP Spirit of St. Louis (replica) |
| 270. | 11-17-01 | Halsted BH-1 Saffire |
| 271. | 11-17-01 | Van's RV-6 |
| 272. | 10-12-02 | Cirrus SR-22 |
| 273. | 12-04-02 | Sikorsky S-38 |
| 274. | 01-05-03 | OMF Symphony 160 |
| 275. | 02-28-03 | Diamond Star DA-4-180 |
| 276. | 03-09-03 | Boeing/Stearman PT-17 Kaydet (N2S-4) |
| 277. | 07-08-03 | Airbus A300-600 |
| 278. | 07-10-03 | Airbus A318 |
| 279. | 10-17-03 | Gulfstream V |
| 281. | 10-24-03 | Nanchang CJ-6 |
| 281. | 10-31-03 | Anderson-Greenwood AG-14 |
| 282. | 11-20-03 | Quicksilver GT-500 |
| 283. | 12-02-03 | SIPA 200 Minijet |
| 284. | 01-17-04 | Bede BD-4 |
| 285. | 04-08-04 | Stinson Detroiter Junior |
| 286. | 04-12-04 | DeHavilland DHC-2 Beaver |
| 287. | 05-27-04 | Beriev Be-103 |
| 288. | 06-05-04 | DeHavilland DHC-3 Otter (turboprop) Floatplane |
| 289. | 06-05-04 | DeHavilland DHC-2 Beaver Floatplane (amphibious) |
| 290. | 07-05-04 | Cirrus VK-30 |
| 291. | 09-24-04 | Zlin 242L |
| 292. | 09-29-04 | Curtiss Wright CW-1 Junior |
| 293. | 10-25-04 | Found Bush Hawk XP |
| 294. | 11-19-04 | Dassault Falcon 900 |
| 295. | 02-04-05 | Liberty XL2 |
| 296. | 04-16-05 | Europa Monowheel |
| 297. | 07-15-05 | Flight Design CTsw |
| 298. | 10-22-05 | Evektor-Aerotechnik Sport Star |
| 299. | 12-04-05 | Piper PA-46-500TP Meridian |
| 300. | 12-18-05 | Lockheed 12A Electra Junior |
| 301. | 12-21-06 | Sky Arrow 650TCN |
| 302. | 3-27-07 | Extra 300 |
| 303. | 5-14-07 | North American TF-51 & P-51D Mustang |
| 304. | 9-10-07 | Canadair Regional Jet CRJ-900 |
| 305. | 10-23-07 | Sopwith 1-½ Strutter |

# Aircraft

## Culver Cadet

| | |
|---|---|
| Engine | Continental A-75-8 |
| Power | 75 hp |
| Length | 17 ft 8 in |
| Height (3-point attitude) | 5 ft 6 in |
| Wingspan | 27 ft 0 in |
| Wing Loading | 10.9 lb/sq ft |
| Power Loading | 17.4 lb/hp |
| Maximum Takeoff Weight | 1,305 lb |
| Fuel Capacity (usable) | 20 gal |
| Rate of Climb (sea level) | 800 fpm |
| Normal Cruise Speed | 120 mph |
| Stall Speed | 45 mph |

# Culver Cadet

## It is little wonder that the Culver Cadet attracted

so much attention when it was introduced in December, 1939. It had a factory-guaranteed cruise speed of 120 mph while emptying the fuel tank at only 4.2 gph. Specific range was an incredible 28.6 miles per gallon. Other 2-place airplanes of that era struggled to achieve 80 mph using the same 75-hp engine. The petite Cadet rapidly became America's sweetheart, the darling of the sportsman pilot.

The story of the Culver Cadet began in 1938 when Knight Culver, Jr., purchased the design rights to the Monosport aircraft and founded the Dart Aircraft Company, which later became Culver Aircraft. The purchase included retaining a young, self-educated, and accomplished designer who would make an indelible mark in general aviation: Al Mooney. (Al's brother, Art, was retained as factory superintendent.)

One of Mooney's assignments was to design an airplane that would take advantage of the new 75-hp, flat-four, Continental A-75-8 engine that rapidly rendered obsolescent the small radial engines that had been so popular. (The A-75 engine was a faster turning version of the 65-hp, Continental A-65.)

The result was the Mooney-designed Culver Cadet (also known as Mooney's "wooden wonder"). It was Mooney's twelfth design, which he designated according to his personal list of designs as the M-12. The structure was predominantly wood because metal was in short supply during that post-Depression, pre-war era. From such aircraft eventually came the cliché claiming with tongue in cheek that "wood airplanes stay together only because the termites are holding hands."

The Culver Cadet LCA made its maiden flight on December 3, 1939 and sold for $2,395. A later version, the Model LFA, had an 80-hp, Franklin 4AC-176-F3 engine, was equipped with an electrical system and starter, and cost $200 more.

Original Cadets were built in Columbus, Ohio, but the factory was relocated to Wichita, Kansas after being purchased by Walter Beech and attorney Charles Yankey.

A total of 359 Cadets were produced from 1939 through early 1942. Production ended so that the company could concentrate on the war effort and building thousands of drones to serve as targets for anti-aircraft practice. The significant differences between the Cadet and the Culver PQ-8 Drone were that the drones had tricycle landing gear and were coated with aluminum paint to make them better radar targets.

Al and Art Mooney eventually formed their own company, which is when Al developed the single-place M-18 Mooney Mite and the 4-place Mooney M-20, the progenitor of an entire family of popular 4-place airplanes. (The 150-hp Mooney M-20 was the first 4-place, production airplane capable of cruising at more than 1 mph per hp.)

Carl Walston became enamored with the Cadet when he was in grade school but did not begin flying until years later in 1961. This is when he lived in New Canaan, Connecticut, was in the securities business, and wanted to use his own airplane to travel from Wall Street to his other offices in the northeastern U.S. For this he used a Cessna 310, a Piper Apache, and an Aero Commander 500. He accumulated 1,100 hours of flight time including 400 were in sailplanes.

When Walston began planning his retirement in Santa Barbara, California, he decided that he would make a dream come true by spending his carefree hours aloft in a Culver Cadet. Although there were more than 100 on FAA's registry, Walston estimated that only 20 or so were airworthy, and none of these rare machines were for sale. Realizing his dream would require that he become involved in restoring a basket case.

His search for a Cadet eventually led him in 1995 to Wallkill, New York, where he purchased N29398 (serial number 191) from a pilot's widow. The airplane had been originally built from scratch and in its entirety in Wichita during the week between Christmas and New Year's Eve, 1940. It was now a collection of bits and pieces.

When his wife, Mimi, saw her husband's purchase, she thought he was nuts. It reminded her of an oversized model airplane kit containing uncountable balsawood parts. The airplane had no log books, no airworthiness certificate, and had not flown since 1957.

Carl Badgett of Winsted, Connecticut, was enlisted to do the fabric and wood work, and Mark Grusauski of Wingworks in Canaan, Connecticut, to do the metal and mechanical work.

The Cadet was restored as much as possible to its original condition, but Walston made two concessions. One was to replace the original full-swivel tailwheel with a steerable unit, and the other was to strengthen the bulkhead behind the seats to accommodate the installation of shoulder harnesses.

Except for the nose bowl and tail cone, all metal parts (of which there are not too many in a Cadet) had to be made from scratch. These included fairings, doors, panels, cowlings, and so forth.

Although he purchased his project for only $7,500, Walston estimates that he has more than $100,000 invested in his dream machine. N29398 finally took to wing on May 16, 2000, its first flight in 43 years.

The fit and finish of N29398, which sports its original colors of Santa Fe red and Diana cream, are impeccable. It is not surprising that the restoration has garnered numerous first-place awards at air shows.

One glance at a Cadet explains why it is so fast and efficient.

The wings and fuselage are exceptionally smooth, reminiscent of something made from composite materials. There are no rivets, fabric stitches, metal joints, or other blemishes to interfere with the airflow. Sheets of mahogany plywood shape the semi-monocoque fuselage, which is then overlaid with fabric to protect the wood.

The cantilever, elliptically shaped wing is similarly constructed from the leading edge to the laminated spruce and mahogany spar. Aft of the spar, the wing is covered with fabric in a conventional manner.

A slot in each wing tip is intended to improve spanwise stall characteristics and low-speed roll qualities. The U.S. Army, however, operated some Cadets with covered slots. These planes reportedly flew better and faster. There is no question that the gap seals used with the ailerons and elevator increase aerodynamic efficiency and performance.

Walston's airplane is equipped with a wooden, fixed-pitch Sensenich propeller, although Cadets were also available from the factory with Freedman-Burnham ground-adjustable propellers.

One negative feature is that the single, 20-gallon fuel tank is only 8 inches forward of the instrument panel and behind the engine, which is not the most crashworthy configuration. A fuel gauge from a Model A Ford below the instrument panel is more nostalgic than reliable. Believe it only when it says Empty.

When I first approached the Cadet, I seriously doubted that there would be enough room in the diminutive airplane for two grown men. I climbed onto the left wing, opened the left door (there is one on each side), stepped onto the seat cushion, and slid in.

I was relieved to discover that there was ample head- and legroom for my 6-foot, 2-inch frame, but cabin width is miserly and makes for shoulder-rubbing intimacy. After Walston flicked the propeller for a manual start and climbed into the cockpit from the right door, I noticed that he had to defer to my not-so-insubstantial width and sat slightly twisted in his seat.

The spartan instrument panel is neatly laid out and contains a center-mounted throttle, which I found a bit too high for comfort.

The top of the pug nose slopes downward significantly so that over-the-nose visibility during taxi is excellent.

The tiny tailwheel and short-coupled fuselage combine to give the Cadet a mind of its own while taxiing. The pilot needs a pair of active feet to keep the aircraft on the straight and narrow. Toe brakes are available to help, but only on the pilot's side.

With only 75 horsepower, the Cadet does not have sterling acceleration during the takeoff roll, but the rudder becomes effective almost immediately, which improves the ease of directional control. A stiff crosswind, however, probably would require some use of differential braking early in the takeoff roll.

The Cadet's 3-point attitude is about the same as the attitude for best climb, so it is unnecessary to raise the tail for liftoff. The airplane flies itself off the ground quite nicely.

Initial climb requires a surprising amount of right rudder to compensate for P-factor considering that you're containing only 75 horsepower.

Like so many other pre-World War II airplanes, a pilot's operating handbook was never published for the Cadet, and many of the performance speeds have been approximated by those who have flown the aircraft. Along these lines, the airplane apparently climbs best at about 75 mph.

One caution: Pilots new to the Cadet should not attempt to retract the landing gear until reaching a safe altitude because the procedure involves more than flipping a switch and begins by using your right hand to shift a near-vertical lever on the floor (between the pilots) from the Locked Down to the Raise position. Then you grip a small wheel and tug it about a dozen times, with each tug turning the wheel 20 or 30 degrees at a time to ratchet the wheels into their wells. (The tailwheel is not retractable.)

I am told that with practice you can raise the gear in 5 seconds.

The downward sloping nose cowl is initially deceiving when leveling off at altitude. When you lower the nose to where you think it should be, the Cadet continues to climb. Leveling off requires putting the nose in what appears to be an exaggerated nose-down attitude that in most other airplanes would cause a shallow dive. One quickly adapts to this quirk.

The elevator-trim crank is on the ceiling between and somewhat behind the pilots. It is similar to the trim control on many early Piper aircraft and at first you'll have to think about which way it should be turned to achieve a given result. Fortunately, trim changes are usually small, and there is seldom a rush to relieve control forces.

The Cadet maneuvers easily and quickly about all three axes, but the controls are not that well harmonized. The elevator is most sensitive, the rudder is next, and the ailerons are least sensitive.

And if you're not in a hurry, you can chug along at 80 mph while sipping only 1.5 gph, a specific range of 53 miles per gallon.

The Cadet reacts quickly to turbulence and tends toward neutral stability about the longitudinal axis. When gusts lower a wing, the aircraft shows little desire to return to a wings-level attitude on its own. The good news is that only light corrective forces with the stick are needed to keep the aircraft on an even keel.

The aircraft does not have a stall warning system, but aerodynamic buffeting provides an ample notice. Buffeting begins at 55 mph, and the Cadet tends to buck a bit as if rebelling against the impending stall, which occurs at 45 mph. There also is a noticeable loss of roll control.

The Cadet has a bad reputation for its stall manners, preferring to almost always fall off on a wing at the break (power-off or power-on). Although recovery is easy and conventional, be careful not to apply excessive aileron to pick up a wing. The little airplane will enter an incipient spin with little additional encouragement.

Although the Cadet was initially approved for aerobatics, some pilots got into trouble, perhaps due to the airplane's sensitivity and quickness. Aerobatic approval was rescinded and intentional spinning prohibited. Too bad. The Cadet loves to spin.

The landing gear should be lowered before entering the traffic pattern to prevent becoming distracted during a critical phase of flight. This might be one reason why the Cadet was not certified for IFR flight. Another might be that the airplane can be a handful in turbulence because the short wings offer limited roll damping.

Gear extension requires first placing the control stick between your knees. Then use your left hand to pull up on the lever while simultaneously placing your right hand on the landing gear wheel. Pull up slightly on the wheel to release the ratchet. Then move the lever from Raise to Drop with the left hand while using your right hand to snub the wheel. This allows the gear to freefall against a dashpot (dampener) and into position. The lever is then moved left to the Locked Down position, which inserts locking pins into place. Finally, restore control of the aircraft from the knees to your left hand.

The original Cadet had an interlocking throttle that prevented the pilot from reducing power to idle with the landing gear retracted. Walston disliked this feature, deactivated it, and replaced the throttle block with a gear-warning horn powered by a 9-volt battery.

Al Mooney had a flair for unusual gear-warning solutions. Retard the throttle of a Mooney Mite with the wheels retracted, for example, and a small, red metal flag at the end of a vertical rod waves like a metronome across the instrument panel to remind the pilot that he might be about to land on his belly.

In a Cadet, a pilot can use the 3-inch-square, Plexiglas viewing lenses on the right and left sides of the cockpit floor of a Cadet to confirm that the wheels are no longer in their wells, but these lenses are essentially worthless. Being able to move the locking pins into place proves that the wheels could not be retracted.

The Cadet does not have flaps, but with a stall speed of 45 mph and the agility to perform steep and effective slips, they are not needed.

Making a full-stall touchdown with the stick fully aft can result in an overflare and landing tailwheel first. The main gear then plunks firmly onto the ground, making one hope that the spindly gear legs and small, 5.00 x 4 wheels are up to the task. The recommended technique is to flare to but not beyond the airplane's normal 3-point attitude while close to the ground. The airplane will land softly on all three wheels, which is much preferable to a full-stall landing. The technique is relatively easy once you become accustomed to the pitch sensitivity.

The classic Culver Cadet is a joy to fly, a wonderful playmate with which to cavort about the sky, and it is doubtful if you can find a production airplane that can cruise at 120 mph and cost so little to operate.

## Fairchild 22

| | |
|---|---|
| Engine | Menasco D-4-87 Super Pirate |
| Power | 134 hp |
| Length | 21 ft 11 in |
| Height (3-point attitude) | 8 ft 0 in |
| Wingspan | 31 ft 10 in |
| Wing Loading | 10.3 lb/sq ft |
| Power Loading | 13.1 lb/hp |
| Maximum Takeoff Weight | 1,750 lb |
| Fuel Capacity (usable) | 36 gal |
| Rate of Climb (sea level) | 1,050 fpm |
| Normal Cruise Speed | 106 mph |
| Stall Speed | 45 mph |

# The Fairchild 22

## Charles W. "Bill" Worman has been infatuated

with aviation since he was six years old and spent much of his youth building and flying rubber band-powered model airplanes. But he truly fell in love with aviation when he was 14.

He was at his home airport, Felts Field, near Spokane, Washington, in 1931 when he saw a sparkling-new Fairchild 22 slide from the sky and alight softly on the summer grass, its polished propeller flickering sunlight.

It was sleeker than any airplane he had ever seen. The eye-catching Fairchild had a thin, straight (no dihedral) parasol wing mounted high on a truss of struts and a trim fuselage that tapered to a distinctive vertical fin. Worman was smitten.

Fast-forward to 1979. While sailing on the waters of Puget Sound, he began to realize that the only thing better than what he was doing would be to fly a Fairchild 22, the object of a lifelong affection. His daydreaming evolved into a goal, and his determination began to take on a life of its own. But Worman did not just want to buy a Model 22. Anyone can do that, he reasoned. "I wanted to restore one so that I could be personally involved with the airplane."

Worman put his plan into action and scoured the country for his dream machine. He found four aircraft, but none was for sale.

He ultimately located one in New Jersey that the seller described as a "project." The aircraft turned out to be a pile of junk, bits and pieces of twisted metal and shattered wood that bore no resemblance to the Fairchild 22 that it was represented to be—no matter how vivid the imagination. Its four-cylinder Menasco D-4-87 Super Pirate engine was in dire need of overhaul.

But this was just what Worman wanted. Although none of the parts could be used to build his new Model 22, he decided that they could be used as patterns from which he could manufacture new parts. He bought the junk in 1979 for $7,000 and negotiated with the seller to throw in a rusted-out, short-bed Dodge pickup truck in which to haul the bits and pieces across the country to his home in Eastsound, Washington, on Orcas Island.

After an exhaustive and discouraging two-year search, Worman concluded that factory drawings were nonexistent. Lacking plans for building the airplane, he arranged with the owner of an airworthy Model 22 near Stockton, California, to take measurements and detailed photographs. He was then ready to begin bringing his dream machine to life.

The notion of building a production airplane without parts or plans might be considered by some as an impossible dream. But such a daunting undertaking surprised no one familiar with Worman's engineering and mechanical expertise.

Worman had designed and manufactured teardrop-shaped Kit Trailers, a business that he sold in 1958 and is still in operation. He then designed and manufactured folding buildings, a business in which he sold his interest and retired to Orcas Island in 1970.

One of the most frustrating challenges faced by Worman while building his airplane was shaping a nose cowl from a sheet of aluminum. He created the necessary mold (made of steel-reinforced concrete) and tried numerous times to bend the metal to match the deep, bowl-shaped mold using rubber mallets, but his attempts failed.

He eventually learned from a friend of a friend about metal bumping. This process involved securing an aluminum sheet to the mold, climbing a 10-foot ladder, and dropping a leather pouch filled with 25 pounds of fine shot onto the target. After repeating this process about 50 times, the aluminum sheet had been bumped into the shape of a Fairchild nose cowl.

Worman is quick to acknowledge that he had plenty of help along the way, people who enthusiastically volunteered their expertise or ran errands. There is a list of about 100 such people proudly and prominently displayed on one wall of his 4,500-square-foot hangar (which contains an elaborate machine shop). Among them is famed author Ernest K. Gann, who lived in nearby Friday Harbor. Also, Worman's friend—respected engineer Victor Ganzer—provided aerodynamic guidance and stress analysis to ensure that the airplane would meet certification criteria. Worman believes that his project prolonged the lives of some older volunteers by providing them with challenge and purpose that they otherwise lacked.

After 10 years and an estimated 7,500 man-hours of labor, Worman's dream took to wing on November 29, 1989. His airplane is so pristine and so much better than new that it would make its original builders green with envy. The only original part of the airframe is the data plate. It shows that NC-13167 is a 1932 Fairchild Model 22-C7B, one of eight versions built by the Kreider-Reisner Aircraft Company in Hagerstown, Maryland, a division of the Fairchild Aviation Corporation.

Worman's airplane originally sold for $3,450, a princely sum for that era. But despite the sticker shock, the Fairchild 22 was a hit with flight schools and became what historians regard as the first popular general aviation airplane. Today there apparently are only six airworthy Fairchild 22s in the world.

Merrill Wien, Worman's close friend, would be checking me out in NC-13167. Since he hadn't flown the aircraft for some time, he first took it around the pattern a few times by himself. As Worman and I watched the antique monoplane shooting circuits and bumps, I noticed a few tears working their way down his cheeks. He explained that this was the first time he had ever seen his airplane fly. During all previous flights, he either was aboard the aircraft or not at the airport when others flew it. This was an emotional experience for him. He said that he did not know "how good the engine sounds and how easy it is to distinguish the parasol-wing monoplane from others in the pattern."

Have I mentioned that Worman is not a pilot? He has been taking lessons in his own 1952 Cessna 170 to gain proficiency in the fine art of taildragging before transitioning to the Fairchild. He hopes to solo the airplane and use it to obtain a recreational pilot certificate. Who says that dreams do not come true?

After his third landing, Wien taxied the airplane directly toward us. This head-on view makes it obvious how the in-line engine contributes to the Fairchild's slender lines. It has much less frontal area than a radial engine and creates much less cooling drag. The inverted engine configuration places the crankshaft high above the cylinders, providing ample ground clearance for the 87-inch-diameter propeller. This eliminates the need for longer landing-gear legs and the added weight and drag that would result.

The Hamilton-Standard propeller is ground adjustable. Clamps near the hub are loosened to adjust blade pitch for the desired performance. Maximum pitch increases cruise speed, and minimum pitch increases climb performance; a mid-range pitch setting results in a compromise between maximum cruise and maximum climb performance. Once the clamps are tightened, the adjustable propeller behaves and is used just like one that has fixed pitch.

The fabric-covered airframe is constructed of chrome-moly steel tubing, spruce, and plywood, not unlike the Aeronca Champions and Piper Cubs that would follow.

The Fairchild 22 has a fuel capacity of 36 gallons, 24 in the nose behind the engine and 12 gallons in a feeder tank in the right wing that gravity feeds into the main tank when a valve in the cockpit is opened. The float-type fuel gauge is a tried-and-true, clear-plastic sight tube sticking up from the nose tank ahead of the forward cockpit.

Also sticking up through the top of the cowling and ahead of the sight gauge is the starter motor.

A single venturi tube on the right side of the fuselage provides vacuum for the turn indicator in each cockpit. This was considered "fully IFR-equipped" until the FAA required artificial horizons and directional gyros in the late 1950s.

A wind-driven generator is mounted on the left lift strut. Should one blade of the diminutive propeller break in flight, the out-of-balance generator could result in airframe damage. To eliminate this threat, the rear-seat pilot can employ a cable-operated brake to arrest generator rotation while in flight.

Although both cockpits are almost identically equipped, the airplane must be soloed from the rear seat to maintain the center of gravity within limits and because that is the only place from which the engine can be started. The Fairchild has an electric starter but does not have an electric fuel pump. A manually operated wobble pump is used for priming.

Otherwise, the airplane is relatively conventional. It has a gross weight of 1,750 pounds, an empty weight of 1,010 pounds, and a useful load of 740 pounds.

After a normal start, Wien and I taxied out and completed the preflight checklist. Although the Menasco engine has a carburetor, it does not have a conventional carburetor heater. Instead, induction air is ducted through a shroud surrounding the number-three cylinder. This heats the air before it enters the carburetor. In other words, carburetor heat is always on—except for takeoff. When the throttle is fully advanced to its mechanical limit, a small door opens that allows ram air to bypass the shroud and enter the carburetor directly. This cooler air boosts maximum power from 125 horsepower (when induction air is heated) to 134 hp for takeoff. It is a clever scheme. The bad news is that induction air is not filtered during either takeoff or cruise. (Retarding the throttle after takeoff also retards the spark.)

Takeoff is unremarkable for a taildragger, but as airspeed increased, I began to feel the exhilaration associated with flying an open-cockpit airplane on a warm summer day.

I was also reminded about why open-cockpit pilots have worn their baseball caps backward since before it became fashionable in the inner city. (Helmets are preferable to caps in the winter.) If the bill of the cap projects forward and catches the wind, there is a good chance that you will lose both the cap and an expensive headset.

Normal climb speed in a Fairchild 22 is 60 mph, but NC-13167 does not climb anywhere near the advertised climb rate of 1,050 feet per minute. It is only half that. I learned later that Worman has his propeller set to optimize cruise performance, which reduces maximum climb rate.

The airplane is a delight to maneuver, although it loses a bit too much airspeed during steep turns even with a wide-open throttle. The ailerons and elevators are light and harmonious, somewhat surprising for a 70-year-old design. This is attributable, in part, to full-span, narrow-chord ailerons that produce surprisingly little adverse yaw. Also, push tubes riding on ball bearings are used to move the ailerons and elevators. The rudder is cable operated, and pitch trim is controlled by a manually operated jackscrew that adjusts the horizontal stabilizer.

It is difficult to get the airplane to "break" nose down during a power-off, 1-G, wings-level stall. The airplane just mushes at an indicated airspeed of 45 mph. Power on or during accelerated stalls, the Model 22 impetuously rolls off toward one side or the other, but restoring control occurs easily and simultaneously with a release of back-pressure.

Even with Worman's propeller adjusted to maximize cruise speed, the Fairchild 22 is not a barnburner. It cruises at 106 mph and has a redline of 116 mph.

The airplane glides and approaches to land at 60 mph. Like most aircraft designed during aviation's Golden Age, it does not have wing flaps but instead slips effectively and without airframe buffeting. Unlike similar aircraft, it does not require as much of a nose-high attitude during a three-point landing. It also is easier to land an airplane with a parasol wing than a biplane because there is so much less wing structure to block the view.

You barely feel the initial touchdown because the long, spring-oleo, shock-absorbing struts compress so slowly. It feels similar to making a good landing in an airplane with trailing-link landing gear.

The Fairchild 22 has toe brakes, but they are so ineffective that you probably could land with them engaged and not notice. It made me wish that the airplane had been equipped with a tail skid instead of the optional tailwheel. (Although a tail skid assists in slowing an airplane—especially on unimproved surfaces—it makes it more difficult to make taxiing turns. The procedure involves pushing the stick fully forward, adding a blast of power to take some of the weight off of the tailskid, and kicking full rudder to yaw in the desired direction.)

The unusually wide landing gear (91 inches), however, makes the airplane relatively stable on the ground and less prone to ground looping.

At 84, Worman says that he has one more construction project left in him. If he can find an engine and the plans, he wants to build another airplane from scratch—a 1917 German fighter from World War I, the Fokker D.VII. He selected the D.VII because of his respect for the design and because he and the aircraft were born in the same year. He hopes to complete the project in less than three years instead of the 10 required to build his Fairchild.

No one who knows Bill Worman will be surprised when another of his dreams comes true.

## Ryan NYP — *Spirit of St. Louis*

| | |
|---|---:|
| Engine | Wright Whirlwind J-5C |
| Power | 237 hp |
| Length | 27 ft 8 in |
| Height (3-point attitude) | 9 ft 10 in |
| Wingspan | 46 ft 0 in |
| Wing Loading | 16.5 lb/sq ft |
| Power Loading | 23.6 lb/hp |
| Maximum Takeoff Weight | 5,250 lb |
| Fuel Capacity | 450 gal |
| Rate of Climb (sea level) | Marginal |
| Normal Cruise Speed (heavy) | 75 mph |
| Normal Cruise Speed (light) | 95 mph |

# Spirit of St. Louis

## The Spirit of St. Louis is perhaps the most famous

and recognizable aircraft of all time. One approaches it with awe and reverence, even if it is a replica. The silver monoplane with the burnished cowling and spinner sits alone on a ramp at Oshkosh, Wisconsin, its nose pointed skyward as if poised for flight.

This is the Experimental Aircraft Association's second reincarnation of the *Spirit*. The first was built to recreate and celebrate the 50th anniversary of Lindbergh's Guggenheim Fund Tour of the United States (July 20 to October 23, 1927). After being flown once by Anne Morrow Lindbergh, it was put on display in EAA's AirVenture Museum.

The original *Spirit* was named by Harold Bixby, a private pilot, St. Louis banker, and one of Lindbergh's sponsors. The city of St. Louis was named for France's Louis IX, an appropriate personage after whom to name Lindbergh's aircraft. "Louis had been a crusader, a pious traveler renowned for his self-assuredness. Maintaining his faith and vision, he withstood intense physical discomfort to reach his holy destination." (From the Pulitzer Prize winning biography, *Lindbergh*, by A. Scott Berg.)

The original *Spirit* was built by Ryan Airlines in an old fish cannery in San Diego, the smell of which did not impress the visiting Lindbergh. A young worker at the factory, Douglas "Wrong Way" Corrigan, obtained trans-Atlantic fame of his own in 1938, when he flew a dilapidated Curtis Robin from New York to Dublin, Ireland. The *Spirit* was a descendent of Ryan's M-2 mail plane and was designed by Donald Hall with substantial input from Lindbergh.

Lindbergh wanted a single-engine monoplane because it "offered less of an opportunity for engine failure" and was "more efficient than a biplane."

He insisted on eliminating excess weight and drag the way a surgeon uses a scalpel to remove cancer. He even trimmed unneeded edges from his charts. Every 6 pounds saved meant another gallon of fuel he could carry. He also declined fuel gauges, preferring to keep track of consumption with his watch. And he carried neither sextant nor radio. He also saved weight by removing the carburetor heater but reinstalled it after an icing encounter between San Diego and New York.

The wheels were widely separated not only to better support his overloaded craft, but to reduce drag by placing them outside the propeller slipstream.

Construction of the *Spirit* took 60 days and cost $10,580. It made its maiden flight in San Diego on April 28, 1927, only 22 days before Lindbergh's historic departure from New York's Roosevelt Field.

Before leaving for Paris, Lindbergh had made 32 flights in the *Spirit* totaling 27.4 hours that included a transcontinental speed record of 21 hours and 21 minutes.

George Daubner, chief pilot for EAA's Volunteer Flying Program, checked me out in the replica. He explained that there are some differences between it and the original.

Lindbergh's *Spirit* was powered by a 223-hp, 9-cylinder Wright Whirlwind J-5C radial engine turning a Hamilton, ground-adjustable propeller. The replica has a 220-hp, 7-cylinder, Continental R-670 because it is more reliable and parts are more readily available. The replica also has an electrical system, avionics, and a starter.

Lindbergh's airplane had five fuel tanks, three in the wings and two in the cabin ahead of the cockpit and aft of the 80-quart oil tank. He developed this arrangement and willingly sacrificed forward visibility because he did not relish the thought of being sandwiched between the engine and a rear fuselage tank during a crash landing. He also wanted the fuselage tank on the *Spirit's* center of gravity so that trim changes and the resultant drag increases would be held to a minimum. Two independent fuel systems fed the engine. During his lengthy flight, he switched tanks hourly.

The replica has two fuel tanks with a total capacity of 106 gallons as well as two sight gauges.

Because the replica does not have fuel tanks in front of the "Lindbergh seat," there is room for a second pilot to sit in front and see through small windows that are revealed when the burnished aluminum panels are removed. This is where Daubner sat during my checkout. I sat in the rear seat and noted with dismay that I could not see through the front windows because Daubner was in the way. This made flying from the rear seat a realistic simulation of what it must have been like for Lindbergh.

Taxiing is easier than it was in the original. The replica has brakes and a fully castoring tailwheel while the original *Spirit* had a tailskid and no brakes. The airports in Lindbergh's day, however, were usually large fields that allowed landing in any direction thus eliminating the need for crosswind operations. Taxiing requires S-turning and the neck of a giraffe to see where one is going.

Lindbergh's takeoff from the muddy, rain-soaked runway at Roosevelt Field was extremely hazardous and was all the more challenging because he had increased the pitch angle of the ground-adjustable Hamilton propeller to improve cruise performance, which prolonged the takeoff roll. It was like using a cruise prop instead of a climb prop.

Lightly loaded, the tail comes up early in the roll, and I am relieved that taking off in the *Spirit* using only peripheral vision is not difficult.

Although optimum climb and glide speeds were never determined for either the original or the replica, Daubner advised that 70-75 mph "seems to work pretty well."

The only way to see ahead in flight is to S-turn while peering out a side window or to boot a rudder pedal. The wing has no dihedral and is so flat that the airplane skids easily toward one side or the other. Lindbergh did not have to worry much about a midair collision in 1927, especially over the Atlantic. Frank Tallman flew a replica for the movie, *The Spirit of St. Louis*, and said that the airplane "is as blind as a nuclear sub under a polar icepack."

The original *Spirit* was equipped with a periscope that extended from the left side of the fuselage through which Lindbergh could see ahead during flight but probably would have been difficult to use during takeoff or landing.

There is an aura about this airplane. You cannot fly it without drifting into thoughts of yesteryear and trying to imagine what it was like to occupy that seat over the Atlantic in 1927. It is like flying through the pages of history.

When Lindbergh began tracking along the 3,610-sm, great-circle route to Paris, he was only 25 years old and had logged fewer than 1,800 hours (including 32 flights in the Spirit).

"A slim, tall, bashful, smiling American boy is somewhere over the middle of the Atlantic Ocean, where no lone human being has ever before ventured." (Will Rogers)

"Modern man realized that nobody had ever subjected himself to so extreme a test of human courage and capability." (Scott Berg)

"A certain amount of danger is essential to the quality of life." (Lindbergh)

Although the front seat of the replica is equipped with standard instrumentation, Lindbergh flew instruments using only a turn indicator, a bubble-type inclinometer, an airspeed indicator, and an altimeter mounted on a plywood panel.

He also had an earth-inductor compass, a telltale sign of which are small, anemometer-like cups spinning about a mast atop the rear fuselage.

The *Spirit* was given a huge wing, 46 feet of span and 7 of chord, to lift the 450-gallon fuel load. This was 10 feet longer than the M-2's wing and increased roll damping dramatically. "The wing drops slowly. The ailerons on the *Spirit* aren't as [effective] as those on the standard Ryan. Hall made them short to avoid overstressing the wing under full-load conditions. It's good enough for a long-range airplane." (Lindbergh)

*The author and actor James Stewart (right) in front of one of the replicas built for the motion picture,* **The Spirit of St. Louis,** *(1955).*

The ailerons are heavy, relatively unresponsive, and create considerable adverse yaw. It helps to have a well-developed forearm and responsive feet.

The control stick is as long as a baseball bat, too tall, I thought, and I tended to grip it low. As my first flight wore on, however, I noticed that my right hand kept inching higher on the stick to gain the leverage needed to combat large control forces.

Considering the larger wing, Hall was dissatisfied with the stability that the small tail surfaces of the M-2 would provide. Larger surfaces would improve stability but increase drag and production time. Lindbergh opted to retain the smaller tail surfaces.

"It's clear that stability is not a strong point with the *Spirit*, but we didn't design the plane for stability. We decided to use the standard tail surfaces to...gain... range." (Lindbergh)

Lindbergh was a master of understatement. The aircraft is dynamically and statically unstable. "It is one of the worst flying airplanes I've ever flown," says Robert "Hoot" Gibson, former space shuttle commander. "It's a challenge to keep the airplane going straight and make it do what you want."

"The *Spirit* is too unstable to fly well on instruments. It is high-strung, and balanced on a pinpoint. If I relax pressure on stick or rudder for an instant, the nose veers off course." (Lindbergh)

You can say that again. After entering a normal turn and neutralizing the controls, you soon notice that although the airplane remains banked, the nose suddenly stops moving across the horizon, and you are in a perfect sideslip.

The rudder and elevator are easier to operate but require constant attention to keep the aircraft on an even keel. The nose hunts left and right, and porpoises like a whale. It is a high-workload airplane that never allows you to relax.

Lindbergh was "thankful we didn't make the *Spirit* stable. The very instability which makes it difficult to fly blind or hold an accurate course at night now guards me against excessive errors." He credits the instability with keeping him awake and alive.

You can fly it with fingertips in smooth air, but the slightest zephyr causes the Spirit to take off on its own. Get a grip, because you'll need it. The *Spirit* has a mind of its own and is a handful.

Despite its idiosyncrasies and rude manners, one nevertheless discovers a growing affection and appreciation for the machine.

Lindbergh carried a driftmeter that could be placed into brackets on one window to determine wind drift at sunrise and mid-ocean. But he never used it because of instability and fatigue. "So simple. So impossible. Why did I ever think I could fly the *Spirit* straight while I lean out to look into the eyepiece of a drift indicator?" (Lindbergh)

Using windows that were stored behind him would have smoothed airflow along the fuselage, but he never used them either. "They'd interfere with the crystal clarity of communion with water, land, and sky [and] insulate me from a strength I'll need before my flight is done, and which, for some reason, cannot penetrate their thin transparency. Fumes drift through the fuselage, and drift away." (Lindbergh)

The wicker porch seat is hard and uncomfortable. Lindbergh used an air cushion. "It's been expanding as I climb to altitude. I open the valve for a few seconds, to lower my position and make sure the fabric won't burst." (Lindbergh)

The rudder pedals are too close and prevent me from stretching my legs. It must have been worse for Lindbergh, who was taller.

It becomes increasingly difficult for me to comprehend how Lindbergh could take off after being awake for 24 hours and then fly this airplane into the unknown for 33-1/2 hours.

The huge wing was designed to carry such a heavy load that it was difficult to stall in our lightly loaded configuration. When the nose does drop slowly at 35 mph, it takes only the slightest release of back pressure to recover.

The only way to keep the runway in sight during a landing approach is to make a slipping turn from base to final and hold the slip until just before touchdown. In the meantime, your head is craned to one side and into the relative wind blowing through the open side window. During the flare for either a three-point or wheel landing, there is only limited peripheral vision upon which to rely.

"I slip down on the final glide, nose high and left wing low — that gives me perfect forward vision. Then I straighten out just before my wheels touch." (Lindbergh)

Wheel landings seem easier than full-stall landings, but you don't always know what type of landing you are going to make until it happens. Daubner says that "you have to be willing to take what you get."

The wheels and fuselage rumble on rollout, and you pray that nothing gets in your way because there is no way that you are going to see and avoid it.

"He took off as an unknown boy from rural Minnesota and landed 33-1/2 hours later [6-1/2 hours less than Lindbergh had anticipated] as the most famous man on Earth and sent the world into an unprecedented frenzy." (National Geographic)

"The *Spirit of St. Louis* is a wonderful plane. It's like a living creature, gliding

*A wicker chair offered Lindbergh little creature comfort during his 33½-hour flight to Paris.*

along smoothly, happily, as though a successful flight means as much to it as to me, as though we shared our experiences together, each feeling beauty, life, and death as keenly, each dependent on the other's loyalty. We have made this flight across the ocean, not I or it." (Lindbergh)

Although a single-place airplane, Lindbergh managed 21 passenger flights that included carrying Henry Ford and his mother, Evangeline Lindbergh. Its final and 174th flight was made on April 4, 1928 after accumulating 489 hours of flight time.

The *Spirit of St. Louis* was donated to the Smithsonian Institution in 1928 and has been on permanent display ever since (now in the National Air and Space Museum).

In her book, *Slim*, by Slim Keith, wife of motion picture producer, Leland Hayward, Keith observed Lindbergh sitting in the cockpit of the *Spirit* in the Smithsonian prior to filming Hayward's movie, *The Spirit of St. Louis*. "Lindbergh had noticed that the primer was out of place, said to himself that 'it shouldn't be this way,' and pushed the knob in with a noticeably tender caress of a gesture."

Paraphrasing aviation writer Jack Cox, "It is difficult for us, 75 years and a cultural lifetime removed from the event, to fathom the impact of Lindbergh's flight. Nothing else in our lifetime, including the first trip to the moon, so profoundly impressed the world. Nothing so dramatically and so instantly changed the course of history."

Lunar astronauts also are in awe of what Lindbergh accomplished. Neil Armstrong said that "[he] flew through miserable weather and stretched the science and art of navigation to find Le Bourget. We could see our destination throughout our entire voyage."

Similar to questions posed to astronauts, England's King George asked in 1927, "Now tell me, Captain Lindbergh. There is one thing I long to know. How did you pee?"

Courtesy Jawed Karim

## Lincoln PT-K

| | |
|---|---:|
| Engine | Kinner K-5 radial |
| Power | 100 hp |
| Length | 25 ft 7 in |
| Height (3-point attitude) | 9 ft 3 in |
| Wingspan | 32 ft 3 in |
| Wing Loading | 5.9 lb/sq ft |
| Power Loading | 17.67 lb/hp |
| Maximum Takeoff Weight | 1,767 lb |
| Fuel Capacity | 28.5 gal |
| Rate of Climb (sea level) | 800 fpm |
| Normal Cruise Speed | 85 mph |
| Stall Speed | 45 mph |

# The Lincoln PT-K

## During the Roaring Twenties, a significant number

of small manufacturers appeared to build aircraft designed to replace the aging trainers left over from the Great War. One of these was the Lincoln Aircraft Company of Lincoln, Nebraska. The company was founded by Ray Page and produced a popular line of aircraft. One was the Lincoln PT-K, so called because it is a Page Trainer with a Kinner engine. (The previous model, the PT, was equipped with a Curtiss OX-5 engine.)

John W. Cook was one of many who received their aerial baptism in a PT-K. He made his first solo in one at Blythe, California before World War II and eventually became a pilot for TWA. He is remembered, along with his friend, Robert Timm, for having established in 1958 and 1959 an endurance record of 64 days, 22 hours, and 19 minutes in a Cessna 172. (Ground-to-air refueling was accomplished by handing a fuel hose to one of the pilots as the pair flew low and slow over a pickup truck.)

As he neared retirement, Captain Cook's sense of nostalgia inspired him to locate and purchase the rag, tube, and wood PT-K in which he had first taken to sky.

Cook located the aircraft but was dismayed at what he found. The PT-K was a basket case, a beleaguered machine that would never again fly unless someone was willing to undertake a complete restoration. Cook accepted the challenge and dedicated himself to resuscitating the biplane. Unfortunately, he died long before the project had been completed.

In the meantime, Dr. Rick Martin, a 2,000-hour private pilot and emergency-room physician at the St. Rose Dominican Hospitals in Henderson, Nevada, had an itch to rebuild an airplane even though he had never done that before. He wanted to learn what makes an airplane tick from the inside out. Martin was inspired by his close friend, Joe Maridon, who had rebuilt a Waco UPF-7 that he uses to sell biplane rides over Las Vegas.

Maridon had learned from an advertising flier that John Cook's widow wanted to sell her husband's Lincoln PT-K. It was not long before he and Martin were in the Cook garage studying a project that obviously had a long way to go and would require a great deal of work. But Martin liked the idea of buying "a piece of history that could be brought to life while learning about airplane building in the process."

It took Martin 4 years to rebuild his PT-K, and he is quick to acknowledge that he had a great deal of help in the process. He is particularly grateful to Al Ball, Dwight Baumberger, Ron Kodimer, Joe and Betty Maridon, Norm Mayer, John McIntyre, Paul Seright, and Dawn Wagenknecht for sharing their labor and expertise.

The airplane is emblazoned in its original colors and many believe that it is better than when new in 1930. It would have made Captain Cook proud.

The 1930 Lincoln PT-K originally sold for $3,865, a princely price in those days. Although Martin paid $22,500 for the project, he has no idea what the airplane is worth today, although he has turned down an offer of $200,000.

The PT-K has a long, thin fuselage, not unlike earlier trainers such as the Curtiss JN-4D Jenny. Its most distinctive visual features are the unusual shape of its vertical stabilizer and its wire-spoke wheels. (The Goodrich tires are borrowed from a Model A Ford.)

Anyone about to fly a PT-K should wear overalls and gloves because of the preflight servicing required. The rocker arms of the 100-hp, 5-cylinder, Kinner K-5 radial engine must be greased before every flight, and the wheel bearings must be greased before every other flight.

One then switches from a grease gun to a can of Marvel Mystery Oil, which must be added to the fuel and engine oil. It also must be squirted liberally into the valve guides before every flight.

The single, 28.5-gallon fuel tank is between the engine and the front cockpit. The PT-K has a maximum-allowable gross weight of 1,767 pounds, an empty weight of 1,200 pounds, and a useful load of 567 pounds. A small baggage area behind the rear seat is limited to 50 pounds, but this must be reduced by the weight of any parachutes being worn.

The front of the "all-weather" cowling has 5 teardrop shaped openings, one in front of each cylinder. The original cowling was equipped with cockpit-controlled shutters that restricted airflow through the openings to keep the engine warm on cold days. Martin has yet to build the shutters, but he is not in a hurry given the desert climate of southern Nevada.

A critical preflight item is thrusting a hand through an access door on the left side of the cowling and opening a valve in the oil line leading from the oil tank to the engine. Oil supply usually is turned off after each flight to prevent oil drainage from the tank into the lower cylinders.

Also, engine oil must be warm before engine start, which means that it must be preheated prior to starting in cold weather.

After stepping onto the lower wing, lowering myself through the 24-by-42 inch cockpit entrance, and settling into the bucket seat, I was delighted to discover that the cockpit is comfortable and roomy even for someone of my sizeable proportions.

Martin's PT-K is equipped with a Bloxham Safety Stick to resolve any problem caused by a student freezing on the controls. The instructor pulls a cable that disconnects the student's control stick from the flight-control system and leaves the stick free and harmless in the student's hand. "Surprise!" There have been times when I would love to have had a Bloxham Safety Wheel, had there been such a thing.

According to aviation historian Joseph P. Juptner, an instructor accomplished the same result during the days of the Jenny by conking the student on the head with a fire extinguisher, but this was frowned upon and considered primitive.

It was uncertain when the PT-K was originally built whether the aviation industry would decide that the pilot should operate the control stick with his right hand and the throttle with his left, or vice versa. So that it could be flown either way, the PT-K was equipped with two throttles in each cockpit, one on the right and one on the left. That's right; the PT-K has four interconnected throttles. Take your pick. Also, the throttles are not gripped conventionally. That is, they are not held with an overhand (palm down) grip. The throttles extend down from their pivot points and are operated with an underhand grip (palm up). This initially feels awkward, but adaptation comes quickly and easily.

The PT-K is equipped with neither a starter nor an electrical system, so the fixed-pitch propeller must be turned by hand. The first step requires turning it a few times to ensure that oil has not leaked into the bottom cylinders and formed a hydraulic lock.

The engine is then primed 4-6 times, and the throttle is pumped 2-4 times or until fuel drips from the carburetor. Although this is undesirable with modern engines, such a "wet start" is standard for the Kinner K-5. After applying pressure to the mechanical heel brakes (rear cockpit only), the pilot is ready to start.

The wood propeller is flicked easily and the engine starts with a delightful crackling sound that seems to echo from the past. This is when the pilot finds out if he has been sufficiently liberal about oiling the valve guides. Unless the windshields become coated with oil and grease after engine start, the pilot did not use enough of the stuff. This is not a good time to stick one's head out of the cockpit and into the propwash (or should I say, oil wash?).

CIGAR (controls, instruments, gasoline, attitude, and runup) serves as a thorough checklist because there is nothing else to do. You never set the altimeter because there is no way to correct a non-sensitive altimeter. (The single hand of the altimeter makes one revolution every 10,000 feet and obviously is not very accurate.)

A sufficiently high oil temperature is critical for takeoff. The engine is not considered warm or safe enough for takeoff unless a full-power, static runup can be performed without oil pressure exceeding 180 psi. If it appears that oil pressure will exceed this value before reaching full power, retard the throttle and wait for the oil to warm further. (Engine oil is changed every 10 hours.)

There is nothing remarkable about taking off in a PT-K as long as one is attentive to directional control. With a 10-mph headwind, the aircraft reportedly can lift off in 6 seconds after a roll of only 100 feet. Climb performance, though, is anemic. One reason that the airplane had little inclination to ascend during my checkout was an ambient temperature of 100 degrees F (a density altitude at the North Las Vegas Airport of 5,270 feet). It was impossible to reach pattern altitude within the confines of the traffic pattern.

The ailerons (two on each wing) are heavy and respond poorly. Sealing the unusually large aileron gaps probably would enhance roll rate and give the PT-K's climb rate a kick in the rudder.

The airplane is not easy to fly; you have to work at it. Particularly disconcerting is that the PT-K approaches being neutrally stable about all axes. If a wing goes down, the nose yaws, or the nose dips, the condition is likely to persist until corrective action is taken.

But one should not complain about the PT-K's handling qualities. According to Maridon, "Designers [of that era] were more concerned that the airplane would actually fly than *how* it would fly."

The good news is that pitch trim (an adjustable horizontal stabilizer) is seldom needed because the nose stays wherever it is put irrespective of airspeed and power variations.

With a wing area of 297 square feet and a light wing loading of only 5.9 pounds per square foot, the airplane responds to every gust and can be a handful in turbulence.

The two rocker-arm push rods behind each cylinder are exposed and can be seen moving rapidly up and down, each one opposite to the other. It is like watching a pair of sewing machines working in opposition. But you don't need to observe the push rods to know that the engine is running.

Although the 372-cubic-inch engine makes a pleasant sound reminiscent of a bygone era, it makes too much. The airplane is very noisy and not because of its blistering airspeed. A short exhaust stack atop each cylinder seems specifically designed to amplify the noise and aim it directly at the pilots. In later years, radial engines were equipped with collector rings that gathered exhaust from all cylinders and directed it beneath the aircraft (and, thankfully, away from the pilots).

The engine in Martin's PT-K is at least as old as the airplane, and Kinner expert, Al Ball, says that it probably belongs more in a museum than bolted onto the business end of an airplane. There is no published TBO for the engine, but Ball says that a Kinner K-5 should get about 500 hours between overhauls.

There also is no pilot's operating handbook for the PT-K and performance information published in some books appears to be more rumor than reality. At the maximum-allowable power setting of 1,810 rpm, the airplane is supposed to step out at 104 mph (not!), and normal cruise at 1,500 rpm is 85 mph. There is no redline airspeed shown in the single page of operating limitations, perhaps because the aircraft could never reach it.

The PT-K reportedly can do a loop from straight and level flight, but this seems doubtful.

The aircraft is mild mannered during a power-off stall and simply enters a mushing descent at 45 mph. Based on this, 60 mph seems a reasonable airspeed for climb, glide, and approach. A pilot does not have to worry about the effects of excess speed on final approach because the airplane has built-in speed brakes: its own drag. Pull the power back and it decelerates quickly.

Although wheel landings are relatively easy, a 3-point landing is not. This might be because Martin replaced the short tailskid with a large Scott 3200 tailwheel that necessitates touching down in a relatively flat attitude, which almost assures a bounce. Once on the ground, be prepared to work the rudder pedals with vigor. The PT-K seems to have an aversion to rolling straight.

Martin has only 20 hours in taildraggers (some in the PT-K) and has yet to solo his airplane. He wanted to fly it to the EAA AirVenture Fly-In Convention in Oshkosh this year because the airplane is likely an award winner. But given the aircraft's limited performance, Martin has been discouraged from doing so because of the difficulty he would have crossing the Continental Divide and the incessant work required to keep the airplane on an even keel (especially in turbulence).

Martin's Lincoln is nevertheless a beautiful example of a pioneering aircraft, and its capabilities should be considered in context. Although the PT-K was manufactured in 1930, it is based on a 1921 design that had languished for the better part of a decade. It was designed only 18 years after Kitty Hawk and 3 years after the end of World War I, and it gives us a wonderful opportunity to fly into the yellowing pages of history and learn what it was like to have been a pilot of that era.

## Aeronca 7AC Champion

| | |
|---|---|
| Engine | Continental A-65-8 |
| Power | 65 hp |
| Length | 21 ft 6 in |
| Height (3-point attitude) | 7 ft 0 in |
| Wingspan | 35 ft 2 in |
| Wing Loading | 7.2 lb/sq ft |
| Power Loading | 18.8 lb/hp |
| Maximum Takeoff Weight | 1,220 lb |
| Fuel Capacity (usable) | 13 gal |
| Rate of Climb (sea level) | 500 fpm |
| Normal Cruise Speed | 85 mph |
| Stall Speed | 38 mph |

# Aeronca 7AC Champion

We were flying low and in formation over the coastal

hills east of Livermore, California, maneuvering for a camera in the warm light of a low sun.

Lengthening shadows began to fill the valleys and hide the few flat spots that could be used for an emergency landing. I was not thrilled about having to rely on an antique engine at such a time. My grip on the control stick tightened slightly and I began to consider my options in case of power loss.

But then a strange thing happened. It was as if the airplane was trying to tell me something. I could almost hear the words. "When I taught you to fly so very long ago, I endured and forgave your ham-fisted blundering. It seemed as though you were trying to break both my back and my spirit. But I never let you down. Not once. I protected you from yourself more times than I can remember. Shame on you for thinking that I might betray you now."

The words were right. I knew that I could trust this airplane without reservation. I felt secure and comfortable as the bond between us renewed. My grip on the stick relaxed and I needed only my fingertips to lead the Champ through an aerial ballet in the disappearing rays of sunlight.

During the summer of 1992, I realized that in a few months I would have been flying for 40 years. I took my first lesson at Clover Field (now called Santa Monica Airport) at the age of 14 in an Aeronca 7AC Champion on November 7, 1952.

Not only did I receive my aerial baptism in N81881 but it also was the airplane that I soloed and earned my private, commercial and flight instructor certificates. But I learned the most about flying when the Champ and I taught others to fly.

I wondered if N81881 was still flying. Or had this number been passed unceremoniously to some other aircraft? Surely, I thought, the old trainer had yielded to the ravages of time. But a search of FAA records showed that the Champ had survived and was registered to James Bottorff of Livermore, California.

I contacted Bottorff to see if I could arrange to once again fly what undoubtedly has been the most meaningful and memorable aircraft of my career. What a wonderful way that would be to celebrate my fortieth anniversary aloft. To my delight, Bottorff agreed to let me fly his Champ. He even seemed to sense and share my excitement.

A hopeless romantic, I suffered some anxiety as I approached the Champ. It was as though I were about to rendezvous with my first love, fearing I would discover that the relationship was not as wondrous as the memories had made it seem.

N81881 was parked in front of Bottorff's hangar. Its door was open, leaning against the aft wing strut, as if inviting me to step in for a nostalgic rendezvous with the past. The Champ had aged more gracefully than I had. It had four changes of fabric, at least as many paint jobs and plenty of affectionate care.

The aircraft had undergone a few changes since the last time I flew it. These included removal of the wind-driven generator and the low-frequency radio, which had the broadcast range of a megaphone. These were replaced with a VHF transceiver powered by a rechargeable, battery pack. Also added were wheel pants, a larger tailwheel, and an increase from 65 to 75 horsepower.

Bottorff was an architect who worked at the Lawrence Livermore National Laboratory. He had liked the idea of an affordable, fabric-covered taildragger with a control stick instead of a wheel. "It seems more like real flying," he said. Bottorff bought N81881 in May, 1985.

He told me that one of the Champ's previous owners was Doren Bean, who also had kept the aircraft at Livermore. In 1980 and while still owner of the Champ, Bean borrowed a Pitts S-1 from his good friend, Jeff Chambliss. During his second flight in the Pitts, Bean had an accident and was killed.

During the subsequent investigation, the FAA determined that Bean did not have a pilot's certificate. The San Joaquin County Sheriff's Department discovered also that Bean had some aliases. One of these was D. B. Cooper. Doren Bean, therefore, might have been the world's first skyjacker (who bailed out of a Northwest Orient Boeing 727 in 1971 with a $200,000 ransom). During a telephone interview, Chambliss told me that Bean had frequently mentioned his exploits as a skydiver, and this explained why many of the locals at Livermore were convinced that the infamous skyjacker played a minor role in the history of N81881.

The squatty, pug-nosed Aeronca Champ is neither glamorous nor distinctive. Its features are almost nondescript and resemble the typical, rubber-band-powered model airplane found in hobby shops. Nor does it go very fast. Aeronca pilots must be content to match the pace of freeway traffic. But the Champ's leisurely stride is a refreshing escape from the frenetic pace of modern life.

Climbing aboard a Champ requires the agility of a contortionist but once inside, the accommodations are comfortable.

But my mother, who was one of my first passengers, did not consider the Champ very comfortable. As I sat in N81881 at Livermore almost 40 years later, I could still hear her scream reverberating throughout the fabric-covered hull. "Stop tilting the airplane," she shrieked. I continued around the traffic pattern using the shallowest possible bank angle, but she would never again fly with me in a light airplane.

The instrument panel is Spartan, and few Champs are equipped with more than is required. The fuel gauge atop the glare shield is the same design that was used in the Model A Ford and occasionally allows fuel to leak into the cockpit. The solution is to replace the indicator with a floating cork-and-wire gauge.

That fuel gauge almost ended my flying career before it had begun. The smell of leaking fuel from the 13-gallon tank made me so airsick that I almost quit after my third lesson.

The Champ can be flown solo from the front or rear seat. Instructors, however, prefer the student in front where he can see the instruments and get the best view of the outside world. The rear perch is the domain of the instructor. From there, he can bop an errant student on the noggin with a rolled-up chart.

I used to take advantage of the rear seat while instructing to sneak short naps on cross-country flights. After all, how far astray could a student get in 15 minutes at 74 knots?

According to a bulletin issued by the Aeronca Owners Club, "cross-country flight in a Champ is slow but possible." If a Champ pilot becomes impatient when flying into a headwind, he simply turns around and heads the other way. It is understood that where we go is not as important as the fun we have in getting there. Champ pilots also become topographical experts. This is because the terrain beneath our wings moves so slowly that we have time to study what other pilots see only as a blur.

When the 7AC is flown solo from the front, 40 pounds of baggage may be carried in the canvas catch-all behind the rear seat. If the rear seat is occupied, only 20 pounds is allowed.

Starting the 65-hp Continental engine is easy as long as someone is available to hold the brakes while the prop is turned by hand (a device known as an Armstrong starter). The engine has no provision for an electrical starter, which is just as well. Most Champs do not have an electrical system either.

The on-off fuel valve, carburetor-heat knob and magneto switches are in a recessed panel on the left cabin sidewall below the window and between the tandem seats. These controls are easily accessible to the rear pilot but the front pilot must crane his neck, twist his torso, and manipulate his double-jointed left arm to use them.

Most pilots accustomed only to tricycle landing gear have no difficulty taxiing a Champ. The steerable tailwheel responds nicely to rudder-pedal movement. Over-the-nose visibility is good so that S-turning to see ahead is unnecessary. The Champ, however, is an outstanding weather vane and tends to turn into the slightest breeze.

I used to win a fair amount of money betting that I could taxi a Champ into a strong wind using only the ailerons for steering. I simply took advantage of the adverse yaw effect of the ailerons, which demonstrates why most airplanes need a rudder.

While taxiing into the wind, I would move the control stick full left. The seemingly contrary little Champ would turn right; full right stick caused it to go left. Using only adverse yaw effect, I could S-turn an Aeronca the full length of a mile-long taxiway.

The Champ's large ailerons also produce considerable adverse yaw in flight and require substantial rudder application. This trainer is intolerant of sloppy flying and demands adroit stick-and-rudder coordination to keep the slip-skid ball under control.

The mechanical brake system obviously was designed by a sadist who disregarded the limited dexterity of the human ankle. Operating the two heel brakes requires resting the balls of the feet on the rudder bars. Next, the heels are brought together until cocked at 45-degree angles. The pilot then jabs at the plywood floor with his heels until they find the tiny brake pedals (which are barely larger than postage stamps). The brakes are not very effective and should be used only at low speed or when out of other ideas.

The parking brake handle is under the right side of the instrument panel but should not be used because it never works.

Immediately above that is the cabin-heat control. I learned never to pull this out completely because the heat is so highly concentrated that it would broil my right foot while the rest of me froze.

The takeoff is relatively easy for a taildragger. Cruise altitude, however, is reached in far less time than is required of more powerful aircraft. This is because Aeroncas are not flown very high. The advertised climb rate of 500 fpm is incredibly optimistic (300 fpm is more like it), but the angle of climb is surprisingly steep (because of the low forward speed).

Aloft, the Champ is as docile and forgiving as any pilot of the late forties could expect. The ailerons are heavy though and when deflected during a stall can induce an unexpected spin. Also, the Champ is slightly deficient in nose-up trim when the rear seat is empty. Otherwise, it is a delightful aerial playmate.

Aeronca never published a pilot's operating handbook for the 7AC but the pertinent number seems to get passed along from one pilot to the next: Climb and glide at 52 knots. If the airspeed indicator seems in error, which it usually is, just fly a comfortable attitude.

Steep turns at Aeronca speeds are remarkable. The Champ can pivot around a pylon in only 10 seconds when in a 60-degree bank, which is impossible in faster machines.

The Champ does not have flaps but because of large and effective control surfaces, it can be slipped from the sky more dramatically and steeply than modern airplanes being slipped with flaps extended.

Anyone who claims that flying has to be expensive has not been introduced to Aeronca economics. The Champ is inexpensive to buy and fly. A refurbished 7AC with new fabric, new paint and a low-time engine can be purchased for less than the price of a medium-priced car and sips only 3.5 gallons of fuel per hour during cruise. Depreciation? There is none. Aeroncas probably will continue to increase in value as they have for the last 20 years.

When I brought the Champ to rest at the end of our flight together, I turned off the mags and watched the wooden propeller tick to a stop as I had so many times before. Memories continued to rattle around like pennies in a drum. I closed my eyes, leaned my head back and remembered with fondness many of the students we had taught to fly, and with relief, many of the mistakes I had somehow survived.

No other airplane taught me as much or as well about flying.

No other airplane ever will.

*Two of the author's favorite airplanes, an Aeronca "Champ" for fun and a Lockheed L-1011 for work.*

# The seeds for the Aeronca 7AC Champion

were sown in 1928 when the Aeronautical Corporation of America developed the Aeronca C-2 and C-3, bathtub-shaped monoplanes. These strange-looking aircraft had little more power than a go-cart and performance to match.

Aeronca failed to produce anything noteworthy until it developed the L-3 Grasshopper liaison aircraft that served a military role during World War II.

In 1943, Ray Hermes used the L-3 as the basis for designing the Aeronca 7AC Champion. The affable Champ—known affectionately as the Airknocker—first flew in 1944, was certified on October 18, 1945, and began rolling off the Middletown, Ohio production line in 1946 with a price tag of $2,295.

In addition to the 65-hp Model 7AC, Aeronca produced the 85-hp Model 7BC and the 90-hp Model 7CC. The 7DC and 7EC also had 85- and 90-hp engines, respectively, but these were equipped with larger dorsal fins.

When production ceased in 1951, Aeronca had manufactured 20,000 aircraft. More than 10,000 of these were Champs of which 7,190 were original Model 7ACs. Almost 1,800 of them are still flying.

Aeronca also produced the Aeronca 11AC Chief, which had side-by-side seating, and the Model 15AC Sedan, which seated four, had a 145-hp Continental engine and performed like a Cessna 170.

In 1954, the newly formed Champion Aircraft Corporation of Osceola, Wisconsin, purchased the Champ's tooling and design rights and began where Aeronca left off. It reintroduced the Model 7EC as the Champion Traveller and in 1956 unveiled the 7FC Tri-Traveler, a 90-hp Champ with tricycle landing gear.

Additional, less-popular models, included the 7GCA Sky-Trac, which had three seats, the agricultural 7GCB Challenger and the 7HC DX'er, which was similar to the Sky-Trac but had tricycle gear.

Next came the unorthodox 7JC Tri-Con, a strange looking Champ with a reversed tricycle undercarriage. This consisted of a large, steerable wheel under the center of the fuselage behind the main gear. This ungainly looking aircraft was an immediate failure as was the final model, the 7KC Olympia, which was bold attempt to restyle the box-like shape of the basic Champ design.

But Champion Aircraft did not give up. In 1961, it introduced the revolutionary Lancer 402 with tandem seating and an engine for each seat. Intended as an inexpensive multi-engine trainer, the Lancer was unable to maintain altitude, any altitude, on one engine.

Perseverance paid off in 1962 when Champion Aircraft introduced an aerobatic version of Aeronca's last model, the 7EC. This beefed-up aircraft was called the Champion 7ECA Citabria and was the forerunner of Bellanca's popular Citabria, Decathlon and Scout aircraft, which were manufactured between 1970 and 1980.

In 1989, American Champion Aircraft Corporation of Rochester, Wisconsin, purchased the rights to the Bellanca taildraggers and began manufacturing the Decathlon in 1991 and the Scout a year later. The Citabria was available around the end of 1993.

Although no longer a household word in general aviation, Aeronca currently is a major manufacturer of aircraft, missile and jet-engine components. The Middletown, Ohio corporation, however, is quick to acknowledge its humble beginning in the era of rag-covered taildraggers.

## Helio Courier H250

| | |
|---|---:|
| Engine | Lycoming O-540-A1A5 |
| Power | 250 hp |
| Length | 31 ft 6 in |
| Height | 8 ft 10 in |
| Wingspan | 39 ft 0 in |
| Wing Loading | 14.7 lb/sq ft |
| Power Loading | 13.6 lb/hp |
| Maximum Takeoff Weight | 3,400 lb |
| Fuel Capacity (usable) | 60 gal |
| Rate of Climb (sea level) | 1,150 fpm |
| Normal Cruise Speed | 152 mph |
| Stall Speed | 26 mph |

# Helio Courier Mark II

*The first thing a writer learns is to start his story* with an attention-getting paragraph, something to arouse the reader's interest. Well, sports fans, how does this grab you? The Helio Courier Mark II can maintain altitude at an indicated airspeed of 28 mph while in a 43-degree nose-high attitude and be fully controllable. It can take off in 300 feet and land to a stop in 245 feet. It can do all of this and cruise at more than 160 mph.

According to John Day, an executive at WHDH-TV in Boston, "The Helio Courier seemed to hover above a spot as our reporters broadcast peak-hour traffic information to our listeners. When we needed to change locations, it got there faster and more economically than a helicopter."

The psychological warfare squadron of the Air Force had need for an aircraft with both high- and low-speed capability. The U-10 (military designation for the Helio Courier) was flown over Viet Cong concentrations in Vietnam at low speed while playing taped propaganda broadcasts over a powerful loudspeaker. The U-10 often dropped 100,000 propaganda leaflets at a time over small, hard-to-reach targets. Load discharged, the U-10 scooted away at redline speeds.

U-10s were subject to ground fire that would have been fatal to a helicopter. But the Helio Couriers were quickly repaired with simple patchwork and returned to their jobs.

In Vietnam, the Helio Courier was affectionately and colloquially known as the "Litter Bug."

If you have a spare acre of unused land in your backyard, you can have your very own "Helio-Port," as did Alan Bemis of Concord, Massachusetts. Bemis used his 425 by 100-foot strip for more than 10 years to cut down on the portal-to-portal time between his home and various destinations, thus eliminating the frustrating, time-consuming, and often dangerous drive to and from the airport.

For many years, the Helio Courier was the only STOL (short takeoff and landing) aircraft manufactured in the United States. It was designed to be an STOL airplane from the wheels up by Lynn Bollinger, Professor of Aviation Research at Harvard University, and Professor Otto Koppen, who taught aeronautical engineering at the Massachusetts Institute of Technology. These men shared belief in the need for a super-safe aircraft capable of operating into and out of short fields yet having the speed, range, and economy of conventional single-engine aircraft.

After intensive study and research, the Bollinger-Koppen team produced its first Helio. What was to be only a taxi test at the Canton Airport in Massachusetts in April, 1949, resulted in the Helio Courier's maiden flight. Modifications and refinements were made to the prototype, which eventually was certificated in 1954 and offered for sale a year later.

Approximately 500 aircraft rolled off the production line in Pittsburgh, Kansas.

At first glance, the Helio gives the appearance of a cumbersome airplane, one that might be underpowered, but this is an illusion. The fuselage, long and lean, is well mated to its 250-hp Lycoming engine. The wings are fully-cantilevered (no struts), which contributes to the cleanliness of the design.

Curiously, the wing was designed for low-drag, high-speed flight, certainly not the crawling approach speeds that helped to establish the Helio Courier's reputation. The airfoil is an NACA 23012, the same one that was used on the North American P-51 Mustang.

At slow speeds, however, the wing does not do much except hold the high-lift devices in place while they produce more than 60 per cent of the total lift.

The wings are equipped with automatically operated, full-span, leading-edge slats. When the aircraft is on the ground, the slats (two per wing) are extended forward and downward on the leading edges of the wings. They have the appearance of smaller wings attached to larger wings. At large angles of attack, low pressure at the leading edge of the wings holds them in this position (open). As the aircraft's angle of attack decreases after takeoff, however, the wing's center of pressure moves rearward and ram-air pressure pushes the slats closed. They are then flush with and form the leading edge of the wing.

With the slats tucked neatly away, the wing becomes extraordinarily clean.

When the Helio's speed is reduced (angle of attack increased) during the approach, the center of pressure above the wing moves forward and the slots are "sucked" open automatically. The pilot does not have to operate them. They are there when you need them and out of the way when you do not.

Photo courtesy Austin John Brown

The slats can be a cause for alarm to novice Helio pilots. During my initiation flight in N6310V, Hunter Blackwell, Helio's engineering test pilot, demonstrated a maximum-performance takeoff from Hanscom Field in Bedford, Massachusetts. The takeoff was dramatic. With about 10 knots of wind on the nose, we lifted off before reaching the runway numbers (less than 200 feet). The exceptionally steep climb is equally impressive.

Although I never saw it, I was certain that there had to have been a control in the cockpit that does to the Helio Courier what the Up button does to the express elevator in the Empire State Building. The angle of climb is staggering. No sooner had I recovered from the initial shock than Blackwell lowered the nose and began to pick up speed. Then came a quick series of loud bangs that I imagined were cracking wing spars. Aware of my anxiety, Blackwell said, "It's the slats!" I responded with a sheepish, "Oh!"

The slats do not open and close slowly; they slam shut. I do not think that I was the first to suffer a panic attack during their first experience with slat retraction in a Helio. But one quickly learns that the banging is an asset because you know that they have closed without need of a cockpit instrument. (They can be observed from the cockpit, too.)

The possibility of a slat sticking closed is remote, but the Helio was required to demonstrate during certification that it could be flown safely with both slats open on one wing and taped shut on the other. There were no controllability problems. Some low-speed potential is lost and the approach must be made at a relatively high speed, about 60 mph. Normal short-field approaches are made at less than 50 mph.

There is nothing new about the Helio's Handley-Page slats. They were designed in 1923 and have been used to lower landing speeds on the Messerschmitt ME-109, the North American F-86 Sabre, the F-100, and a host of other aircraft.

When the slats pop out at 50 mph, the angle of attack at which the wing stalls almost doubles. The slats are literally auxiliary wings that appear automatically when needed most.

Blackwell pointed out the ease with which a climb can be made at the optimum angle of climb airspeed. "After takeoff, allow airspeed to increase to the point where the slats begin to close. Hold precisely that airspeed. If the slats are closed, you're too fast; if they're fully open, you're climbing too slowly. At precisely the right point, the slats should be wiggling in and out."

The slotted wing flaps extend over 66 percent of the trailing edge, contributing greatly to the Helio's low-speed capability. The flaps are lowered to their maximum of 40 degrees by turning a large crank on the cockpit ceiling between the pilots' seats. At first, this cranking seems a nuisance. But there is a good reason for everything in the Helio, and the flap crank is no exception.

Blackwell explained, "Suppose you're skimming over a dense jungle at 50 mph indicated, preparing to land in a 300-foot clearing. If the flaps were controlled by an electric switch or a Johnson bar, there would always be the possibility of inadvertent flap retraction. During this type of approach, flap retraction and the resultant loss of lift could be catastrophic."

The elevator trim tab is operated by a smaller handle, concentric with the flap crank. Trim changes are made in the same manner as on many of the older single-engine Piper aircraft.

Because the flaps occupy so much of the trailing edge, there is little room for long ailerons. Instead, the ailerons are quite wide (large chord) and resemble squares rather than the customary narrow rectangles typical of other aircraft.

In most aircraft, the use of right or left aileron to begin a roll results in adverse yaw that requires the use of coordinating rudder. But adverse yaw on the Helio Courier is almost non-existent because of its Frise ailerons.

When such an aileron is deflected upward, the lower leading edge (lip) of the aileron moves downward into the airflow beneath the wing. The drag created by this lip extending into the relative wind counters the additional drag of the opposite, downward-deflected aileron. This effect, called "proverse yaw," eliminates most of the need for rudder input during turn entry and recovery.

It seems strange to see fabric-covered ailerons on such a sturdy and otherwise all-metal aircraft, but Blackwell explained, "If the aileron were made of aluminum, it would be off balance. Since most of the wide aileron is behind the hinge point, lead weights would have to be added to fill the ailerons' leading edges.

"The addition of such dead weight simply isn't justified."

The final stroke of low-speed genius incorporated in the Helio wing are 4 "interceptors," two of which are on the top of each wing at the point of maximum camber and behind the outboard slats. The interceptors consist of curved blades that operate in conjunction with the ailerons and are like small spoilers. With the control wheel neutralized, the interceptors are recessed within the wings. If left aileron is applied, for example, the interceptors above the left wing rise into the airstream and kill some of that wing's lift (just as small spoilers would do). The result is enhanced roll control and high roll rates at minimum flying speeds.

The interceptors are recessed half an inch below the surface of the wing so that they do not extend above the upper wing surface and have no effect during normal, relatively minor aileron operation in cruise flight.

Now step away from the Helio and take a cold, hard look at this machine. You will notice that the main landing gear is located exceptionally far forward. It is actually attached to the engine firewall and for good reason. So much of the weight of the aircraft is located behind the main gear that even when flown at the maximum-allowable forward center of gravity, the Helio can be landed with the brakes locked without nosing over, an interesting way to really make a short-field landing. The landing gear is tough and resilient, too. The Helio can be flown in and out of freshly bulldozed fields without a whimper.

The reason for such unusually long landing gear legs is to allow ample space between the large-diameter propeller and a field full of destructive rocks and pebbles.

Because so much aircraft weight is behind the main landing gear, the Helio is slightly more prone to ground loops than other taildraggers. Using the cockpit-controlled tailwheel lock is recommended during takeoff and landing until experienced in the airplane.

Photo courtesy Austin John Brown

The Helio does not have a conventional horizontal stabilizer. It has instead a stabilator or "flying tail," the first American airplane to have this feature.

There are 2 doors for climbing into the Helio, and inside are 6 roomy seats, a cavernous interior that can hold a ton of cargo with a full load of fuel. The instrument panel is one of the largest you will find in a single-engine airplane.

The Helio was built employing the concept that accidents are bound to happen because of the hazardous duty for which the airplane was designed. This is why it was equipped with shoulder harnesses long before they became required. What cannot be seen is the crashworthiness of the seats and welded-steel tubular cocoon that protects the cabin. Each is stressed for 15 Gs of deceleration.

A Helio pilot once experienced an engine failure shortly after takeoff from a jungle clearing. He landed straight ahead and into a population of thick trees and vines that took a positive stand against the powerless aircraft. The Helio was totally demolished, but the pilot climbed down and walked away unscathed amid the excited cries of the monkeys and birds that inhabited said trees.

Attempting to stall a Helio Courier is ludicrous. It simply cannot be done, which is why the airplane does not have a stall-warning indicator.

Power off, the nose can be raised until the elevator hits the stops. The Helio will porpoise slightly and settle down at an indicated airspeed of 50 mph and a 1,000 fpm sink rate. Thanks to the interceptors, excellent lateral control can be maintained at all times, even with the control wheel held fully aft.

Do not try a full-power stall in a Helio. The nose goes up and up until the nose is pointed almost straight up. Finally, when there is insufficient power to support the aircraft, the Helio begins to slide downward tail first.

A partial-power stall with full flaps produces a buffet, but this is not from stalling. It is from downwash above the wing striking the tail.

If you feel like spinning, go ahead and try. With the control wheel held fully aft, kick full rudder in either direction. The Helio will begin to autorotate. This is technically a spin but is not quite the same because a wing has not stalled. No dive or forward movement of the yoke is required to recover. Simply crank in opposite aileron (or rudder) and the interceptors will do the work. With full right rudder, for example, applying left aileron stops the "spin" and can be used to turn in the opposite direction.

Flying a Helio Courier is an extraordinary experience. You can shoot an ILS approach at 40 mph or make a precautionary landing due to weather in almost any clearing. If you get tired of touching down on a runway and stopping by the numbers, you can land the Helio across the runway, just for a change of pace.

## Interstate Arctic S-1B2 Tern

| | |
|---|---|
| Engine | Lycoming O-320-A2B |
| Power | 150 hp |
| Length | 24 ft 3 in |
| Height | 9 ft 9 in |
| Wingspan | 36 ft 0 in |
| Wing Loading | 9.2 lb/sq ft |
| Power Loading | 11.0 lb/hp |
| Maximum Takeoff Weight | 1,650 lb |
| Fuel Capacity (usable) | 41.5 gal |
| Rate of Climb (sea level) | 800 fpm |
| Normal Cruise Speed | 110 mph |
| Stall Speed | 39 mph |

# Interstate S-1B2 Arctic Tern

## The flag of Alaska is a field of blue containing

the 7 stars of the Big Dipper, the handle of which points to an eighth star, Polaris. But according to Bill Diehl, President of Arctic Aircraft Company in Anchorage, this bright star in the northern sky is not Polaris. Instead, he says, it represents a star soaring across the Alaskan skies, the Interstate S-1B2, a modern, more powerful version of the Interstate Cadet, which also is known as the Arctic Tern.

For those unfamiliar with the Cadet, it is a member of that nostalgic family of low-powered taildraggers that taught the lessons of flight to untold thousands of pilots in the late thirties, throughout the forties, and into the early fifties. Other such aircraft include the Aeronca 7AC Champion, the Piper J-3 Cub, and the Taylorcraft BD-12.

Although the original Cadet was powered by a modest 65-hp engine, the S-lB2 has a 150-hp Lycoming O-320 engine giving the aircraft a quantum increase in performance, yet it retains the high-lift wing and NACA 23012 airfoil that gave the Cadet such remarkable slow-flight, short-field agility.

Because the emphasis today is on airplanes with nosewheels, satellite navigations systems, and speed, it might seem anachronistic for a manufacturer to enter the market with a 2-place tandem taildragger, but there seems to be a growing demand for these small, fun machines, especially in Alaska where the tailwheel is the rule rather than the exception.

Bill Diehl used to own a war-surplus L-6 liaison airplane, a 102-hp version of the Interstate Cadet that was developed for the Army Air Force at the outbreak of World War II. Diehl felt that with certain improvements, the L-6 could become a successful, lightweight bush plane capable of carrying respectable loads into and out of Alaska's small, isolated bush strips that sometimes are little more than rough clearings.

He also believed that the L-6 could be redesigned as a fully aerobatic trainer and fill a variety of roles.

When Diehl learned that the manufacturing rights to the Interstate could be purchased from the Call Aircraft Company in Wyoming, he pursued his ambition with typical Alaskan perseverance. The rights to the Interstate became his in 1969. From an acorn of an idea, an oak tree began to grow. A redesigned, newly-manufactured Interstate made its maiden flight only a year later.

Changes made to the L-6 design included boosting the maximum-allowable gross weight, adding horsepower, increasing structural integrity, and expanding wing and flap area. Diehl also added Horner-type fiberglass wingtips, reduced drag, replaced the 3-piece windshield with wrap-around Plexiglas, redesigned the cowling, used stronger, more contemporary components, and generally gave the aircraft a major facelift and some streamlining.

Anchorage might seem an improbable place to manufacture airplanes, but not when you consider that this is where the Arctic Tern has the greatest potential for success. Also, Diehl contends that since Alaska is so aviation oriented—20 percent of the population is licensed to fly—he has a labor pool already familiar with airplanes. He admits, however, that shipping parts and raw material to Alaska increases manufacturing costs.

"Big Diehl," as he is called by his friends, introduced me to N49128, the second production Interstate. At first blush, it looks like every other taildragger of the pre-war era. It is almost nondescript except for the distinctive shape of the vertical fin.

A close inspection, however, reveals unusual features that may qualify the S-1B2 as the easiest and least expensive aircraft in its class to maintain, important not only to the bush pilot who occasionally needs to make emergency repairs in the field but to any pilot who has an aversion to sending monthly support payments to his local repair shop.

For example, removing either of the two 20-gallon fuel tanks from its wing takes less than 10 minutes. Simply unscrew a panel on the bottom of the wing, loosen a few bolts, and the tank drops out. In other aircraft, this is a major and costly procedure. Want to replace an instrument? Simple. Whip out a dime and twist a few fasteners at the top of the hinged instrument panel. It then plops in your lap exposing everything to which you might want access. With that same dime you can remove the entire cowling in only a minute.

Maintenance also is simplified because nothing is buried beneath floorboards or side panels. Everything, including control cables, brake cables and fuel lines, is fully exposed and easily accessible. These features might blemish the aesthetics, but this is, after all, a utility aircraft.

The wing spar is Sitka spruce. When I questioned Diehl about using a wood spar, he grinned, indicating that I must not know much about bush flying, something I candidly admit.

"Suppose," he said, "that you screw up a landing in the boondocks and slam a wing into a tree. If you bend a metal spar, it stays bent. But a resourceful pilot can field-splice a wooden spar and return to civilization."

Such is Alaskan spirit and resourcefulness. "And," he continued, "if you can't repair the wing and have to spend the night, you can sleep in the Interstate's 6-foot-long baggage compartment."

I peered and ultimately crawled into this cavernous compartment. It runs almost the entire length of the fuselage aft of the rear seat. Diehl was right. I am tall and had no difficulty stretching my frame on the plywood floor. With such a voluminous compartment, it would be easy to overload the S-1B2 and exceed the maximum-allowable aft center of gravity. The FAA insisted that a red line be painted across the floor designating the point aft of which no load may be carried in flight. I doubt, however, if the FAA would fuss if you allowed a few fishing poles to cross the red line and extend into the restricted zone.

Maximum-allowable gross weight of the aircraft is 1,900 pounds. Deducting 1,100 pounds of empty weight leaves a respectable 800-pound useful load.

Other exterior features offer further evidence that the Arctic Tern is intended for unimproved strips. The horizontal stabilizer and propeller have unusually high ground clearance for a taildragger and the large, high-flotation tires allow the airplane to be landed safely on unexplored beaches or riverbeds.

Cockpit entry requires hauling yourself in; there is nothing graceful about it, but once inside, the accommodations are comfortable. The door is a seaplane type that drops flush against the fuselage, needed by the pilot wanting to equip the Arctic Tern with floats. A conventional door is undesirable on a seaplane. It would get in the way when trying to hand-prop the engine from behind in case of a dead battery.

I would soon be flying the airplane over some of Alaska's spectacular wilderness, and Diehl handed me a bag of survival gear. In addition to other useful amenities, it contained 2 large bottles of mosquito repellent, enough to kill a caribou. If stranded in the bush without repellent, a swarm of mosquitoes could drive a man insane to the point of death.

I climbed into the front seat with a set of sectionals and an anticipation of excitement. What more could I want? I had an aerobatic bush plane without a Hobbs meter, full fuel tanks, and all of Alaska to explore.

Taxiing toward Anchorage International's Runway 31, I scanned the spartan instrument panel. Everything needed is there but there are no extras except for an electric auxiliary fuel pump. This, according to Diehl, is needed only when gravity fails, an FAA certification requirement.

Cockpit visibility is outstanding. The greenhouse design of the original L-6 liaison aircraft has been retained, resulting in large windows and a skylight that spans almost the entire cockpit roof. The rear-seat passenger does not feel as though he is sitting in a hole as he does in so many other taildraggers with tandem seats. The wide, rear bench-type seat accommodates 2 small passengers behind the pilot, but they will be cozy. At such times, the rear control stick can be easily removed to increase legroom and prevent possible control interference.

After a normal engine runup, I extended the semi-slotted Fowler flaps to the first notch by pulling on the Johnson bar located next to the left sidewall some distance forward of my knee. Some torso bending is required for this, and is no problem on the ground. In the air, however, there is a tendency to unwittingly move the control stick forward as a pilot reaches for the flap handle.

With the throttle wide open, the 82-inch propeller snarled, and by the time I thought about raising the tail, the Interstate was off the ground. Ground roll was approximately 150 feet.

Landing distances are about the same as those needed for takeoff under similar conditions, which is comforting to know when operating in and out of critically short fields. This means that a proficient pilot can get out of almost any field on which he can land. This is not true when flying most other aircraft because they typically need more distance for takeoff than for landing.

The spunky airplane climbs well, too. At the best rate-of-climb speed of 60 mph, it goes up 1,000 fpm. Best angle-of-climb speed is 48 mph.

At 2,500 feet, I headed southwest and followed the snow-patched cliffs that plunge precipitously into the icy waters of the Turnagain Arm, so called because when Captain Cook sailed up this dead-end finger of water, he was forced to "turn again."

I experimented with various power settings to find a compromise between power and noise. Like other aircraft in its class, the Interstate is not quiet.

The cabin heater could use some redesigning, too. When you pull the knob, your right shin gets scalded, but the rest of the cockpit remains cold.

At 75-percent power, the S-1B2 cruises at a true airspeed of 110 mph while burning 9 gph. This results in a no-wind range of about 450 mile plus reserve. By slowing and leaning, range can be stretched to 650 sm.

The fuel system has a unique safety feature, a reserve tank similar to that of early-model Volkswagens. The reserve tank is actually the bottom 4 gallons of the left wing tank, which holds a total of 20 gallons. The recommended fuel-management procedure is to initially use the left tank. This allows you to burn only 16 of its 20 gallons. When this runs out, switch to the right tank for an additional 20 gallons. When this is gone, you are assured that an additional 4 gallons remain at the bottom of the left tank, but it is useable only by moving the fuel-selector valve to the reserve position. By then, it is time to find a place to land.

I arrived over the gravel strip at the foot of the Portage Glacier but was in no hurry to land. The glacier is an awesome spectacle. It is a thrill to soar above this glistening blue-white river of ice as it winds and carves its way between snow-capped sentinels of towering majesty.

Downwind and abeam the approach end of the strip, I chopped power and extended the flaps to the first notch, retrimmed, and then pulled the handle to the second and final notch. At this point, the Arctic Tern seems to halt abruptly in midair, behaving somewhat like a bird trying to use its wings to back up upon discovering that it is about to fly into the cat's mouth. I added power and allowed the airspeed to settle at 50 mph, safely above the 39 mph, 1-G stall speed. A moment later the well-mannered airplane plunked onto the gravel runway tailwheel first and rolled to a stop next to a small, glacial river.

The Arctic Tern is an honest, straightforward airplane. It has no adverse flight characteristics, and can be looped and rolled with ease. The controls respond nicely during slow flight, and the aircraft is a joy to fly in all flight regimes, especially when over our 49th state.

## Goodyear Blimp "Columbia"

| | |
|---|---|
| Engines | 2 Continental IO-360-D |
| Power | 210 hp ea |
| Length | 192 ft |
| Height | 59 ft |
| Width | 50 ft |
| Envelope Surface Area | 21,600 sq ft |
| Envelope Volume | 202,700 cu ft |
| Maximum Takeoff Weight (sans helium) | 12,320 lb |
| Fuel Capacity (usable) | 294 gal |
| Rate of Climb (sea level) | 2,400 fpm |
| Normal Cruise Speed | 35 kt |
| Minimum Speed | 0 kt |

# Goodyear Blimp "Columbia"

## A Goodyear blimp is one of the most recognizable

aircraft in the world. Yet when people see one over the Super Bowl or Dodger Stadium, most believe they are looking at the Goodyear blimp, not realizing that there are four. Known technically as a Goodyear Model GZ-20, each is named after a winner of an America's Cup Yacht Race: America (based in Houston), Enterprise (Pompano Beach, Florida), Columbia (Los Angeles) and Europa (Rome, Italy). As familiar as they may be, only a few pilots really understand them.

Unlike most aircraft that have fixed or rotary wings to create lift, a blimp is lifted by the buoyancy of helium, which is 86 percent lighter than air. On a standard day at sea level, a cubic foot of this inert gas can raise slightly more than an ounce of weight. Although hydrogen is lighter and can lift more, its flammability makes it impractical.

When there is exactly enough helium in a GZ-20's 202,700-cubic-foot envelope to support the aircraft, it is said to be in equilibrium; its net or static weight is zero. The engines can be shut down, and the blimp will float at constant altitude and zero airspeed.

In lighter-than-air lingo, a blimp is statically heavy when gross weight exceeds the lifting ability of the onboard helium. For each 50 pounds of static weight, a GZ-20 sinks about 100 fpm. One way to maintain altitude when statically heavy is to dispose of ballast (consisting of 25-pound bags of shot). Also, fuel can be dumped, but only from the auxiliary tanks. The preferred way to preserve altitude, however, is to use engine power to build forward airspeed and apply up-elevator to raise the nose. Because the envelope of a GZ-20 is shaped like a symmetrical airfoil, it can develop enough dynamic lift to maintain altitude when the blimp is as much as 800 pounds heavy (maximum allowable static weight). At maximum heaviness and a cruise speed of 32 knots, an 11-degree, nose-up attitude is needed to maintain altitude.

When a blimp is light, however, it simply rises like a child's helium-filled balloon, unless forward airspeed and a nose-down attitude are used to create negative dynamic lift.

Maneuvering a blimp in flight has been compared to handling a submerged submarine; each is controlled only with power, elevators, and rudders. Turning a blimp is remarkably simple but initially disconcerting to airplane pilots accustomed to coordinating ailerons and rudder. A blimp has no ailerons. An airship pilot simply stretches a leg and shoves a rudder pedal to its forward limit. After what seems an eternal delay, rudder deflection takes hold and the ponderous nose sluggishly begins to slue along the horizon. Although maximum turn rate is little more than 3 degrees per second, the turn itself is incredibly tight because of the slow airspeed.

Because the blimp's car (or gondola) and its useful load hang beneath the envelope, a blimp has an exceptionally low center of gravity. Consequently, the airship acts like a giant pendulum. During turns, centrifugal force pulls on the car and rolls the blimp into a shallow bank, which is why ailerons are unnecessary.

During turbulence, pendulum effect keeps the blimp on an even keel. Since the envelope is so long and resilient (there is no internal framework as there is in a dirigible or rigid airship), the blimp pitches very little, even in heavy turbulence. This is why lap belts are neither required nor installed in Goodyear blimps.

The elevators are controlled by what appears to be a mammoth elevator trim wheel next to the pilot's right leg. Raising the nose requires pulling the top of the wheel rearward and vice versa. The process, though, can be a laborious, two-handed effort. Pitch control, especially in turbulence, requires almost constant hauling and tugging. Shoving the nose down feels as though you are trying to hold a basketball underwater.

Goodyear pilots usually fly their blimps in a somewhat statically heavy condition, which helps them to descend for landing. Consequently, cruising at 40-percent power and 30 knots requires a 5-degree, nose-high attitude. Raising the nose to 20 degrees without adding power produces a 400 fpm climb; pushing the nose 20 degrees below the horizon results in a 600-fpm descent. Curiously, these gross attitude changes have almost no effect on airspeed. This is because the blimp's static weight is so light (usually 100 pounds or so) and its drag so great.

The complexities of handling a blimp become obvious during climb and descent. When the aircraft gains altitude, outside air pressure naturally decreases. Consequently, the helium expands and increases pressure against the 21,600 square feet of the neoprene-coated, 2-ply Dacron envelope. If this internal pressure increase goes unchecked, the material could stretch to intolerable limits, weaken, and possibly tear. (Envelopes are replaced every 10 years, cut into large tarpaulins, and donated to schools to protect their athletic fields from rain or snow.)

The simplest way to relieve this internal-pressure increase would be to open a valve and allow some of the expanding helium to escape. But considering that a GZ-20 carries tens of thousands of dollars worth of the stuff, this would add unacceptably to the already high operating cost. Venting helium during climb would result in a more serious problem. During descent, the remaining helium would compress because of the increasing outside air pressure and become insufficient to provide needed buoyancy. Also, there might not be enough helium left to maintain the envelope's shape at lower altitudes resulting in the airship pilot's ultimate embarrassment: returning to base with a limp blimp.

To compensate for changes in altitude, temperature, and atmospheric pressure, a large, air-filled balloon, or ballonet, is installed inside and at each end of the sausage-shaped envelope. During climb, the pilot opens a pair of valves that allows air from within the ballonets to escape the envelope at the same rate that the helium expands. This allows pressure within the envelope to remain approximately constant.

When the helium compresses during descent, the ballonets are replenished with outside air and expand within the envelope to take up the slack. (Air scoops positioned behind the pusher propellers provide the air pressure necessary to keep the ballonets properly inflated.)

It is natural to presume that considerable internal pressure is required to keep the envelope inflated and shaped, but this is not so. The pressure differential between the inside and outside of the bag is normally only 0.04 to 0.07 pounds per square inch, barely enough to make your ears pop. This pressure difference is so slight that a bullet hole in the envelope would produce such a slow leak that it might not even be noticeable during a normal flight.

(During preflight inspections, the pilot removes a panel from the car's ceiling, climbs into a tight, dark compartment, and inspects the envelope's innards through a viewing lens. Pinholes of light in the envelope are leaks that need patching.)

Pressure differential must not be allowed to fall below 0.04 psi. Otherwise, the envelope will begin to lose rigidity. Excess pressure, of course, can damage the rubber-coated fabric. To prevent this, an emergency helium relief valve opens automatically at 0.10 psi. Redline envelope pressure is 0.12 psi. Airship pilots spend considerable time monitoring and controlling envelope pressure, a factor as critical to them as airspeed is to airplane pilots.

In addition to using ballonets to compensate for changes in helium volume, these air-filled compartments (each of which occupies up to 14 percent of the envelope's total volume) also are used as trim devices. Assume that the airship is slightly heavy and needs to be flown nose high to maintain altitude. The pilot could roll back the elevator wheel, but holding the necessary control pressure for very long would be fatiguing. Instead, the pilot further inflates the aft ballonet. This forces helium inside the envelope to be squeezed forward. As a result, the center of buoyancy moves forward and lifts the nose above the horizon. By reversing the procedure, a blimp can be made to fly nose low.

There is nothing exciting about a GZ-20's 30-knot cruise speed (the never-exceed speed is 43 knots), but do not underestimate its climb performance. Since almost all of a blimp's maximum-allowable gross weight of 12,320 pounds is supported by helium, very little power is devoted to producing lift. Consequently, most of the power produced by the 2 Continental IO-360D, 210-hp engines can be devoted to rocketing the blimp skyward at an impressive 2,400 fpm (maximum allowable). The GZ-20 could climb at 3,400 fpm, but the helium would expand faster than the ballonets can be deflated, risking excessive envelope pressure. Also, a 3,400-fpm climb requires more than the maximum-allowable, 30-degree pitch angle.

In theory, a blimp can be pointed straight up, but this would impose an unacceptable strain on some of the cables that support the car from the roof of the envelope. Also, the engines are not configured for inverted flight (nor are the seat-beltless passengers).

One advantage of airship operation is that it is almost impossible to violate center-of-gravity limitations. This is because the blimp is so long and the entire 3,281-pound maximum useful load is concentrated in the car at its middle. (CG range is stated in feet, not inches.)

Flying a blimp at altitude in smooth air is a joy, especially on a warm day with the side windows slid open and your elbow propped on the sill. The cabin is extraordinarily spacious, and the view hither and yon is Cineramic, except when looking up. Then there is an ominous, Dacron overcast everywhere, a constant reminder of the blimp's mammoth dimensions. (GZ-20s are 192-feet long, but consider that the Hindenburg was four times as long and 30 times as voluminous.)

Although the GZ-20 is certified and equipped for IFR flight (including radar), it usually is flown only VFR. Flying through a rain shower is often desirable, however, because this is the only way to wash a blimp. (Clinging raindrops add 300 pounds to the static weight.) The U.S. Navy once speculated that the undulating bag of a blimp would not collect structural ice. But the Navy was wrong. Goodyear's blimp America, flying between Dallas and Houston, once picked up an estimated ton of ice. (A safe but severely overweight landing was made at Houston, even though the blimp came to rest with the nose burrowing into the ground. The ice melted at the warmer ground temperature.)

Wind poses more frequent but less serious problems. Because a blimp flies so slowly, a 20-knot headwind can be catastrophic, reducing cruise speed from 30 to 10 knots and normal range from 396 to 132 nautical miles. (With the auxiliary tanks full, a GZ-20 carries 294 usable gallons and has a still-air range of 850 nm.) This explains why airship pilots, like glider pilots, usually fly only upwind of an airport during local flights. Otherwise they might not be able to return should the wind pick up. Endurance, of course, is not affected by wind. By shutting down one engine and operating the other at 3 gph, a Goodyear blimp can remain aloft for more than 4 days.

Although the propellers cannot be feathered, the drag created by windmilling blades at such slow speed is inconsequential. Also, the engines are mounted so close to the aircraft centerline that no yaw results from shutting one down.

A double engine failure has more ominous consequences. The blimp suddenly becomes little more than a balloon. Although ballast usually must be dumped to maintain altitude, a pilot's attention ultimately must be focused on landing. Descending is easy enough; just release some helium. But unless a ground crew is available to hold down the blimp and prevent it from blowing away, the airship pilot must pull a rip cord to tear open a 20-foot-long panel that allows the entire load of helium to escape. And the pilot had better be prepared to jump out and run like crazy to avoid being smothered by the collapsing envelope.

A conventional landing with power is far less dramatic. It is executed precisely into the wind because there is no way to land one of the world's largest weather vanes against a crosswind. To help a pilot line up directly into the wind, one of the ground crewmen (there are more than a dozen) stands in the landing area and holds up a portable wind sock that is mounted atop a pole. Although shifting winds are difficult to handle, airship pilots claim that light, variable, and calm conditions are worse. This is because the controls lose effectiveness below 7 knots, yet the airship must be brought to a halt before ground crewmen can grab the lines hanging from the nose and prevent the blimp from drifting away. Ideal landing conditions include a steady, 10-knot wind. The touchdown itself is simply a matter of driving the blimp onto its single-wheel landing gear and using reverse power (when necessary) to slow the craft. (Goodyear blimps do not have brakes.)

Before the blimp crew deplanes (deblimps?), ground crewmen must add ballast to the car. Otherwise, the reduced payload would allow the blimp to simply float away (along with those hanging on to the lines) and become a pilotless hazard to navigation.

A normal takeoff requires less effort. Most departures are made at fairly light static weights (between 100 and 200 pounds). Several ground crewmen grab a railing that encircles the car and heave the blimp into the air like a medicine ball. When the blimp is a few feet above the ground, full power and nose-up elevator are applied. That is all there is to it. But do not be shocked by the initial climb attitude of up to 30 degrees. Other categories of aircraft might be in danger of stalling, but not blimps. (They cannot stall and have no minimum airspeed.)

When a GZ-20 is loaded heavily (up to 800 pounds of static weight) for special-purpose missions or long cross-country flights, a conventional, rolling takeoff is required. This is amusing to watch because the bending and flexing of the envelope is apparent every time the tire hits a rut or a bump. Acceleration is painfully slow and the takeoff roll of 700 feet (at maximum heaviness) seems to take forever. Pilots must be cautious during liftoff not to raise the nose excessively. A 7-degree rotation results in a tail strike.

When a GZ-20 has completed its daily and nightly chores, the tip of its nose is nuzzled into a locking cup at the top of a 32-foot-tall mooring mast. A blimp is not tied down conventionally because such a broad surface cannot be restrained in a crosswind. Instead, the blimp becomes a ponderous wind sock and pivots restlessly about the mooring mast in response to even the slightest zephyr. So even when not flying, a blimp is still quite unlike an airplane; it is never really at rest.

*Author's Note:* The America, the Enterprise, and the Columbia have been replaced with newer aircraft, the Spirit of Goodyear (based in Akron, Ohio), the Stars and Stripes (Pompano Beach, Florida), and the Spirit of America (based near Los Angeles). Goodyear no longer maintains an airship (blimp) in Europe.

## McCulloch J-2 Gyrocopter

| | |
|---|---|
| Engine | Lycoming O-360-A2D |
| Power | 180 hp |
| Length | 16 ft 0 in |
| Height | 8 ft 6 in |
| Disk Diameter | 26 ft 0 in |
| Disk Loading | 2.8 lb/sq ft |
| Power Loading | 8.3 lb/hp |
| Maximum Takeoff Weight | 1,500 lb |
| Fuel Capacity (usable) | 20 gal |
| Rate of Climb (sea level) | 700 fpm |
| Normal Cruise Speed | 105 mph |
| Minimum Speed in Level Flight | 30 mph |

# McCulloch J-2 Gyrocopter

## Looking like a bumblebee with tail fins, the

McCulloch J-2 Gyrocopter has an unpowered rotor and is part helicopter and part airplane with some virtues of each.

It looks like a recontoured Volkswagen "Beetle" with a conning tower and rotor blades, or perhaps like a helicopter with tricycle landing gear but no tail rotor, or perhaps like an airplane with the twin-boom empennage of the Cessna Skymaster and the stubby wings of a bumblebee.

It is initially tempting to compare the J-2 with either a helicopter or an airplane, but it is neither. It is a hybrid with traits of both and other traits that cannot be duplicated by either a helicopter or an airplane.

I was introduced to the McCulloch J-2 many years ago when invited to its debut in Lake Havasu City, Arizona. There I attended the manufacturer's gyroplane school and obtained became rated in the machine. At the time, there were only 50 to 75 pilots in the country with gyroplane ratings, and most of them had not seen one since before World War II.

According to the FAA, the J-2 is technically a gyroplane although these machines also are informally known as autogyros and gyrocopters. The McCulloch is a 2-place, enclosed-cabin, rotary-wing aircraft that uses a free-wheeling rotor lift (as compared to a helicopter whose rotor is powered). Thrust is obtained from a rear-mounted engine with a pusher propeller.

Lift is created by the rotor using the principle of autorotation, which requires movement of the gyroplane through the air (see the sidebar on pages 74–75). Unlike a helicopter, the J-2 cannot hover. Because the rotor is not powered, it generates no torque as do powered rotors. Hence, there is neither a tail rotor nor are there any of the yaw-control problems associated with a helicopter.

Attitude is controlled conventionally with stick and rudder, but instead of moving ailerons and elevator, which the J-2 does not have, the stick controls the tilt of the rotor disk (like the cyclic control of a helicopter). The rudder pedals are conventional and operate the rudders, one on each tail boom. A right turn, for example, is entered by moving the stick to the right and simultaneously applying right rudder pressure. This tilts the rotor disk to the right, which causes the gyroplane to turn in that direction. It turns for the same reason that airplanes do; lift is directed in the desired direction.

The rudder performs the same function as in an airplane; it corrects for undesirable yaw.

An advantage of the J-2 over an airplane is that its "wings" (meaning its rotor blades) have airspeed before the takeoff roll begins. After the pilot starts the engine, he accelerates the rotor by coupling it momentarily to the engine via a clutch and transmission (like that of an automobile with stick shift), a procedure discussed later. A 180-hp Lycoming 0-360-A2D powers the J-2 and is controlled with either of 2 throttles. One is a standard push-pull type on the instrument panel; the other is a motorcycle-type of grip-and-twist throttle on the spin-up lever (discussed later).

The walk-around is straightforward except for checking the rotors and the rotor dampers.

The stubby wings offer the fixed-wing pilot more psychological lift than aerodynamic. Each contains a 12.1-gallon fuel tank, 10 gallons of which are useable.

Empty weight (including unusable fuel and a navcom) is 1,049 pounds. This provides a useful load of 451 pounds. With full tanks, this allows only a 331-pound payload. (Maximum baggage of 95 pounds is stored under the bench-type seat.)

Because of balance considerations, the J-2 may not be flown unless gross weight is at least 1,250 pounds. A lightweight pilot flying with partial fuel must carry ballast.

The J-2 has 2 large entry doors, one on each side, so getting in and out is gentile. Headroom is generous but shoulder room leaves a bit to be desired. Except for the rotor spin-up controls, the cockpit resembles a typical, uncomplicated airplane. Its small instrument panel is centered between 2 glove compartments and has only the necessary gauges. There is room for more instruments, but the J-2 is not certified for night or instrument flight. One unusual instrument is the dual-reading tachometer that shows both rotor and engine rpm.

Taxiing is done with engine thrust and the rudder pedals, which control the steerable nosewheel. Because the center of gravity is relatively high, sharp turns must be avoided at fast taxi speeds. When taxiing across rough terrain, the rotor should be spun to at least 100 rpm to prevent the otherwise motionless blades from flapping and damaging the rotor assembly.

After a conventional runup, the J-2 is taxied into takeoff position and held there with toe brakes—it does not have a parking brake—for the rotor spin-up procedure. Here is where things get unconventional.

*Continued on Page 76*

# *Autorotation — How it Works*

Most confusing about gyroplane aerodynamics is how free-wheeling rotor blades can advance against the relative wind. Common sense suggests that unpowered blades should move in the opposite direction (with the wind).

The rotors of a gyroplane (and a helicopter) are simply rotating wings. Like a wing or a propeller, the cross-section of a rotor blade is an airfoil.

As the relative wind flows across such an airfoil (Figure 1a), lift is produced. A rule of aerodynamics is that lift acts perpendicular to the relative wind. Because a rotor blade is no more than a revolving, high-aspect-ratio wing, lift is shown (in this case) as a vertical force. A necessary result of lift is drag, which is shown acting parallel to the relative wind. The resultant of lift and drag is shown in the figure acting aft of the axis of rotation. This is a retarding force that causes the rotor blade to decelerate.

Figure 1b solves the mystery of autorotation, the phenomenon of inducing forward movement (rotation) against the relative wind.

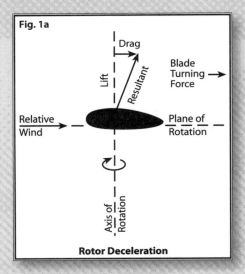

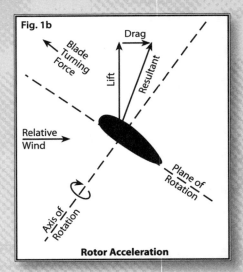

In this case, the plane of rotor rotation is mechanically tilted aft by the pilot applying back-pressure to the control stick. Lift and drag remain perpendicular and parallel, respectively, to the relative wind. The resultant acts forward of the axis of rotation. This force literally pulls the rotor blade forward with respect to the axis of rotation.

If this seems confusing, tilt the diagram so that the plane of rotation is horizontal and the relative wind comes from ahead of and below the airfoil (a requirement for autorotation). The resultant force then leans forward, making it easier to understand how the rotor is pulled forward and advances against the relative wind.

A crude analogy can be made between autorotation and tacking a sailboat into the wind. Both are possible only when advances into the wind are made at a small angle.

In reality, Figure 1a shows what happens when the control stick is pushed forward. Aerodynamic forces reduce rotor rpm. Simultaneously, gyroplane airspeed increases because of reduced drag.

Figure 1b demonstrates why back pressure on the control stick produces increased rotor rpm. Also, gyroplane airspeed decreases because of increased drag.

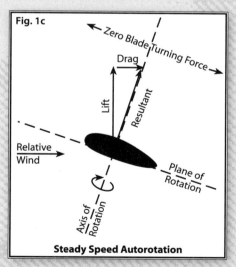

**Fig. 1c**

Zero Blade Turning Force →

Drag

Lift

Resultant

Relative Wind

Plane of Rotation

Axis of Rotation

**Steady Speed Autorotation**

Figure 1c shows steady-state autorotation. The resultant of lift and drag is parallel to the axis of rotation and rotor rpm remains constant.

This, by the way, is exactly what happens when an airplane spins; the unstalled or outside wing is pulled forward and forces the aircraft to autorotate.

With the throttle retarded, the transmission engagement lever on the cabin's rear bulkhead is raised, gearing the rotor shaft to the transmission. Next, the spin-up lever (left of the pilot's seat) is slowly and firmly depressed, a chore that requires a strong left arm and applying 60 pounds of force. Engaging the spin-up lever connects the engine to the transmission through a drive-belt system and simultaneously changes the pitch of the rotor blades from 5 to 0 degrees to reduce drag during spin-up.

After the rotor accelerates to between 100 and 150 rpm, the motorcycle-type grip throttle is twisted slowly until rotor speed increases to 450 rpm. The spin-up lever is then raised, mechanically releasing the clutch and disengaging the rotor shaft from the transmission. A red light on the instrument panel extinguishes to confirm that the rotor is freewheeling. The disengagement simultaneously returns the rotor blades to a 5-degree pitch angle.

The rotor is now up to speed and freewheeling. The blades are "biting" the air at the proper angle and are creating about 1,300 pounds of lift before the J-2 has even begun to move.

As the rotor takes on the load, the fuselage suddenly rises on its landing gear and catches the new J-2 pilot off guard, leaving him with the feeling of sitting on a kneeling camel that stands up unexpectedly.

Takeoff power is applied before rotor rpm has a chance to decay. Directional control is a bit tricky because the J-2 is so light on its wheels. Also, the aircraft tends to ride more on the nosewheel than on the mains (like a wheelbarrow). Because all but about 100 pounds of its weight is off the ground during the takeoff roll, the J-2 is well suited for taking off on rough terrain.

Some rotor rpm is lost during the takeoff roll but is quickly recaptured at 40 mph when the nose is raised to the liftoff attitude and the rotor disk's angle of attack increases. If the nose is raised too much or prematurely, considerable drag is created by the tilted rotor disk, decreasing aircraft acceleration and prolonging takeoff. At liftoff, the J-2 wants to yaw and roll to the right. When you learn to anticipate this, it is easily avoided with timely stick and rudder inputs.

This yaw-roll tendency on liftoff is caused by a combination of asymmetrical propeller thrust and engine torque. Although present in fixed-wing airplanes, it is not as noticeable because of the lateral damping effect of the wings. This yaw/roll combination acts to the right and not the left because the pusher propeller turns opposite to a tractor propeller.

This lengthy description of the takeoff belies its brevity. Although rotor spin-up takes 20 seconds, the takeoff roll itself can be as short as 3.2 seconds. Everything happens so quickly that a new J-2 pilot feels as though he is being launched by catapult. The rapid acceleration is due to so little rolling friction and an exceptionally low power loading (8.3 pounds per horsepower), less than that of most popular lightplanes.

Taking off at maximum gross weight and during standard, sea-level conditions requires only 540 feet.

Those who remember the Umbaugh autogyro may recall that it could make a jump takeoff without any ground roll. What followed, however, was a losing race with time to see if it could accelerate fast enough to remain airborne. Including ground roll, the J-2 can take off and climb over a 50-foot obstacle in 600 ft, less than the Umbaugh needed after its jump takeoff.

One drawback of the J-2 is that it is not certified to take off above 4000 feet msl, which eliminates much of the West for J-2 operations. Another problem with the J-2 is that it compares unfavorably with a Piper Super Cub, for example. The venerable PA-18 not only gets off the ground in less distance but carries a heavier load faster, higher, and farther. The Cub also cost much less to buy and operate.

A Super Cub flown at minimum speed, however, has sluggish control response. Its wing is on the verge of stalling. Any mishandling could result in control loss, a characteristic of most airplanes.

The J-2 does not have such low-speed problems. Its "wing" is at cruising speed (rotor rpm) irrespective of indicated airspeed thus providing positive control response at all times.

Although the J-2 cannot stall, reducing airspeed to below 30 mph results in a gradual descent. Further airspeed reduction increases sink rate. At 0 mph, the J-2 is in level-flight attitude and descends at 1,400 fpm. The effect is fascinating and delightful. You feel as though you are strapped under an open parachute. There is no sensation of falling, but you are aware that the aircraft has no forward speed. Pull back a bit more on the stick, and the J-2 goes backwards.

During this parachute-like descent, full right or left rudder makes the J-2 revolve slowly about its vertical axis to provide a truly panoramic view.

During a vertical descent, the stick is held neutral. Moving it in any direction confirms that the control response of a gyroplane does not depend on indicated airspeed.

Recovery from this intriguing maneuver should begin at least 500 feet agl and results in an additional 200-foot altitude loss. Simply lower the nose 30 degrees and apply full power. Without power, recovery requires about 300 feet.

The J-2s climb performance is unimpressive, sensitive to small increases in weight and temperature. Climb rate at maximum gross weight seldom exceeds 500 fpm. Fully loaded at 5,000 feet, the J-2 climbs at barely 200 fpm. Best angle and best rate-of-climb speeds are 62 and 70 mph, respectively.

Because weight has a profound effect on gyroplane performance and allowable payload, McCulloch took great pain to save every ounce and explains the choice of a wooden propeller instead of a metal one.

The J-2 cruises at 105 mph and rides more smoothly than a helicopter because freewheeling blades create less vibration than powered rotors.

It takes an hour of flying the J-2 to get used to the differences between its flight characteristics and those of an airplane. Most pilots initially tend to overcontrol laterally because there are no wings to dampen roll. Also, the J-2 has neutral pitch stability, meaning that it does not pitch down automatically to recapture lost airspeed the way the airplanes do. Changing speed requires positive stick forces, thus the fixed-wing pilot initially undercontrols in pitch.

Turning the J-2 is conventional, but bank angle should not exceed 60 degrees. There is insufficient reserve power available to maintain altitude during steeper turns. This maximum angle of bank decreases to about 45 degrees at 4,000 feet. If maintaining altitude is not important, bank angles up to 90 degees can be made as long as G-loads are kept positive.

Helicopter pilots are cautioned not to revert to habit and depress the J-2's spin-up lever in flight as though it were a collective pitch control. Depressing that lever would change the pitch of the rotor blades from 5 to 0 degrees and provide the unexpected thrill that accompanies a sudden loss of all lift.

During flight there is no reason to be concerned about maintaining a given rotor rpm such as when flying a helicopter. Aerodynamic forces automatically maintain rotor rpm within its 300-to-480 rpm limit at all times.

Landing the J-2 is childishly simple. Airspeed during the approach is controlled by pitch (as with an airplane) at 60 mph. Rate of descent is controlled with power. At a height of 5 or 10 feet, begin a normal flare to reduce sink rate. Airspeed then decreases rapidly because of the increased rotor drag. Touchdown occurs at 25 mph followed by less than 100 feet of roll. It is that easy.

With a 10-knot headwind, landing roll is less than 50 feet. Landing over a 50-foot obstacle requires a 500 feet.

The J-2 is virtually impervious to a crosswind because of its high disk loading (2.8 pounds per square foot of rotor disc area). A minor problem arises however, from the poor rudder response at landing speeds. Considerable downwind rudder is essential after the main gear touches, to prevent weathervaning into the wind. Unless the pedals are neutralized before the nosewheel touches, a quick downwind turn will occur because of the direction in which the nosewheel is cocked.

The J-2 is an exceptionally safe aircraft, but acceptance was handicapped by the poor safety record of its predecessors, the Umbaugh and numerous homebuilt autogyros.

The Umbaugh suffered from lateral instability, a characteristic that made side slipping dangerous. When you try to raise the low "wing" of an Umbaugh with top rudder, the condition becomes aggravated. The aircraft rolls farther into the slip, increasing the possibility of lateral upset and inverted flight. The Umbaugh should have been sent back to the drawing board, but instead was equipped with a horn that sounds when a slip exceeds limits. Recovery has to be executed gingerly with stick only.

The J-2 is laterally stable and can be slipped in either direction without adverse results. When top rudder is applied, the J-2 responds obediently and rolls to a wings-level attitude.

A maximum effort pullout from a dive at $V_{NE}$ (109 mph) results in only 4.5 Gs, the maximum attainable under any condition. The blades cone slightly and accelerate to maximum-allowable rpm, but that is all. The J-2 decelerates to zero airspeed and begins a vertical descent.

There are two ways to get into trouble in a J-2. One is to develop a high sink rate at low airspeed near the ground. The other is to fly inverted, at which time the blades slow down and wrap themselves around the fuselage.

An engine failure obviously results in a forced landing. This is when a helicopter has the edge because it can land in an area barely larger than its rotor diameter and without forward speed. The J-2 would be safer than an airplane because it can land in less distance and at a snail's pace. Crashworthiness is better, too, because the fuselage frame is stressed to 20 Gs.

The McCulloch J-2 failed to become a marketing success because it is such a hybrid, a cross between a helicopter and an airplane that is incapable of matching the performance of either. But it sure is fun to fly.

# A Brief History of Gyroplanes

The man responsible for the autogyro was Juan de la Cierva, an accomplished aeronautical engineer and member of the Spanish aristocracy. His first three experimental models failed, but on January 9, 1923 his fourth flew near Madrid, Spain for 80 seconds.

Cierva's autogyro consisted of a conventional airplane fuselage above which was mounted a 4-bladed, freewheeling rotor. The blades were hinged, allowing them to flap while revolving.

In 1928, Cierva sold the right to manufacture his aircraft in America to Harold Pitcairn. The Pitcairn PCA-2 (essentially a de la Cierva design) was America's first certified, rotary-wing aircraft.

On April 8, 1931 a Pitcairn powered by a Wright Whirlwind engine was flown by Amelia Earhart to 18,415 feet. A month later she flew it across the United States.

Pitcairn's only noteworthy American competitor was the Kellett Autogyro Corporation, which produced the KD-A1 Autogyro (the military YO-50). Between Pitcairn, Kellett, and manufacturers in England, France, Germany, and Russia, about 500 autogyros were been built when their civilian production lines came to a grinding halt at the onset of World War II.

With the exception of homebuilt and experimental autogyros, there was little effort to revitalize this almost forgotten class of aircraft until the mid-1950s. Enter Raymond E. Umbaugh.

This loquacious and colorful character promised—in addition to the moon and all mineral rights thereof—an autogyro that would revolutionize general aviation. Unfortunately, his efforts were poorly funded and his impossible dream of an autogyro in every garage became a nightmare to those who believed and invested in his company. A Muncie, Indiana firm, Air and Space Manufacturing built a few Umbaugh Model 18s of which only a few survive.

As a result of Umbaugh's fiscal fiasco, he and his autogyro were frequently raked through the red-hot coals of the aviation press as well as those of the courts where the wrangling over Umbaugh's "questionable" stock promotion lasted for years.

Unfortunately, the words "Umbaugh" and "autogyro" became synonymously linked.

The FAA finally adopted "gyroplane" as the formal name for this class of rotorcraft.

The McCulloch J-2 gyroplane was the brainchild of Drago K. Jovanovich, a rotary-wing aircraft pioneer. He was responsible for developing 12 different prototype helicopters. Some of these were produced for commercial and military markets.

Jovanovich formed the Jovair Corporation through which he built and flew the prototype J-2 in 1962. The project languished without financial support.

In 1967, industrial magnate Robert P. McCulloch, president of the dynastic McCulloch Corp, became interested in the J-2 and purchased the manufacturing rights. In May, 1968 the McCulloch Aircraft Corporation was added to the swelling list of McCulloch subsidiaries.

In the early 1940s, McCulloch was the largest stockholder in Pan American Airlines, and during World War II he manufactured reciprocating engines for all U.S. drone aircraft. Later he became prominent in superchargers. The corporation's vast real-estate holdings and sales efforts required that prospective customers be flown to distant developments. The result was McCulloch International Airlines, a certified, supplemental air carrier. The best known of all McCulloch interests was the McCulloch Oil Corporation.

## NASA's Space Shuttle Orbiter

| | |
|---|---|
| Engines | 3 internal liquid-propellant rockets |
| Power | 488,800 pounds of thrust each |
| Length | 122 ft 2 in |
| Height | 56 ft 8 in |
| Wingspan | 78 ft 1 in |
| Wing Loading (landing) | 95.2 lb/sq ft |
| Maximum Takeoff Weight | 265,000 lb |
| Useful Load | 90,000 lb |
| Rate of Climb (@ 130,000 ft) | 132,000 fpm |
| Orbital altitude | 100-312 nm |
| Normal Cruise Speed (typical) | 14,800 kt (in orbit) |
| Stall Speed (landing) | 150 kt |

# The Orbiter (Space Shuttle)

## Like the moon floating serenely across the sky,

a spacecraft in Earth orbit is in a constant struggle to escape gravity and streak boundlessly toward outer space. It is an exquisite blend of forces that allows an orbiting projectile to free-fall toward our planet at exactly the same rate at which the Earth's curvature falls away. Such is the magic of orbital mechanics.

While sailing in silence above the atmosphere where one can watch meteors burning below and where there is virtually no drag or weight, a NASA orbiter, which is about the size of a Douglas DC-9, can be made to assume any attitude without regard to its flight path. The nose can be pointed straight up and belly forward, straight down in knife-edge flight, or in any attitude in between.

Attitude in space is controlled by an autopilot or by a human pilot using a short control stick called a rotational hand controller. As in conventional airplanes, the stick is moved left and right to control roll, and fore and aft to control pitch. It is twisted clockwise and counterclockwise, however, to control yaw.

Aerodynamic flight controls obviously are ineffective in space. Moving the control stick signals a combination of control jets to operate. These are small rockets that make the orbiter roll, pitch, and yaw. There are 44 such steering jets on the shuttle, 16 on the nose and 28 on the tail.

The runway at the Kennedy Space Center in Florida is half a world away, one hour from touchdown, and we are about to vacate circular orbit, which can be a minimum altitude of 100 nm msl and a maximum of 312 nm. The orbiter is turned tail first, its nose pointed opposite to our direction of travel. Two 6,000-pound-thrust rocket engines are fired for two to three minutes, and the orbiter responds with a speed reduction of 118 to 326 knots (depending on orbital altitude). Tugging relentlessly, gravity finally wins the struggle. The orbiter begins an initially gradual descent.

An orbiter's cockpit has the general appearance of an airliner's, but many of the switches and controls have unfamiliar markings and labels. Patches of Velcro are glued everywhere, handy places to secure small objects that would otherwise float about the cockpit during orbital weightlessness. The commander, who makes the landing, sits on the left, while the pilot (who is really the copilot) sits on the right.

As in most aircraft, the primary instrument for monitoring attitude is the attitude indicator. The AI in an orbiter, however, is much more sophisticated than those found in most other aircraft. It consists of an enclosed sphere (colloquially called an eight ball) that is gimbaled to display movement about all three axes.

A three-cue flight director (called guidance needles) is contained within the attitude indicator to command computer-generated roll, pitch, and yaw control inputs.

## TOUCHDOWN: T MINUS 32 MINUTES 14 SECONDS, 14,800 KNOTS (TAS), 400,000 FEET MSL.

We encounter the upper fringes of the atmosphere (entry interface) 4,200 nm from destination. Sink rate is 30,000 fpm. The orbiter begins to make the transition from a spaceship to a glider. The steering rockets are now used to establish zero roll, zero yaw, and a typical angle of attack (alpha) of 40 degrees.

The angle at which the shuttle enters the atmosphere is critical. If it is excessive, the glider could skip off the top of the atmosphere like a flat rock off water or stall as the increasing air density takes a firmer grip. Recovery from either event is unlikely. Too small an angle of attack results in excessive speed and frictional heating that can damage the leading edges of the wings. Damage also can result from excessive dynamic pressure and G-load.

## T MINUS 28:42.

The orbiter has four hydraulically actuated elevons, two on the trailing edge of each wing. These combine the pitch and roll functions of elevators and ailerons and are commonly used on delta-wing aircraft. The elevons start to become effective at an indicated airspeed of 25 knots, which occurs between 250,000 to 280,000 feet. Most of the steering rockets are deactivated when the elevons become fully effective at 108 knots.

## T MINUS 26:56.

The flight directors give the first roll commands for the purpose of steepening the descent profile when on-board computers sense that the orbiter has too much energy (altitude). Rolling steeply left and right reduces the vertical component of lift, which increases sink rate. Rolling increases skin temperature, but not as much as would lowering the nose (decreasing alpha) and increasing airspeed. Roll maneuvering results in very little heading change because the turn rate at such high airspeed is so minimal. The pilot and commander monitor the actual vs. desired descent profiles on one of the CRT displays on the main instrument panel.

## T MINUS 26:04.

Our glider is descending at Mach 19.0 to 25.0, and the friction of the atmosphere causes skin temperatures to peak. During hypersonic flight (more than Mach 5.0), the aircraft has a glide ratio of 1.05:1; at subsonic speeds, it improves dramatically to 5.1:1, a far cry from a typical jetliner's at 20:1 or a retractable piston single at 10:1.

Although an autopilot normally makes the descent from orbit and is used to enter the atmosphere, it also is capable of making the entire approach and landing. Shuttle commanders enjoy the little actual flying involved in a shuttle mission and typically take over manually at Mach 1.0. When hand-flying an orbiter, a pilot never needs trim because the fly-by-wire control system automatically displaces the control surfaces as necessary to obviate the need for trim. (A manual backup trim, however, is available.)

## T MINUS 12:54.

The angle of attack gradually begins to decrease, and the speed brake opens to 81 percent. The speed brake is incorporated into the rudder, which is made to split open along its trailing edge.

## T MINUS 10:33, MACH 7.3, 142,000 FEET, 50 NM.

The aircraft has been guided by inertial navigation, but now the destination TACAN (the UHF military equivalent of a Vortac) is within range and will be used for guidance during most of the arrival.

## T MINUS 8:44, MACH 5, 120,000 FEET.

The dual, relatively fragile pitot probes are deployed from the fuselage. Had they been extended earlier, they would have overheated, softened, and failed. The rudder, which previously had been blanketed by the large angle of attack of the wings, is now activated. It automatically compensates for adverse yaw effect, acts as a yaw damper, and provides rudder trim as needed. The remaining control rockets, which have been used to control yaw, are now deactivated.

## T MINUS 6:44, MACH 2.6, 83,000 FEET.

Control guidance has thus far been provided by the dual flight directors. But now the heads-up displays (HUDs) are activated. Each is a transparent panel that is situated in a pilot's field of vision as he looks out the front windshield (like a sun visor). The pilot looks through the HUD to see the outside world while simultaneously viewing a plethora of performance and status data that is holographically displayed on the HUD.

© Patrick McCabe - Fotolia.com

Two of the many symbols on the HUD are of particular interest. One represents the velocity vector of the orbiter and shows where the aircraft is going. The other shows where the computers want the aircraft to go. The pilot's job is to roll and pitch the aircraft so as to superimpose one symbol on the other so that the actual path of the aircraft coincides with what the computers want. If the computers want the pilot to lower the nose and turn left, for example, one symbol moves down and toward the left, and the pilot responds by moving the controls so that the second symbol "catches up" with the other. It's essentially an easy-to-use flight director, an extraordinarily sophisticated video game. More good news is that the pilot does not have to worry about airspeed. As long as he follows the pitch and roll commands issued by the HUD and the flight director, airspeed takes care of itself.

### T MINUS 3:57, MACH 0.9, 46,000 FEET AGL.

The speed brake now receives computer-generated commands and modulates automatically to manage airspeed.

The "traffic pattern" consists of joining the heading alignment cone that is tangent to the final approach course at a point seven miles from the runway threshold. HUD and flight-director guidance is provided to join the cone, which essentially leads the orbiter into a spiraling descent that leads to intercepting the final approach course.

This is the last opportunity for on-board computers to manage orbiter energy. If the aircraft is too high, the pilot is given roll commands that result in widening the turn; if the aircraft is too low, the turn is tightened. (A normal 360-degree turn results in an altitude loss of about 38,000 feet.)

### T MINUS 1:31, 280 KNOTS, 15,000 FEET

The turn toward final approach is almost complete, and a transition is automatically made from TACAN to guidance by a microwave landing system. MLS is similar to an ILS, except that on-board computers can use MLS data to establish and display a variety of localizer and glideslope angles (as compared to the fixed localizer and glideslope of a conventional ILS).

### T MINUS 1:14, 300 KNOTS (IAS), 12,000 FEET.

We intercept the MLS localizer and roll onto the straight-in final approach. The initial reaction to seeing the runway for the first time is that there is no way to lose 12,000 feet of altitude in the remaining seven miles and still cross the runway threshold in a position to land.

Astronauts seldom have to worry about weather during an approach. Landing minimums are an 8,000-foot ceiling and a 5-mile visibility; maximum-allowable crosswind component is 15 knots (launch or landing).

We have intercepted the outer glideslope (diveslope might be a more accurate term), which guides us earthward at 18 or 20 degrees, depending on the orbiter's landing weight. (A normal ILS glideslope descends at only 3 degrees.) Our aim point on this segment of the descent is 7,500 feet short of the runway threshold. (If all is going as planned, the HUD symbol representing the velocity vector of the orbiter will be superimposed on this aim point.)

### T MINUS 0:33, 300 KNOTS, 2,000 FEET.

The symbols on the HUD and the flight director needles now urge me to begin a 1.3-G pull-up to make the transition from the outer glideslope to the much shallower, 1.5-degree inner glideslope. I raise the nose somewhat aggressively to recover from the 18- or 20-degree dive and superimpose the symbol representing the velocity vector of the HUD onto the runway at a point abeam the precision approach path indicator lights. This is the touchdown target, and it is 2,500 feet beyond the threshold. Airspeed begins to decay from 300 to 220 knots.

## T MINUS 0:20, 288 KNOTS, 300 FEET

The pushbuttons used to lower the landing gear are depressed. A go-around is obviously not an option should the gear fail to operate, and astronauts are not trained for a gear-up landing. NASA's philosophy is that the landing gear will operate. If hydraulic pressure fails to do the job, an automatic backup system of explosive discharges will.

## T MINUS 0:10, 261 KNOTS, 30 TO 80 FEET.

I raise the nose of the orbiter so as to superimpose the speed-vector symbol on the far end of the runway, which is clearly visible through the HUD. The goal is to cross the runway threshold at 26 feet. Airspeed bleeds to a touchdown speed of 195 to 205 knots, depending on gross weight.

## T MINUS 0:00.

The orbiter touches down at a sink rate of 200 to 300 fpm. The speed brake immediately deploys to its full-open position (a 99-degree rudder split), and the drag chute is deployed between 190 to 195 knots.

I begin derotation (NASA's expression for lowering the nose) at 185 knots with a steady application of the thumb-operated, elevator "beep" trim. This lowers the nose at the desired rate without having to use any elevator input. I apply the brakes at 140 knots or with 5,000 feet of runway remaining, whichever occurs first. The toe brakes have antiskid protection, and nosewheel steering operates conventionally through the rudder pedals. The drag chute is jettisoned at between 40 and 60 knots to prevent it from damaging the exhaust nozzles on the tail. The orbiter comes to rest in a nose-low attitude like an anteater rooting for food. The nose gear strut is unusually short to save weight.

The computers aboard the orbiter are capable of establishing an approach to almost any large airport in the world (using Vortac data when MLS is not available). Although the typical landing roll consumes 10,000 feet of concrete, a shuttle commander can in a pinch set down on a 6,000-foot-long runway.

My "pulsemeter" is still pegged after this, my first landing in NASA's only full-motion orbiter simulator, which is equipped with a realistic visual system. It is at the Johnson Space Center in Houston. Astronaut Charles "Charlie" J. Precourt is seated to my right. He leans toward me and asks with a grin, "Why are you holding the brakes?" So real is the experience that I am still depressing the pedals, a habit bred during 46 years to prevent undesirable forward movement of conventional aircraft caused by idle thrust.

Precourt is NASA's chief astronaut. He was the flight engineer on STS-55, the pilot on -71, and the commander of STS-84 and -91. (STS stands for space transportation system.) A seemingly natural linguist, he also learned Russian for and did all of the docking with the Russian space station, Mir, during his last two missions. An avid general aviation enthusiast, Precourt also built and flies his own Rutan Long-Eze.

*The author (left) and "Charlie" Precourt, NASA's Chief Astronaut at the time.*

By the time an astronaut becomes a commander, he will have made 800 to 900 landings in the simulator and at least 1,000 approaches in the shuttle training aircraft. These are a quartet of Gulfstream G-IIs that have been extensively modified to duplicate the steep, high-speed approach-to-landing profile of an arriving orbiter. According to Precourt, this kind of experience probably would enable a commander to make a dead-stick approach and landing without computerized guidance and energy management, although he would prefer not to have to put this theory to test. (Each orbiter has five independent guidance computers, a redundancy that makes it extremely unlikely that any shuttle commander will ever be challenged in this manner.)

Although events occur rapidly during the approach and landing, my impression is that the average general aviation pilot could land an orbiter (as long as he first receives a few hours of instruction, nothing goes wrong, conditions are favorable, and Precourt is in the right seat). Someone skilled at video games might be more adept. Arriving in an orbiter is mostly a matter of using a joystick to match symbols on the HUD. This, however, is a simplistic view. Flying an orbiter while wearing a bulky spacesuit and coping with the effects of increasing body weight after days of weightlessness complicates matters.

In addition to a year of vigorous and intensive training, one of the most challenging aspects of becoming an astronaut for me would be learning NASA's acronyms, of which there are literally thousands. Two of the most amusing are WOW (weight on wheels) and WONG (weight on nose gear).

But I will not have such an opportunity, despite how this incredible experience enflamed my desire for an actual flight. Perhaps in another life.

## Transavia PL-12U Airtruk

| | |
|---|---|
| Engine | Continental IO-520-D |
| Power | 300 hp |
| Length | 20 ft 10 in |
| Height | 9 ft 2 in |
| Wingspan | 39 ft 4 in |
| Wing Loading | 15.0 lb/sq ft |
| Power Loading | 12.7 lb/hp |
| Maximum Takeoff Weight | 3,800 lb |
| Fuel Capacity | 96 gal |
| Rate of Climb (sea level) | 600 fpm |
| Normal Cruise Speed | 130 mph |
| Stall Speed | 60 mph |

# Transavia PL-12U Airtruk

*There was nothing unusual about my approach to*
Nyngan Airport in Australia's Outback. But my airplane looked so unusual that the local press came to investigate the curious craft that had slipped from the sky to visit their remote community.

What they saw evoked quizzical expressions, poorly disguised chuckles, and a deluge of questioning. There is no disputing it. The Transavia PL-12U Airtruk is a strange-looking airplane. Like an Airbus A380, it has two passenger decks. The pilot and one passenger sit on top in tandem, but the passenger faces aft. Three additional passengers share the lower deck, and they too face rearward.

The Airtruk appears ungainly, resembling a Volkswagen that has been modified to look like a Cessna Skymaster with one engine. But instead of having a single horizontal stabilizer, the empennage consists of 2 independent T-tails, each supported by its own slim boom. A pair of stub wings adds to the curiosity.

Fascinating aircraft have lured me all over the world. Variety helps to maintain my passion for flight. It took only one glance at the photograph of an Airtruk to inspire my trek to Australia. There I developed an intimacy with what might have been the world's most unusual general aviation airplane.

Gil Forrester, Transavia's general manager, welcomed me to Sydney. He is amicable, quiet, and polite to the point of formality, not what you would expect of a transplanted New Yorker. He was committed to the Airtruk and defended the homely-looking airplane against any insult, implied or direct.

Forrester volunteered that the Airtruk was conceived as an agricultural aircraft, which explains some of its unorthodox features. The designer, Luigi Pellarini, was concerned with function, not aesthetics.

In the agricultural configuration, the pod-shaped fuselage contains a cavernous 220-gallon hopper that carries up to a ton of agricultural material. The unique tail assemblies are 11 feet apart, allowing a loading truck to approach safely from the rear and eliminate the need for the pilot to shut down the engine. The stub wings contribute 20 percent of the lift and preclude the need for the main wings to have greater span.

Swinging the McCauley 88-inch, constant-speed propeller is a Continental IO-520-D, 300-hp engine. Although the Airtruk is not eye-pleasing, agricultural pilots rave about its performance, maneuverability, and safety features. The PL-12 also produces an efficient, 90-foot-wide swath pattern and has comparably low operating costs.

The Airtruk was remodeled and certificated as a passenger aircraft, marking what might have been the first time that an agplane went through such an evolutionary change.

Before I could fly the Airtruk, I had to obtain an Australian pilot's license, a procedure that involved studying a manual, Australian Air Legislation, and passing a written exam. Most Australian regulations are similar to ours, but some are unique. Flight plans, for example, are required for all flights in excess of 50 miles; an alternate airport is needed for flights to certain major airports at night; en route position reports are required every 30 minutes; a smoke puff rising from the airport indicates a wind change, and so forth.

Bureaucratic procedures behind me, I drove to the Transavia plant in Seven Hills. There I met the company's chief pilot, Roy Mitchell, who checked me out in the Airtruk.

As we approached the PL-12U, I could hardly believe my eyes. The aircraft is more provocative in person than in photographs I had seen. No question, the Airtruk is a unique breed of airplane.

Because the Airtruk has only one set of flight controls, Mitchell suggested that I sit behind him in the upper passenger deck while he flew the airplane to nearby Hoxton Park Airport where there was a runway more suitable for my first solo. The factory strip is little more than a 1,000-foot clearing surrounded by towers, cranes, and tall industrial machinery. I felt somewhat apprehensive as we taxied out. There was no way for me to get to the single-place cockpit should the pilot become incapacitated. Adding to my anxiety was the helpless feeling of being unable to see out the front window.

Before I had a chance to think about opting out, Mitchell had the Airtruk barreling along the dirt runway. After a ground run of only a few hundred feet, the nose pitched up rapidly, and I found myself staring back and down at the retreating ground at uncomfortably steep angle.

Seconds later, a large tower passed beneath and behind. Maybe this sitting backwards isn't so bad, I mused. By the time you see a hazard, it's gone. Also, the human anatomy can better endure the deceleration of a crash landing when sitting backward than when facing forward.

Mitchell's dramatic takeoff and climb emphasized that the Airtruk is a STOL airplane. The wings (all four) have the same airfoil (NACA 23012) as the Helio

Courier. Stall fences keep the Frise ailerons effective during stalls. At light weights, takeoff roll is only 255 feet but increases to 600 feet at maximum weight.

During cruise, I twisted in my seat and tried talking to Mitchell, but I could not overcome the din. The noise level reminded me of the B-25 Mitchell bomber. In the Airtruk, communication is via written note, even though pilot and upper-deck passenger are seated back to back.

Feeling lonely and slightly claustrophobic, I clambered down into the lower passenger deck and spent the rest of the short flight enjoying the roominess of this compartment.

I soon felt the power ease and watched with concern as the flaps extended. When the left flap comes down, it blocks the lower cabin door, making it impossible to open. Not wishing to be a prisoner in an Airtruk, I scampered back to my lonely perch on the upper deck where there is a door through which I could evacuate.

After parking at the ramp, Mitchell motioned for me to climb into the cockpit. He squatted on the right wing and briefed me on systems, procedures, and what to expect during my first flight as pilot. This reminded me of being checked out in single-place airplanes. You must listen attentively during such instruction because your first use of the controls will be while alone.

The cockpit is laid out like a military fighter. The throttle, propeller, and mixture controls are clustered on the left sidewall. Also on the left between the seat and the sidewall are the trim wheel, flap handle, ignition switch, and fuel controls. In flight, the left hand can get a little busy, but the right hand is always free to fly.

Cockpit visibility is wonderful, like being in a control tower. Sitting above the pistons instead of behind them allows the pilot to look down and ahead at a steep angle to see potholes and other ground hazards only a few feet ahead. It also is nice not to be sandwiched behind the engine, a factor that increases crash survivability. A disadvantage is that you cannot easily relate the position of the nose to the horizon. Attitude is best maintained visually by glancing at the wings.

Mitchell advised me to hold the stick forward during takeoff to keep the nosewheel firmly on the ground. "The rudders," he cautioned, "are out of the propwash and unusable for ground steering until you've gathered airspeed. If the nosewheel isn't held down, directional control is initially marginal."

Taxiing for takeoff, I noticed that the Airtruk porpoises slightly because of the landing gear's relatively short wheel base. Increasing taxi speed dampens this effect.

A brisk crosswind swept across the taxiway, and I noticed it had almost no effect on ground handling. The stubby fuselage offers little keel surface to the wind. Similarly, the Airtruk exhibits almost no weathervaning tendency during a crosswind takeoff.

The preflight check and runup were conventional. I taxied onto the runway, reviewed Mitchell's instructions, and pushed the throttle home. By the time I remembered his caution about holding down the nosewheel, the Airtruk had pushed the ground away and clawed skyward at what first appeared to be a dangerous climb angle but later proved to be a normal Airtruk climb. You do not need to rotate for liftoff; the nose rises positively and without assistance.

At altitude, I retarded the throttle and noticed something strange. Reducing power does not cause the nose to drop the way it does in other airplanes. Conversely, adding power does not cause the nose to rise. I then realized that the elevators, too, are out of the propwash. Power changes have little effect on pitch. If a pilot wants the nose to move, he must move it.

I coerced the Airtruk into a few stalls, power-on and power-off. The airplane does not stall in the conventional sense; it simply mushes along in a nose-high attitude with little tendency to buck or roll. With power off and the stick held fully aft, the Airtruk sinks about 1,000 fpm, depending on weight.

Maximum-allowable gross weight of the passenger model is 3,800 pounds. The agricultural model is approved for 290 pounds more because it has a jettison system enabling the pilot to dump a 2,000-pound payload in 3 seconds in case he cannot clear an impending obstacle. Passengers, of course, cannot be jettisoned, but would not this be a novel way to silence a loquacious, backseat pilot?

I extended the flaps fully (30 degrees) on final approach and recalled that, in addition to their normal function, they create a venturi effect between the main and stub wings, thereby increasing the lift of all wings simultaneously.

Landings are easy. After the mains touch, though, it is difficult to hold off the nosewheel.

Becoming familiar with any airplane requires a few days of leisurely flying away from the watchful eyes of an instructor. My opportunity came a few days later when Gil Forrester asked if I would fly one of their executives to Cobar, a small community 349 miles into the barren Outback of New South Wales.

Half an hour after takeoff, we were over the Great Dividing Range, a north-south spine of low-lying mountains that keeps the moist Pacific air of Australia's east coast from reaching the arid Outback.

The Airtruk is no hot rod and cruises at only 130 mph. What it lacks in speed it makes up for in load-carrying ability. The Airtruk has an empty weight of 1,849 pounds and a useful load of 1,951 pounds. It is one of only a few aircraft that can carry a load greater than its own weight. Range without reserve is 870 miles.

I noticed another strange Airtruk quirk as I leveled off at altitude. As airspeed increases, up-elevator and nose-up trim must be applied to maintain altitude, a clue that the aircraft is mildly unstable longitudinally.

As we progressed deeper into the Outback, the Airtruk became bludgeoned by afternoon thermals. The aircraft does not do well in turbulence and requires constant pitch and roll corrections. Left to its own devices in turbulence, the PL-12 behaves like a drunk trying to pirouette on a volley ball. The Airtruk wants to pitch and roll every which way and exhibits little tendency to return to its trimmed attitude.

I was informed later that extending the flaps to the first notch—7 degrees is allowed at any airspeed—shifts the center of lift and increases stability. Also, the Airtruk has a spring-loaded trim augmenter that could have been used because of the relatively aft location of the center of gravity during my flight.

We soon passed over some of Australia's expansive sheep ranches. The one below reportedly had so many drovers that the cook there has to ride a bicycle around the frying pan to turn all the sausages.

After sending a position report to Dubbo Radio, I was given a destination notam: "Caution. Kangaroos on the runway."

The Airtruk droned on, and I began to appreciate where in the world I was. It explained why the full moon looks so unusual. The man in the moon is upside down when viewed from the Southern Hemisphere, as are the zodiacal constellations. My familiar compatriot of the night sky, Polaris, was hidden beyond the horizon, and the sun is in the northern sky. Adding to the confusion, winds blow the wrong way, clockwise around a low and counterclockwise around a high.

Outback navigation before GPS required dead reckoning and a pair of sharp Mark IV eyeballs. A nervous ADF occasionally added a confirming wiggle. Radio aids in the Outback were as common as oases in the Sahara.

On the ground at Cobar, I turned the hand crank on the payphone and closed my flight plan. Australian flight service stations encourage pilots to keep in touch and accept collect calls. When a pilot needs a briefing or wants to close a flight plan, he tells the telephone operator that his call has "air-move" priority. The government picks up the tab, or at least it did in those days.

I checked into a local motel and inquired about a good restaurant. I realized that I was really in the Outback when a freckle-faced teenager told me that the Shell station down the road has the best food in town.

Sydney is just another big city, but the Outback is the romanticized, story-book Australia that beckons the visitor. Cobar, like so many Outback towns, had the placid atmosphere of a small, 1950s town in the Midwestern U.S. Ice cream parlors were cooled by large overhead fans, malts were still served in stainless-steel shakers, and flypaper took me back to my youth.

The Airtruk was the only lightplane manufactured in Australia at that time, and although it lacks creature comfort and speed, this flying truck satisfied a variety of utilitarian roles. In addition to reportedly being a good crop duster, the PL-12U would serve well as a firefighter. When the aircraft carries freight, the lower deck can be filled with 80 cubic feet of outsized cargo or a pair of medical patients on 6-foot stretchers. Ample room remains for the pilot and a passenger on the upper deck. This workhorse is also rugged, designed to operate on terrain that would tear away the landing gear from lesser aircraft.

The Airtruk has been used as a rainmaker, too. When the monsoon season in Southeast Asia once failed to produce needed rain, the King of Thailand said, as kings sometimes do, "Let there be rain." And with the help of 9 Airtruks that deposited the proper chemicals into the humid, cloudless skies, there was rain. The king was very happy.

## Champion 402 Lancer

| | |
|---|---|
| Engines | 2 Continental O-200-A |
| Power | 100 hp ea |
| Length | 22 ft 3 in |
| Height | 8 ft 2 in |
| Wingspan | 34 ft 6 in |
| Wing Loading | 14 ft 4 in |
| Power Loading | 12.3 lb/hp |
| Maximum Takeoff Weight | 2,450 lb |
| Fuel Capacity (usable) | 52 gal |
| Rate of Climb (sea level) | 642 fpm |
| Normal Cruise Speed | 120 mph |
| Stall Speed | 43 mph |

# The Champion 402 Lancer

## The Lancer is, in almost every respect, a most unusual

airplane. It has 4 throttles and 4 mixture controls but only 2 engines. It seems that its designers could not decide whether to use wheel or stick controls because the Lancer has both, a joystick in the rear cockpit and a wheel up front. It looks like a Grumman amphibian. But with fixed tricycle landing gear, the notion of a water landing is outlandish. To top off the list of curious features, the Lancer has a gear-position switch complete with green "safe" and red "unsafe" lights.

That the Lancer can even get off the ground is almost miraculous. The basic design is cluttered with a proliferation of struts to brace the wings and 2 husky, 5-foot-long main landing gear legs that seem to belong on a much larger airplane. A nose wheel, 8 flying wires to support the horizontal stabilizers, 4 external landing gear braces, an ultra-large pitot tube, and an assortment of other oversized protuberances add to the drag. No wonder that the Lancer's single-engine ceiling is below sea level!

With a maximum gross weight of only 2,450 pounds, the Lancer is one of the lightest production twins ever built in the United States. It certainly is the only one with fixed-pitch propellers and a fuselage of chrome-moly steel tubing, wood and fabric.

The Lancer was born in the early 1960s when the Champion Aircraft Company had what it considered a better idea, to manufacture a small, economical twin that could be used exclusively to train multi-engine pilots. With a price tag of only $12,500 (including a combustion cabin heater and night lights), Champion offered two engines for little more than the price of one. The idea sounded great on paper but did not sell or fly very well. The Lancer was given burial rights after only 100 had been produced.

The mini-twin was doomed to failure because, ironically, the aircraft was too expensive to operate profitably. It was economical as a multi-engine trainer, but that is where the Lancer's advantage ended. A flight school cannot afford to buy a twin solely for training. The aircraft also needs to help pay its way as a rental or charter airplane. But no one in their right mind would rent or charter a Lancer when a Cessna 152 carries the same load at the same speed and flies as far in more comfort for half the operating cost.

The Lancer is a highly modified version of Champion's Tri-Champ, an outgrowth of the pre-war Aeronca 7AC Champion and forerunner of the Citabria. It retained tandem seating, a 2-place cabin, and the characteristic swayback fuselage of the original Aeronca "Champ." To this was added enlarged control surfaces and stabilizers, a streamlined nose section, and a beefed-up wing to which was attached a pair of 100-hp, Continental 0-200-A engines, the same dependable powerplant found in the Cessna 150. A trim tab for the rudder and mechanically operated flaps also were added.

When you first approach a Lancer, you get the impression that this homely-looking aircraft is a homebuilt, that it really could not or should not be a production airplane. Everything about the Lancer seems an afterthought.

The preflight requires nothing unusual except having to drain 6 fuel drains and determine that the numerous inspection plates are in place. Each engine has large augmenter exhaust systems that birds find ideal for nesting.

Each wing contains a 26-gallon fuel tank. The fuel caps can be checked for security by a tall man reaching up and over the leading edge of the wing, but looking inside the tanks requires a ladder. Although the engines are mounted relatively high off the ground, the oil can be checked without a ladder through access doors on the starboard sides of the nacelles.

Entry to the cabin is made a la Citabria by grabbing something sturdy and hauling yourself in. Once seated, you become a bit disoriented. You feel as though you are in a single-engine "Champ," but the plethora of knobs, controls and instruments surrounding you give the impression that you are in a Douglas DC-6. Hanging from the left side of the ceiling is a pair of throttles and mixture controls for each pilot and a single pair of carburetor heat controls to be used by both. The ceiling-mounted controls take advantage of the short linkage to the engines and using them gives the feeling of being in a multi-engine seaplane, which usually has similarly mounted ceiling controls.

A pair of elevator and rudder trim-tab controls is next to each seat on the left sidewall of the cockpit, the same locations normally occupied by the front and rear throttles of a single-engine "Champ" or Citabria. Unfortunately, the location of these trim controls can easily be mistaken for throttles. It is alarming to visualize how a new Lancer pilot might execute a missed approach by reacting to single-engine habit and shoving forward on the trim controls instead of raising his hand to operate the ceiling-mounted throttles.

The Lancer would respond, not surprisingly, with a sudden dive to the right caused by the rapid application of nose-down and right-rudder trim.

The front cockpit has a wheel control, presumably to give the multi-engine student the feeling that he is in a "real" twin. A joystick is provided for the rear pilot. The mock gear-up and -down switch on the front instrument panel helps the student to develop habits needed in more complex twins that really do have retractable landing gear.

The heel-operated brakes are reminders of the Lancer's heritage, the Aeronca "Champ." Anyone who has ever flown the "Airknocker" has a dispassion for these medieval pedals, and the Lancer pilot finds them no less difficult to operate. One improvement, though, is that the brakes are hydraulic, not mechanical. Unfortunately, the instructor in the rear does not have any brakes at all. He must ensure that his student has coordinated heels with which to operate the front brakes before getting under way.

The single, 4-position flap handle is operated like a Volkswagen parking brake and is on the floor ahead and to the left of the front seat.

A maze of instruments, switches and controls literally surrounds the pilot, and there is no apparent method to the madness of whoever designed the cockpit layout. While flying the Lancer, a pilot must crane his neck and stretch his arms in almost every direction. For example, the magneto switches are above, left, and behind his pilot's head. The mixture controls are easier to reach but can be mistaken for carburetor-heat controls. A wrong move and it gets awfully quiet. Crane your head up and right to see the ammeters and then do a 180-degree swivel to see a fuel gauge.

The cockpit does have some niceties, however. The circuit breaker pertaining to each electrical device is located adjacent to the switch that controls that device. The circuit breakers are not grouped together and hidden in a remote corner to improve the decor of the instrument panel.

Instructors in most other tandem-seat aircraft have to stretch their necks to look over the student's shoulder for a peek at the instruments on the main panel. Not so with the Lancer. A small console in the ceiling above the student's head contains a grouping of three instruments solely for the instructor's convenience: an altimeter, airspeed indicator, and a blank space to install whatever other instrument the owner would like to make available to the instructor.

Photo courtesy 1000aircraftphotos.com

Loading the Lancer presents no particular problems as long as you do not load it very much. The aircraft has a useful load of 660 pounds. Deducting 335 pounds for niceties such as fuel and oil leaves 325 pounds for both pilots and baggage (behind the rear seat).

Cockpit visibility is not bad; it is miserable. The instructor in the rear hole will want a collision-warning device installed in the overhead console, and the student gets an instant case of tunnel vision created by the engines projecting so far forward. It is a safe bet that whoever designed the Lancer used to design horse blinders. The sloping nose section, however, does provide excellent forward visibility for the student.

Preconceived notions begin to disappear when you begin to taxi. The engines sound deceptively powerful, throaty. The aircraft feels big and heavy. Nosewheel steering is only moderately effective after the almost-Herculean effort it takes to apply full rudder travel while taxiing. A little differential power makes steering easier, especially when rounding tight corners.

One joy that comes from flying the Lancer is observing the startled faces of those who watch you taxi by. Chances are they have never seen one before, and it is amusing to watch them scratch their heads in bewilderment. It is not so much fun, however, when an old pro waves at you with his Rosary beads.

The runup is conventional: Check the magnetos at 1,800 rpm; rudder and elevator trim—neutral; fuel pumps—on; flaps to the first notch (8 degrees); pilot courage "in the green."

As soon as the takeoff roll begins a new Lancer pilot is ready to abort and head for the barn for a pair of noise-canceling headsets. The Lancer is loud. It does accelerate well, though, and is ready to fly at 73 mph after a 700-foot roll.

Once airborne, the Lancer continues to feel and fly like a heavy airplane, and there is an initial tendency to overcontrol laterally. This apparent instability disappears once you get used to the sensitivity of the large ailerons. And these ailerons demand substantial use of rudder to prevent slipping all over the sky. The Lancer is a stick-and-rudder airplane and anyone lacking in seat-of-the-pants coordination must have some basic flying skills before this aircraft can be flown smoothly.

The Lancer achieves its best rate-of-climb (about 600 fpm) at 75 mph with flaps up and the throttles fully forward. During one of my test flights in the Lancer, I attempted to coax the aircraft to 10,000 feet but gave up after spending almost 17 minutes trying to climb much above 9,000 feet.

During a full-power climb, propeller synchronization is perfect. But once power is reduced to cruise, you are reminded that the Lancer has fixed-pitch propellers. Every change in bank or pitch results in an "out-of-sync" condition. An instructor may wish for constant-speed propellers on this twin, but these are good lessons for the multi-engine student.

In straight-and-level flight, the Lancer does on two engines what the Cessna 150 does on one. At 5,000 feet and an ambient temperature of 20 degrees C, indicated airspeed is 108 mph and true airspeed is 119 mph. This Mach 0.18 flight results from using 65-percent power. Total fuel consumption at this power setting is 10 gallons per hour. Pushing the throttles to the firewall increases fuel flow but does little to improve forward speed, a result of the Lancer's high-drag profile.

The Lancer has the same docile and forgiving stall characteristics as its single-engine counterpart, the "Champ." It is difficult not to feel an impending stall, and recovery requires only the slightest release of back pressure. There is no tendency to drop a wing one way or the other. P-factor produced by the non-critical right engine, however, does produce a slight left yaw during power-on stalls.

After flying the Lancer for a few hours, I had the impression that the flaps had the same function as the landing gear switch, that they did not do anything. Although the flaps do not reduce stall speed, they do steepen the descent profile.

Photo courtesy 1000aircraftphotos.com

It is difficult to speak of the Lancer's single-engine performance with a straight face because the Lancer does not have single-engine performance. According to the flight manual, the Lancer descends 250 fpm (at sea level) with one engine shut down and the other developing maximum power at maximum-allowable gross weight.

The single-engine performance improves slightly at lighter weights, but I cannot conceive of a condition that would enable the Lancer to maintain altitude—any altitude—with "one turning and one burning." (Perish the thought of an engine fire in a fabric-covered airplane.) It is simply too much to expect of a 100-hp engine.

Although the following procedure is not exactly kosher, there is one way to maintain altitude in the Lancer, provided the engine failure occurs at altitude.

First, go through the engine shutdown procedure: mixture control to idle cutoff, fuel-selector valve off, throttle closed; ignition and generator off.

The next steps are not in the book: Retard the throttle of the operative engine, establish an 80-mph glide, and slowly raise the nose. There is no problem in reducing airspeed to below the Lancer's minimum-controllable airspeed of 73 mph ($V_{MC}$) because the operating engine is not developing power and cannot create directional-control difficulties.

As airspeed decreases, the rpm of the windmilling, dead engine will decrease. Continue decreasing airspeed until the Lancer stalls. By this time, the windmilling propeller will have stopped and the drag created by windmilling will have been eliminated.

Next, lower the nose and accelerate to more than 73 mph. Power from the operative engine can then be applied because sufficient rudder effectiveness exists above this speed to keep the airplane pointed straight ahead.

Using this procedure raises the single-engine ceiling from below sea level to more than 2,000 feet msl.

Although the Lancer cannot maintain altitude with a windmilling propeller, this deficiency does not prevent the aircraft from being a decent trainer. A student can still be taught the principles of controlling direction with an engine out, the significance of $V_{MC}$, and the problems associated with reduced performance following an engine failure.

Perhaps the most important thing that a multi-engine student can learn when flying a Lancer is not to fly one again.

## Antonov AN-2 Colt

| | |
|---|---|
| Engine | Shvetsov ASh-621R |
| Power | 1,000 hp |
| Length | 40 ft 8 in |
| Height | (3-point attitude) 13 ft 2 in |
| Wingspan | 59 ft 9 in |
| Wing Loading | 15.7 lb/sq ft |
| Power Loading | 12.1 lb/hp |
| Maximum Takeoff Weight | 12,125 lb |
| Fuel Capacity (usable) | 310 gal |
| Rate of Climb (sea level) | 551 fpm |
| Normal Cruise Speed | 103 kt |
| Stall Speed | <30 mph |

# Antonov AN-2 Colt

## There is no way that a photograph of an Antonov

AN–2 Colt can prepare you for an in-person encounter. It is a behemoth, presumably the world's largest single-engine biplane, and it dwarfs every other single in its vicinity. A massive caricature of an airplane, it has the appearance of something intended for the flintstones.

The "Ant" was designed by Oleg Antonov to serve a variety of utilitarian roles. It made its maiden flight in the Soviet Union on August 31, 1947, and its small ASh-2 750-horsepower radial engine was quickly replaced with the more substantial 1,000-hp Shvetsov engine driving a huge four-blade, constant-speed propeller. (The Shvetsov is a licensed copy of the dependable Wright R-1820 Cyclone that powered many DC-3s.)

Its appearance suggests that Antonov was more interested in rugged simplicity than graceful lines. The airplane was intended to operate under harsh conditions in remote locations. Although there is nothing beautiful or fragile about the Colt—some call it ugly—Russian pilots holding the big biplane in high esteem affectionately refer to it as *Anushka* (Annie).

The Soviets built more than 5,000 Colts, but production was moved to Poland in 1960 where PZL-Mielec built some 12,000 units. China also produced many (called Y-5s) beginning in 1957. The production run spanned an incredible 50 years (1947 to 1997), during which 20,000 to 24,000 units took to wing.

Although the introduction of a biplane in the postwar era might seem anachronistic, the extra wing area was an excellent way for Antonov to provide the prodigious quantities of lift needed to operate a 12,125-pound machine out of unimproved strips less than 1,000 feet long. The extra span also allowed him to hang an assortment of high-lift devices on the narrow-chord wings. It was a matter of form following function.

The entire leading edge of each upper wing is cuffed with corrugated slats that open automatically at large angles of attack and close as the angle of attack is reduced (a result of the center of lift's movement). Bungee cords hold the slats closed when the aircraft is on the ground. The upper wings also are equipped with electrically operated, slotted flaps and ailerons that droop 16 degrees when the flaps are deployed. In effect, the upper wings have full-span flaps. The lower wings do not have ailerons but are configured with full-span flaps that operate in conjunction with the upper-wing flaps.

The Colt is all-metal except for the fabric-covered horizontal stabilizer, control surfaces, and those portions of the wings aft of the forward spars.

The AN–2 featured in this chapter is owned by Robert Haley, a line-maintenance planner for United Airlines who became interested in eastern European aircraft after purchasing a Yak 18T several years ago. He then founded Red Sky Aviation in Livermore, California, which specializes in importing and selling these exotic aircraft.

N707WA rolled off the Polish assembly line on November 4, 1968, and bears the paint scheme of the Soviet airline, Aeroflot. (Aeroflot was once regarded as the world's largest airline because it included in its fleet thousands of AN–2s used as crop dusters, utility transports, and cargo haulers in the Siberian hinterlands and other remote areas.)

Preflighting a Colt includes some unusual items. One is the engine-driven air compressor that is used to operate the pneumatic brakes and to pressurize a 490-cubic-inch air bottle installed in the fuselage. The 710-psi bottle is used to inflate tires and oleo struts (depending on gross weight and type of runway surface).

There are three fuel tanks in each upper wing with a total usable capacity of 310 gallons. Access to the filler caps without a very tall ladder requires climbing up the side of the fuselage using four kick-in steps and walking along a catwalk on top of the fuselage. If the Colt cannot be refueled from above the wing with a conventional hose, a ground-fueling valve accessible through the left side of the cowling allows fuel to be pumped into the tanks from barrels on the ground using the ship's electrical power.

The entry door on the left side of the fuselage is actually a section of a much larger cargo door that is 4.4 feet wide and 5 feet tall and can be opened when loading outsized items. A door in the aft bulkhead of the cabin leads to the long, voluminous tail cone. Although this area may not be used for cargo, it can accommodate light loads such as live chickens and ducks. The wide, spacious cockpit is separated from the cavernous, 12-seat cabin with an accordion-style door. The entire roof of the cockpit can be quickly unlatched, removed, and used as an emergency exit.

Soviet engineers did not have much regard for ergonomics. Switches and controls are scattered helter-skelter and do not accommodate a normal scan pattern. Flying on instruments in the Colt would be a challenge, especially for an American pilot unable to interpret the Cyrillic markings and adapt to the numerous metric indications. The instrument panel in Haley's airplane is completely original except for the added Bendix-King transponder. Standard equipment includes a humongous ADF, a radio altimeter, and a heated clock (don't ask).

The ventilation system includes a small, rubber-bladed fan on each side of the cockpit. These are quite handy when sitting in this greenhouse of a cockpit. The windows consist of 28 glass panes, and the side windows bulge outward a foot so that either pilot can see straight down with the wings level. Looking aft, a pilot can see almost straight back.

The propeller is almost 12 feet in diameter and should be pulled through by hand if the engine has been idle for more than an hour or so. Although Arnold Schwarzenegger could do it alone, it is much easier for a crew of three to attack and keep the prop moving through 20 blades.

Starting the Shvetsov (or Wright, if you prefer) is complicated and best accomplished by a pilot with three hands. Confusing matters is a "mixture-corrector lever" that moves aft to enrich and forward to "make weaker." The carburetor-heat control also operates "backwards."

A spring-loaded toggle switch is positioned up to energize the inertia-wheel starter. You can tell that the wheel has reached maximum rpm when the distinctive whining sound reaches a constant pitch and no longer draws electrical power. (A fully charged battery permits only three or four start attempts.) You then release the toggle and push up on another to engage the starter. After four blades pass before your eyes, turn on the ignition, operate the electrical primer, and hope that the engine starts before the inertia wheel poops out (in which case the procedure is begun anew).

The big radial seems to awaken one cylinder at a time, belching and coughing copious clouds of smoke guaranteed to create IFR conditions for anyone standing behind.

Prior to my arrival in Livermore, I had asked Haley to clean the aircraft in preparation for photographs that would be taken. He replied that, "it would be clean until after the first engine start." The airplane sprays as much oil on the fuselage as it burns. (Engine oil consumption is four to five quarts per hour, and oil capacity is 132 quarts.)

"Washing it," he added, "is like bathing a brontosaurus."

The rudder and fully castoring, self-centering tailwheel are controlled with a rudder bar instead of pedals. The brake handle is on the control wheel, and it appears and is operated much like a hand brake on a bicycle. Squeezing the handle with the rudder bar neutral applies pneumatic brake pressure to both wheels. But engaging the brakes when the rudder bar is angled more than 15 degrees causes pressure to be applied only to one. Apply right rudder and only the right brake operates, and vice versa.

As the airplane trundles along the taxiway, there is much moaning, creaking, and rattling, as if it were some mechanized, prehistoric beast. Intermittent use of the air brakes adds hissing and wheezing to the orchestral mix. The lumbering Colt has a personality of its own and sounds like an 18-wheeler being maneuvered into a tight parking space.

The huge, supercharged Shvetsov on the nose limits forward visibility, so some taxiing S-turns are in order. Considering the almost 60-foot wingspan, I expected some difficulty taxiing in tight quarters but was pleasantly surprised. The upper wing is so high that it easily passes over other aircraft that would otherwise be in the way, and the lower wing is short enough to pass between them.

A before-takeoff checklist is essential and directs you to every nook and cranny in the cockpit. Finally, check the mags at 2,000 rpm and the prop at 1,900; set the flaps to 15 degrees; and the Colt is ready to rumble.

Haley suggested that I not push forward on the control yoke during the takeoff roll. "Just let it go and she'll fly off by herself. There's no need to raise the tail."

I opened the throttle for a 1,000-hp takeoff setting of 2,200 rpm and 1,050 mm (41.3 inches of manifold pressure). Before there is time to think about it, the "Ant" levitates in three-point attitude, all wheels rising from the ground simultaneously. I had such a handful of airplane that I didn't have a chance to glance at how many knots we had. I did know, however, that we didn't have enough, so I lowered the nose to gain speed.

In normal climb at 1,800 rpm and 800 mm (31.5 inches) there is substantial torque and P-factor. This explains why the Colt has such a seemingly oversized tail.

The duties of the copilot include constantly fidgeting with the engine knobs, electrically operated shutters for the external oil cooler, and the electrically operated cowl flaps to keep engine temperatures under control. A pilot flying alone would have his hands full. Although essentially a single-pilot airplane, the Soviets required that a flight engineer sit in the right seat to operate the engine and its systems.

The U.S.-designed engine thankfully turns the "right" way as compared to most Russian engines that turn the "wrong" way (counterclockwise when viewed from behind). My right leg has been conditioned for many years to push against P-factor and no doubt is the stronger of the two. I question if my left leg could have contained the Colt's right-turning tendency for very long during slow flight with a high power setting had the engine turned the other way.

The aircraft has electric trim about all three axes, but no trim-position indicators. Instead, a light for each illuminates only when the tab is neutral. At other times, trim position is largely guesswork.

At its maximum gross weight at sea level, the Colt climbs its best (551 fpm) at 78 knots. Although its cruise speed of 100 knots (1,600 rpm and 700 mm) is unimpressive, its ability to haul a useful load of 4,510 pounds out of an unimproved strip less than 1,000 feet long is very impressive. Fuel burn during cruise is 45 to 50 gph, a specific range of only 2 nm per gallon.

The AN–2 has a sluggish and delayed roll response. It also has an overbanking tendency during turns that requires "holding off" bank with "top" aileron. The Colt could use the additional ailerons found on the lower wing of many other biplanes. After an hour of flying in formation with a photo airplane, my forearm ached and my right leg throbbed. I am convinced that the Soviets developed this airplane as a training aid for their Olympic wrestling and weightlifting teams. Pitch control is more authoritative and lighter, but I was nevertheless grateful for the electric elevator trim.

Stall speeds are difficult to determine because there is no identifiable stall warning or break, nor is there a stall-warning indicator. Controlled descents can be made at

25 KIAS with the yoke held fully aft. According to the pilot's operating handbook, "an inadvertent stall is impossible."

During an approach to a full-power stall (if there is such a thing in the Colt), you can run out of right rudder and not be able to arrest the left yaw.

The AN-2 has a best glide speed of 65 knots, but landing approaches are usually made with power because this is better for the engine.

During the approach, wing flaps are deployed incrementally by pressing with your left thumb a spring-loaded button on the left side of the throttle. It's a handy feature that enables you to lower the flaps (40-degree maximum) without removing a hand from the throttle or control wheel.

Your first arrival is likely to be made with a thud, as mine was, because it is initially difficult to adjust to flaring a single at a height of 20 or 30 feet. The slats deploy automatically during the flare and if things work out properly, the Colt sort of "squishes" onto the ground in three-point attitude. It is something like landing on a wet sponge.

Crosswind landings can be a problem, though. The aircraft touches down so slowly (28 knots, according to GPS) that the rudder has lost much of its effectiveness.

The AN–2 is a workhorse, not a sportplane, and is not fun to fly. Nor is it as much difficult as it is different. Everything seems to happen in slow motion. The name, Colt, is a misnomer that belies its behavior, which is not perky.

The mixture control does not have an idle-cutoff position. The engine is shut down with a separate stop lever that cuts off the fuel supply to the carburetor. If the airplane won't be flown for a while, postflight duties include removing the spark plugs from the bottom cylinders. This allows oil to drain into a can instead of pooling in the cylinders.

Haley claims that despite its size, the AN–2 is trouble free, relatively easy to maintain, and does not require special tools. His aircraft has a total time of 17,000 hours and has been fully reconditioned.

The bad news is that although *Anushka* is fully certified in numerous countries, the FAA only allows it to operate here in the Experimental category, a subject of much controversy. This imposes restrictions that make the Colt impractical for most potential owners.

There are only a few dozen of these gentle giants in the United States, and only a handful are kept airworthy. The AN–2 is a primitive, simple, utilitarian workhorse that turns heads wherever and whenever it lands.

## SIAI Marchetti SF.260C

| | |
|---|---|
| Engine | Avco Lycoming O-540-E4A5 |
| Power | 260 hp |
| Length | 23 ft 3 in |
| Height | 7 ft 11 in |
| Wingspan | 27 ft 5 in |
| Wing Loading | 22.4 lb/sq ft |
| Power Loading | 9.35 lb/hp |
| Maximum Takeoff Weight | 2,430 lb |
| Fuel Capacity (usable) | 62 gal |
| Rate of Climb (sea level) | 1,800 fpm |
| Normal Cruise Speed | 185 kt |
| Stall Speed | 60 kt |

# SIAI Marchetti SF.260

## It is not surprising that the U.S. Air Force

considered the SIAI Marchetti SF.260 as an Enhanced Flight Screener (EFS) to replace its aging fleet of T-41s, military version of the Cessna 172. With a maximum speed at sea level of 196 knots, it is the fastest piston-powered, naturally aspirated, single-engine, aerobatic airplane in production.

The 260 is a sleek, sensuous-looking aircraft. Its carbureted, 260-hp Avco Lycoming engine nuzzles within a slender cowl. Its sliding, teardrop canopy and shapely lines give the impression of a mini-Mustang poised on tricycle gear. The aircraft is an artistic blend of aerodynamics, ballistics and allure.

When approaching some airplanes, form gives way to flaw, but not in this case. The Italian craftsmanship is superlative and withstands scrutiny. Access doors and panels fit snugly, paint is without runs, blemish or overspray, and the thin, laminar-flow wings have flush-riveted, butt-jointed panels.

The quality of an SF.260D is more than skin deep. Before assembly, every structural member is individually etched, alodined, and coated with anti-collision primer.

Inspection plates are secured by nut plates, not sheet-metal screws. Fuel and oil lines are either fire-shielded or made of stainless steel. Each of the four rudder pedals has its own master brake cylinder. Circuit breakers are push/pull (instead of the less expensive flush-mounted type that cannot be used to deactivate electrical circuits). The list of standard equipment is lengthy for a civilian single. That is because the SF.260D is manufactured on the same production line as its military counterpart.

The airplane has been designed for ease of maintenance. By removing six nuts, for example, the entire instrument panel slides aft and into the cockpit on telescoping rails. The components are so accessible that all maintenance can be performed while sitting in either of the pilot's seats.

Cockpit entry is made from narrow wingwalks on either side, but a pilot should mount from the right, because this is where he will sit. The aircraft is essentially a trainer for fighter pilots (who operate the stick with their right hand and the throttle with their left). The captain sits with the center-mounted control quadrant to his left. (A second throttle is mounted on the left sidewall for an instructor.) Although some pilots initially complain about sitting on the co-pilot's side (that is also where the flight instruments are), most pilots make the transition easily.

The interior was designed by the famous automotive design studio, Pinin Farina. Head and leg room is good. With the seat fully aft, my six-foot, two-inch frame was fully stretched to reach the rudder pedals and my arms fully extended to reach the molded stick grip. Shoulder room for two wide people, however, is only marginally acceptable.

There is a rear bench seat for a third passenger, but it is suitable only for a short person on a short flight, or for baggage. The SF.260D has a maximum-allowable gross weight of 2,430 pounds and an empty weight (equipped) of 1,755 pounds. This leaves room for a maximum payload with full fuel (372 pounds) of only 303 pounds, which is the airplane's most serious shortcoming.

The 2,430-pound restriction, however, is not due to structural limitations. The SF.260D is certified in the aerobatic category (+6 to –3 Gs), and the military version has a gross weight of 2,866 pounds without much loss of performance.

The weight limit is a result of the FAA's requirement that single-engine aircraft in the landing configuration not stall above 61 KCAS, which happens to be the SF.260D's stalling speed at 2,430 pounds. Any increase in gross weight would, of course, increase the 1-G stall speed beyond the 61-knot limit.

If the USAF, however, opts for the SF.260, it could—as a military operator—take advantage of the heavier gross weight and accept the higher $V_{so}$ of 66 knots.

Aircraft systems are unremarkable except for a few noteworthy items. The fuel-selector valve, for example, cannot be turned off inadvertently because there is no Off position. (In typical military fashion, an independent push/pull shutoff valve is located beneath the panel.) Fuel can be drawn from the tip tanks (18.3 gallons useable on each side) together or one at a time (to control lateral balance). But the two 12.7-gallon wing tanks only can be used individually. Since each of these tanks supplies fuel for only about an hour, fuel management can be a bit demanding. Total useable capacity is 62 gallons.

The panel-mounted landing-gear lights (three green and one red) are supplemented by a mechanical indicator on the floor similar to many Beech Bonanza and Mooney models. A gear-horn cut-out switch is provided to silence the alarm when throttling back during aerobatic maneuvering, but the horn cannot be muted when the flaps are extended beyond 30 degrees, which normally occurs only prior to landing. Gear and flaps are electrically operated.

Other features include a canopy jettison system and bright annunciator lights that warn of alternator failure, low fuel pressure, unsafe landing-gear position and impending stall.

*Continued on Page 122*

# In 1970, I was invited by the Federation

*Aeronautique Internationale* to attend its annual conference in New Delhi. I was to have been honored there for having broken a world speed record in 1969 for piston-powered airplanes weighing less than 2,205 pounds (1,000 kg) at takeoff.

Flying an unmodified SIAI Marchetti SF.260, I averaged 199.48 KTAS around a 100-km, closed-circuit course.

Although grateful for the invitation, such attention was misdirected. This is because my speed mark was not attributable to superior airmanship. Any competent pilot could have done the same. Instead, the new record was a triumph of design, and the person who deserved the accolades was the SF.260's designer, Stelio Frati.

Frati has always had a passion for performance and surgically removes drag from a design as if it were a cancer. Sleek lines and darting silhouettes are his trademark. In his own words, "I cannot understand how one can design an ugly airplane [when] it costs no more to build a beautiful one."

Although the Italian designer had produced many noteworthy designs, he did not develop a low-wing monoplane until 1951, when he created the F.4 Rondone (Swift), a 90-hp, two-place aircraft clocked at 147 knots.

His first commercially successful design was the F.8L Falco (Hawk), which had a maximum speed of 184 knots using only 160 hp. It currently is available only in kit form.

Frati's first all-metal design was to become his most famous. In the early 1960s, he designed the SF.250 (the SF represents the designer's initials), a three-seat sporting machine that was remarkably similar in form to the Falco. But only a prototype was built. SIAI Marchetti was so impressed with the SF.250's potential as a military trainer that it purchased the manufacturing rights from Frati's company, Aviamilano, and increased the power. The result was the SF.260, which first flew in 1966.

Since then, more than 1,000 SF.260s have been sold to the military services of 28 countries where they have been used as *ab initio* trainers (SF.260M), weapons trainers and attack aircraft (SF.260W) and coastal surveillance aircraft (SF.260SW). In addition, more than 100 civilian versions have been sold (of which 70 are in the United States) including some used by a few European air carriers as proficiency trainers.

In the late 1960s, SIAI Marchetti added leading-edge cuffs to the outer 20 percent of the wing's span (to tame reputedly ill-mannered stall characteristics), added wing dihedral, increased the height of the rudder and vertical fin, incorporated a canopy jettison system and modified the wing with hard points to carry such external loads as drop tanks, rocket pods and launchers, 7.62-mm machine guns and small bombs. These changes resulted in the SF.260B.

Additional improvements, which included lagging balance (or servo) tabs on the ailerons to lighten lateral stick forces and a more sophisticated 24-volt electrical system, resulted in the SF.260C.

An improvement in the wing spar (which allows aerobatics to be performed at the maximum-allowable gross weight), a stronger nosewheel strut, and a short-stroke canopy jettison handle are the major differences between a C- and a D-model.

Engine start and preflight are conventional, but the anticipation a pilot feels is not. There is something exciting about just taxiing an SF.260. Perhaps it is the throaty sound resonating from the unmuffled engine. Or perhaps it is simply knowing that you are about to fly a very special airplane. (It is a noisy one, too; noise-attenuating headsets are a must.

With the slotted flaps set at 20 degrees and full throttle, the diminutive warbird accelerates like a squeezed watermelon seed. Rotate at 65 knots, lift off at 70, retract the gear, milk up the flaps at 90, and settle back for an 1,800-fpm ride to altitude.

The *creme de la creme* is the SF.260's handling qualities. The controls, activated by both rods and cables, are very responsive, well harmonized and exhibit no noticeable system friction (due to the liberal use of ball bearings). Pilots unaccustomed to such light controls tend initially to overcontrol in roll and in pitch. They should not grip the stick; instead, they should rest their right forearm on their right thigh and maneuver the airplane with fingertips. Finesse is used, not muscle. A pilot does not fly an SF.260; he makes love to it.

Small control deflections result in large attitude changes. Yet the aircraft can be maneuvered (except for takeoff, steep climb and landing) with feet flat on the floor. Rudder input seldom is required. The SF.260D flies the way it looks like it should fly: beautifully.

It has been said that one man's passion is another man's peril, and this certainly is true of the SF.260. Experienced pilots are delighted with its control sensitivity, but others may fail to survive it. It takes little effort to build Gs (the aircraft has a shallow stick-force gradient) or flick into a steep turn. Consequently, pilots must learn to avoid inadvertently entering high-speed (accelerated) stalls. Such traits, however, should not pose a problem for *ab initio* military students. This is because they would not have to overcome habits of complacency that would have been developed had they initially flown aircraft requiring less attention.

Aerobatic flight best demonstrates the handling qualities of the machine. Move the stick to one side and the earth tumbles at 150 degrees per second. From level flight at cruise speed, the SF.260 will perform a high, sweeping loop without a net loss of altitude. The airplane is certificated for all aerobatic maneuvers—including snap rolls—as long as the tip tanks are empty, the rear seat is unoccupied and the canopy is closed. (The canopy may be open six inches at airspeeds below 120 knots.)

The SF.260D also is a good cross-country machine because it crosses country so quickly. Cruise speed at 5,000 feet using 77-percent power is 185 knots. Throttling back to 66-percent power at 10,000 feet yields 178 knots. Range at 9,000 feet using 62-percent power is 755 nm with a 45-minute reserve. (During my flight testing of the aircraft, resultant cruise speeds were never less than those quoted by the pilot's operating handbook.)

And because of its high wing loading of 22.35 pounds per square foot, the Marchetti's sharp wing cuts through turbulence like a hot knife through butter, which gives the impression of a heavier aircraft.

At the opposite end of the speed spectrum, the D model has milder stall characteristics than the original 260 because a leading-edge cuff added to the outer 20 percent of the wing's span. The stall is preceded by an attention-getting, aerodynamic buffet. But this occurs so close to the "break" that it does not serve as an adequate warning. The stall warner, however, does give timely notice and must be regarded seriously because of the ease with which a 260D enters a high-speed stall. The stall itself demonstrates no unusual traits. The ailerons are so effective during a deep (stick fully aft), prolonged stall that a wings-level attitude can be maintained without rudder input.

One reason for such roll effectiveness is that the ailerons are enhanced by lagging balance (or servo) tabs. Another is the small, airfoil-shaped vane attached to the upper, inboard side of each tip tank. These energize the air flowing over the Frise-type ailerons.

Stall recovery requires only a slight release of back pressure. A pilot must be careful not to shove the stick forward excessively because this can result not only in stall recovery, but also in the first half of an inadvertent, outside loop.

Spins are conventional but are steeper and more rapid than in most general aviation aircraft. Although recovery can be made simply by releasing the controls, the aircraft is aerodynamically clean and accelerates rapidly to the 236-knot red line. A more aggressive recovery, therefore, is required. (A 3-G pullout results in a 1,500-ft. altitude loss.)

Landings require planning because the slippery 260 is reluctant to slow down. Although 20 degrees of flap can be extended at 130 KIAS, the landing gear and additional flap must not be deployed until 108 KIAS. The aircraft has a respectable glide ratio (10:1), but with the gear out and the flaps extended 50 degrees (maximum), it plummets like Wall Street stock just after I buy it. Approaches should be made with power.

Traffic pattern speed is 95 KIAS to protect against maneuver-induced stalls. When on final approach and further turning no longer is anticipated, reduce to 85 KIAS until nearing the threshold.

Landings are softened by the trailing-link landing gear, but consistently good landings require a familiar hand and a conscious effort to avoid overcontrolling (especially in roll during gusty conditions).

After a few circuits and bumps, one realizes that elevator trim rarely is required. You can take off, cycle the gear and flaps, vary power and land without even thinking about the trim wheel. When trim is needed, only a slight amount is used; a little movement goes a long way.

An aerobatic fanatic has a choice of two 260-hp engines: the carbureted Lycoming, which is limited to 10 seconds of inverted flight, or the fuel-injected, Lycoming AEIO-540. This option includes inverted wing tanks and a Christen inverted oil system that allow the SF.260D to be flown upside down until either the fuel or the pilot is exhausted, whichever occurs first.

(The ultimate option is the SF.260TP, a turboprop version of the SF.260D. The TP, which has been in military service for years, was recently certified by the FAA as a civilian aircraft and is powered by an Allison 250B-17C, 420-shp engine that is derated to 350 shp. The TP has a 3,600-fpm climb rate and a maximum speed of more than 250 KTAS at 10,000 feet.)

The SIAI Marchetti SF.260D obviously is not for everyone. It is a machine for the discriminating pilot in search of style, performance and panache, something guaranteed to make his adrenaline flow. It is also one of the most seductive lightplanes ever developed.

## Israel Aircraft Industries Model 201 Arava

| | |
|---|---|
| Engines | 2 Pratt & Whitney PT6A-34 |
| Power | 750 shp ea |
| Length | 42 ft 6 in |
| Height | 17 ft 1 in |
| Wingspan | 68 ft 6 in |
| Wing Loading | 32.0 lb/sq ft |
| Power Loading | 8.3 lb/shp |
| Maximum Takeoff Weight | 12,500 lb |
| Fuel Capacity (usable) | 417 gal |
| Rate of Climb (sea level) | 1,713 fpm |
| Normal Cruise Speed | 161 mph |
| Stall Speed | 64 mph |

# IAI's Arava 201

## "I have an appointment with Shimon Shamir."

The burliest of four armed security guards at the entrance to Israel Aircraft Industries turned and suspiciously ran his eyes over the two Americans standing before him. He paid particular attention to the Nikon camera slung casually over my shoulder.

"One moment," he said gruffly. "Let me have your passports, and stand aside."

He picked up the telephone, dialed, and after a short pause began speaking excitedly in rapid-fire Hebrew. Unable to understand this revitalized ancient language, I turned toward the nearest window of the security shack in time to see a TWA Boeing 707 thunderously departing Israel's Ben Gurion International Airport.

As the roar of the turbines faded over the Mediterranean, the guard's raised voice predominated once again. The only words recognizable to me during this end of the conversation were "Schiff" and "Nikon."

Trying to maintain a facade of nonchalance, I studied what was visible of Israel Aircraft Industries' vast research and manufacturing complex. It was no secret that within these buildings was the extraordinary scientific and technological talent responsible for developing the Kfir advanced combat aircraft, the Gabriel sea-to-sea, guided-missile system, the Dabur patrol boat, and a host of other sophisticated defensive/offensive devices needed to provide Israel with a strong military posture in the Middle East.

IAI began humbly in 1953 with only 70 employees working in temporary quarters. Since then it has emerged into a first-class aerospace organization that has been a major factor in the survival of the Jewish state during its brief, turbulent history.

But survival requires more than arms and armies. Israel also is fighting an economic war and desperately needs to remedy a serious trade deficit. This is one reason why IAI entered the fiercely competitive arena of manufacturing and marketing civilian aircraft. It began this ambitious program in 1967 by acquiring the Jet Commander 1121 from Rockwell Standard. Since then the business jet has been stretched and extensively reengineered resulting in the Model 1123 Commodore Jet, the Model 1124 Westwind, and eventually the Model 1125SP Astra.

Eager to manufacture an Israeli-designed aircraft, IAI opted to build a light, twin-turboprop transport for which it felt there would be a large market in developing nations. The aircraft was to have military, commuter, and executive potential. The result was the Model 201 Arava, Israel's first indigenous design.

Named after the desert valley extending from the southern tip of the Dead Sea to the Gulf of Eilat, the Arava first flew in November, 1969 and entered production in 1971.

Five years and almost 50 military versions later, IAI entered the civilian market, and this was the reason for my visit to the Holy Land. Accompanying me was Jack Chrysler, whose expertise with a somewhat similar craft, the DeHavilland DHC-6 Twin Otter, would be helpful in evaluating the Arava.

Several minutes after the security guard had terminated his conversation, Shimon Shamir of the Arava sales force arrived to settle the matter of allowing my camera on the premises. Apparently Shamir had the necessary clout because the Nikon was permitted. This, we were told later, was a rarity. It was not that anyone was afraid that we would photograph some top-secret project. These were well hidden from view. What could be seen were a variety of military and civil aircraft from an assortment of distant countries undergoing major maintenance and/or modification. It was these activities, and for whom they were performed, about which IAI was sensitive and preferred not to have memorialized on film.

As we drove toward the flight line, I spotted a rather unorthodox looking aircraft. When I inquired about this strange machine, our escort responded coolly, "You didn't see that."

In the distance, however, I did see the Arava being readied for flight. It has the appearance of a bumblebee or a stubby cigar slung under a thick rectangular wing (take your pick). But what the Arava lacks in aesthetics is adequately offset with rugged practicality.

The basic design began with a fuselage that had a circular cross-section because, even though this is more expensive to build than a rectangular fuselage, circular is more suitable for pressurization and/or stretching, possibilities for future models. Fuselage length and diameter were dictated by the need to carry a fully-armed jeep or to comfortably seat 20 passengers.

To accommodate such outsized cargo as a jeep, a large door was required. This resulted in the conical swing-tail that opens more than 90 degrees toward the starboard side of the fuselage. The geometry of the tail cone also minimizes drag and allows short-field takeoffs and landings at exaggerated, nose-up attitudes without risking a tail strike.

A high wing was chosen to keep the 3-bladed Hartzell propellers clear of ground obstacles and debris when operating from unimproved runways. Double-slotted, electrically operated flaps span 61 percent of the wing, which has a thick, high-lift, NACA 63-series airfoil. This leaves room for only relatively short-span Frise ailerons.

To augment roll control at slow speed, a scoop-type spoiler (like those found on Helio Couriers) is positioned forward of each flap. These are linked to the ailerons and each spoiler rises automatically and only when its respective aileron is deflected up more than 5 degrees.

The twin-boom configuration allows a truck to back up under the high elevator and park immediately adjacent to the Arava's cabin floor, thus permitting straight-in loading through the open swing-tail. Or, a small vehicle can be driven up a portable ramp directly into the aircraft.

Airstairs were planned for future models, and the 113-cubic-foot cone of the swing tail would serve as an easily accessible baggage compartment.

An added benefit of the twin-boom configuration is that this places a rudder directly in the propwash of each Pratt & Whitney PT6A-27 turboprop engine. This increases rudder effectiveness at slow airspeeds and provides a respectably low minimum single-engine control speed ($V_{MC}$) of 78 mph.

The Arava's designers decided against retractable landing gear believing that the added performance would not be justified by the increased weight, cost, and maintenance. The idea was for the Arava to have maximum reliability, simplicity, and ruggedness, goals that appear to have been adequately met.

Shamir introduced us to Menahem Schmul, an Arava test pilot, who received his aerial baptism in the Israeli Air Force. Schmul did an about face, presented 4X-IBH (a new Arava destined for Mexico), and inquired abruptly, "Shall we fly?"

We nodded, and Schmul led us to the left side of the tail cone where we climbed a small portable ladder through the passenger door into the spacious cabin.

I was immediately impressed with the utility of the 7-foot, 8-inch-wide cabin. The Arava was the only commuter-type aircraft certificated under U.S. Federal Aviation Regulations Part 23 that was capable of 4-abreast seating.

Although Part 23 limits the Arava to a maximum takeoff weight of 12,500 pounds, IAI sought an exemption from the FAA to operate the aircraft at 15,000 pounds. This is the limitation observed by operators in 8 other countries where deliveries had been made. (During the Yom Kippur War, the Arava scampered in and out of short, unimproved strips while weighing in excess of 17,000 pounds.) During our flight, the aircraft was loaded with full fuel tanks (417 gallons) and sufficient ballast to establish a takeoff weight of 12,500 pounds.

Schmul buckled himself into the left seat because he was required to have access to the single steering wheel used to control the hydraulically-powered nosewheel. Engine start was conventional, and as we trundled toward Ben Gurion's Runway 21, the simple pre-takeoff checklist was completed.

After being cleared to line up, Schmul extended the flaps to 25 degrees, locked the brakes and commanded 750 shp (783 eshp) from each engine. When the toe brakes were released, the Arava lunged forward, quickly gobbled up 600 feet of sea-level runway and was rotated positively to a jet-like attitude of more than 15 degrees. At 75 mph, the "bumblebee" clawed skyward at an extraordinarily steep angle.

After lowering the nose and retracting the flaps, Schmul established a more conventional climb at 1,700 fpm.

At altitude, Schmul demonstrated how comfortably the aircraft can be maneuvered at the lower limits of the design envelope. He then relinquished the controls to give Chrysler and me an opportunity to become more intimately acquainted with this Israeli workhorse.

The aircraft exhibits conventional and predictable handling characteristics, but flying the aircraft for long periods can be fatiguing due to the physical effort needed to move the control surfaces. The Arava is not flown with fingertips.

Since a heavy hand is needed to control pitch (especially during large power and/ or speed changes), liberal use of the electrically-operated pitch trim is necessary. Rudder and aileron tabs are also electrically activated. One wonders, however, how an Arava pilot would fare during an electrical failure because none of the trim tabs can be operated manually. At such a time, a pilot would be wise to cruise at the trimmed airspeed (the speed at which trim or electrical failure occurred) rather than change speed and be forced to exert considerable control forces for the remainder of cruise flight.

It is difficult to determine the precise flaps-down, power-on stall speed because the Arava does not stall in the conventional sense. When indicating about 50 mph (which seems to be the slowest achievable airspeed), the Arava simply holds its head high and gradually settles, all the while exhibiting exceptional roll control. It is difficult to imagine losing control of this forgiving airplane. A flaps-up, power-off stall results in a mild break at 79 mph.

To escape the beehive of international arrivals and departures at Israel's main airport, we established cruise power at 5,500 feet and pointed the nose toward

Jerusalem's less-hectic traffic pattern. True airspeed was 165 mph. At 10,000 feet, the Arava cruises at 182 mph.

The wide, spacious cockpit is a comfortable working environment and there is ample room for the various instruments and controls, which are arranged neatly and logically.

The thoroughly rugged design of the machine extends also to the cockpit. All handles, knobs, and switches are heavy duty, built to last. The noise level is appreciably high, but the din is not as assaulting as in similar utility craft.

Once in the pattern at Jerusalem, it was difficult to devote total attention to Schmul's instructions regarding short-field landings. The Western Wall, holiest spot on Earth for Jews, passed by on the right. Then there was the Dome of the Rock Temple, the Mount of Olives, Mount Zion, and a host of other biblical pylons that are difficult to ignore during low-altitude turns. But soon the windshield was filled with Jerusalem's single runway.

Schmul dragged the Arava over the boundary at 60 mph with the immense flaps fully extended. Raising the nose imperceptibly, he allowed the aircraft to hit the tarmac (excessive flaring uses too much runway) whereupon he simultaneously applied maximum reverse pitch, stomped on the binders, and did a one-eighty on the tarmac. Total runway used was less than 600 feet. It was a convincing demonstration and removed any doubt about factory claims that the Arava operates routinely from a 950-foot-long, jungle strip in Ecuador located at 5,000 feet msl.

Chrysler and I took turns shooting touch-and-goes, and we found the Arava easy to maneuver and land using conventional techniques. Developing proficiency in short-field operations, we concluded, requires practice.

During a coffee break at Jerusalem, I finally was allowed to uncover my camera, but not without first being cautioned about where not to point it. Nearby, armed security guards ensured that I paid attention to this admonishment. Aerial photography in Israel, by the way, was verboten at the time.

Although IAI felt confident about penetrating the commuter market with the Arava, it was also planned to introduce the airplane to the bush country of Alaska and Canada. Perhaps it is there that Israel's "Flying Boxcar" will have an opportunity to demonstrate its potential as a versatile utility aircraft. The Arava can carry 17 fully-armed paratroopers or haul 2.5 tons of cargo from fields that would tear the landing gear from more fragile aircraft. On floats, the Arava would be quite a performer.

The aircraft was designed to fill a variety of civil and military roles, so if a customer wanted an Arava to be configured as an ambulance, a tanker, a gunship, a hunter-killer in anti-submarine warfare, or for counter-insurgency missions, IAI was willing to provide the hardware. It apparently performed those roles quite well.

## Saab MFI-17 Safari

| | |
|---|---|
| Engine | Avco Lycoming IO-360-A1B |
| Power | 200 hp |
| Length | 23 ft 4 in |
| Height | 8 ft 6 in |
| Wingspan | 29 ft 1 in |
| Wing Loading | 20.6 lb/sq ft |
| Power Loading | 13.2 lb/hp |
| Maximum Takeoff Weight | 2,645 lb |
| Fuel Capacity (usable) | 48 gal |
| Rate of Climb (sea level) | 810 fpm |
| Normal Cruise Speed | 129 mph |
| Stall Speed | 67 mph |

# Saab Safari

To my list of Scandinavian favorites such as Ursula Andress, Ingrid Bergman, Britt Ekland and Ann-Margret (I am definitely showing my age), I now add another Swedish star performer, the Saab Safari.

This is a versatile aircraft designed to do it all. The Safari is aerobatic (+6 to −3 Gs), is rugged enough to land on a winding dirt road you would not want to drive on, can haul a litter case in its expansive baggage compartment, is easily convertible from tricycle gear to taildragger, and—if you are so inclined—can carry 660 pounds of wing-mounted, anti-tank missiles and 135-mm rockets.

Or the Safari can turn its swords into plowshares. In 1974, a small fleet of Safaris were flown to famine-ravaged Ethiopia to participate in a unique airlift. Taking off from small clearings at density altitudes above 10,000 feet, the Safaris air-dropped desperately needed food to remote villages accessible only by pack mule or helicopter. Approaching the village centers at 70 mph and 10 to 15 feet agl, the pilots dropped burst-proof sacks of grain and inner tubes filled with water to within a few feet of their targets. During this operation, each Safari delivered 7 tons of food per day.

At the other extreme, six 8-man life rafts can be attached to underwing hardpoints and dropped precisely where needed during air-sea rescue.

When not working, the Safari is an ideal playmate. It has everything except speed. Full power from its 200-hp, fuel-injected Lycoming results in a maximum sea-level speed of only 147 mph. Normal cruise (75% power at 8,000 feet) is 132 mph. Speed, or lack of it, is the Safari's deficiency. But Bjorn Andreasson, the Safari's Swedish-born designer, was not interested in speed. The goal was to develop a rugged, utilitarian machine that could withstand the rigors of adverse bush conditions and still possess exceptional handling characteristics for use as an *ab initio* trainer.

From a design standpoint, the Safari is not a beautiful airplane, partially because of its strut-braced wings that sweep forward 5 degrees. This forward sweep, however, is not a designer's fetish. Andreasson wanted the pilots to sit on the center of gravity without their outside view being impaired by the low wings. So he moved the wing roots aft and out of the way. This was countered by moving the wingtips forward. The forward sweep also improves short-field performance by reducing spanwise flow, which decreases induced drag and improves wingtip flow patterns.

The wings are mounted at the height of the pilots' shoulders so that when looking aft, you can see above and below the wings. Additionally, a small chunk of wing is removed from each forward wing root to further enhance visibility. To offset this slight loss of lift, a small slot is built into the leading edge near each root.

The wing is tough, too. When bent to simulate a 17-G load, nothing broke and the ailerons were still operative.

Another eye-catching feature of the all-metal Safari is the square cross-section of the aft fuselage. (The side panels are slightly curved to prevent "oil canning.") This utilitarian shape was employed to hold down construction costs, surprising when you consider that everything else about the aircraft is expensive. The Safari is built to exceed military and NATO specifications. Saab claims to have applied the same quality standards to this aircraft as it applied to its Mach 2 Viggen.

Emphasis also is placed on crashworthiness. The longitudinal structural members of the cockpit are bent slightly outward, for example. During a crash, these members fold outward (away from the cabin) and act as shock absorbers. (The pilots are held in place by 5-point, inertia-reel shoulder harnesses stressed for 20 Gs.)

The integral fuel tanks are between the forward and aft wing spars and, therefore, receive significant crash protection.

Should a pilot flip a Safari on its back and be unable to open the canopy, the cockpit seat backs are designed to fold out of the way. This allows the pilots to escape through the baggage compartment and out the rear door.

One inadvertent testimony to the Safari's crash survivability occurred in Africa. No one can explain what inspired the pilot to enter a loop immediately after takeoff, but he did. With obviously insufficient airspeed, the aircraft stalled and impacted the ground nose first. The pilot extricated himself from the tangle of metal and walked away from the wreckage dazed but uninjured.

Mechanics, too, are delighted with the Safari. Large access panels on the cowling allow a really close inspection of the engine. When the cowl is fully removed, the engine can be tilted nose down to expose the entire accessory section.

A large door aft of the baggage compartment allows easy access to the electronics compartment.

One philosophy of the Safari design is to make maintenance as unnecessary and as simple as possible. And if the maintenance technician has a friend handy, he can remove the nosewheel, relocate the main gear legs and install a tailwheel in 2 hours. *Voila!* A trike that converts to a taildragger. Conversion reduces empty weight by 30 pounds (from 1,410 to 1,380 pounds) and increases airspeed by a few knots.

I was introduced to the Safari at Malmo, Sweden's Bulltofta Airport, which is where Saab assembled these aircraft and performed flight-test activities. Leif Salmbert, one of Saab's test pilots checked me out in the airplane.

My friend, Jack Chrysler, was with me to serve a necessary but unglamorous purpose: the third occupant. Without a whimper, he crawled through the baggage compartment door and into the lone, aft-facing seat. Chrysler stated later that he wasn't at all uncomfortable facing aft and studying the tail surfaces even during steep arrivals and departures, and unusual maneuvering.

The observer's seat is easily and quickly removable, leaving ample room for 220 pounds of cargo or a supplemental ferry tank for long-range flights.

The cockpit is magnificent. All instruments, switches, and controls are logically placed, within easy reach, and are so self-explanatory as to preclude the possibility of any design-induced system mismanagement.

`In addition to conventional instrumentation, the panel features a fire-detection system for the engine, a rarity on small, piston-powered singles. There also is a substantial annunciator panel that warns of a host of other possible problems (such as an overheated 24-volt, NiCad battery or an unlocked canopy). Other lights warn when the auxiliary electric fuel pump is on and when the fuel selector is off.

The cockpit is roomy and comfortable. The seats are balanced on gas-spring cylinders which makes positioning them (up and forward or down and aft) an effortless operation. Once the seats are in place and the rudder pedals have been adjusted to the length of your legs, you discover the dual, military-style control-stick handgrips bristling with buttons.

Each stick (the right one is easily removable) has four buttons to operate the electric pitch trim, transmitter, intercom, and rocket launcher (or whatever loads are attached to the bottoms of the wings).

A pilot also has the option of flying right-handed using the left, sidewall-mounted throttle or left-handed using the center, console-mounted throttle.

Cockpit visibility is outstanding, better than some helicopters. This is due to Andreasson's unorthodox wing, the military-style canopy, and a relatively low instrument panel. The view is remarkably good.

Excellent ground ventilation results from taxiing with the aft-hinged canopy raised somewhat. (Personally, I preferred a sliding canopy.) Shutting and locking the heavy canopy is effortless because it, like the seats, is balanced on gas-spring cylinders.

The first surprise comes during takeoff. Because pitch control is so light, it is initially easy to rotate excessively. Instead of relying on feel, a pilot should wait until almost 60 knots before applying back pressure.

At maximum-allowable gross weight at sea level, the Safari scampers to liftoff in only 675 feet. The best rate-of-climb airspeed (80 knots) produces an 810-fpm climb rate, but holding 60 knots results in a very steep climb over obstacles.

All primary controls are light, responsive and extraordinarily well-harmonized, a surprising accomplishment for such an all-purpose machine.

Only two control peculiarities are noticeable. At large angles of attack, the cruciform-mounted stabilator is lowered into the propwash and results in a medium-frequency nibble felt through the control stick. Also, the rudder seems somewhat deficient. Because of this, it is difficult to maintain a steep or even moderately-banked slip. There is sufficient rudder, however, to recover from a fully-developed spin in half a turn. Perhaps the rudder is not really needed at all because the ailerons produce negligible adverse-yaw effect, and the Safari makes a hands-and-feet-off recovery from a 20-turn spin in only one turn. Altitude loss per spin is about 350 feet.

Hesitation rolls are relatively easy due to the light control forces required and the aerodynamic contribution of the slab-sided fuselage. Roll rates vary from 700 degrees per second at 80 knots to 1,200 degrees per second at 145 knots.

Inverted flight is limited to 10 seconds unless the optional, inverted oil system is installed.

Power-off stalls are conventional and mild. Power-on stalls, however, do not "break" in the normal manner. Instead, the Safari just bucks while maintaining a more-or-less level attitude during which the ailerons remain effective. When entering an accelerated stall during a coordinated, steep turn, the Safari cooperates nicely by breaking out of the turn.

One of the Safari's long suits is its exceptionally strong, dynamic longitudinal stability. Reduce the power or increase it, and the nose repositions automatically and promptly to maintain the same airspeed; virtually no trim change is required. As a matter of fact, the transition from a power-off glide (with flaps extended to 20 degrees) to a full-power missed approach can be executed "hands off."

Conventional approaches (flaps 38 degrees, 75 knots) and landings are childishly simple, but be careful about steep, short-field approaches with full flaps (38 degrees) and power off at 60 knots. The aircraft sinks like a brick. Like most airplanes in a high-drag, low-airspeed configuration, considerable power is needed to avoid high sink rates near the ground.

Without power, additional airspeed is required to assume a more reasonable descent profile. Best glide speed (flaps up) is 84 knots and results in a 9:1 glide ratio.

The Safari is a sprite, spirited, multi-purpose aircraft that was designed to compete as a military trainer against the Scottish Bulldog, Italy's SIAI Marchetti SF.260, and New Zealand's CT-4. But it was also available to civilians, and I envy those who took advantage of the opportunity. The Safari is a unique airplane with lots of ability and utility.

## Lockheed U-2S

| | |
|---|---|
| Engine | General Electric F118-GE-101 |
| Power | 17,000 lb thrust |
| Length | 63 ft 0 in |
| Height (3-point attitude) | 16 ft 1 in |
| Wingspan | 103 ft 0 in |
| Wing Loading | 41.6 lb/sq ft |
| Power Loading | 2.4 lb/lb thrust |
| Maximum Takeoff Weight | 41,000 lb |
| Fuel Capacity | 2,915 gal |
| Rate of Climb (sea level) | 4,920 fpm |
| Maximum Cruise Speed | 510 kt |
| Stall Speed | 75 kt |

# The Lockheed U-2 "Dragon Lady"

Maj. Dean Neeley is in the forward, lower cockpit of the Lockheed U-2ST, a two-place version of the U-2S, a high-altitude reconnaissance aircraft that the Air Force calls "Dragon Lady." His voice on the intercom breaks the silence. "Do you know that you're the highest person in the world?" He explains that I am in the higher of the two cockpits and that there are no other U-2s airborne right now. "Astronauts don't count," he says, "They're out of this world."

We are above 70,000 feet and still climbing slowly as the aircraft becomes lighter. The throttle has been at its mechanical limit since takeoff, and the single General Electric F118-GE-101 turbofan engine sips fuel so slowly at this altitude that consumption is less than when idling on the ground. Although true airspeed is that of a typical jetliner, indicated airspeed registers only in double digits.

I cannot detect the curvature of the Earth, although some U-2 pilots claim that they can. The sky at the horizon is hazy white but transitions to midnight blue at our zenith. It seems that if we were much higher, the sky would become black enough to see stars at noon.

The Sierra Nevada, the mountainous spine of California, has lost its glory, a mere corrugation on the Earth. Lake Tahoe looks like a fishing hole, and rivers have become rivulets. Far below, "high flying" jetliners etch contrails over Reno, Nevada, but we are so high above these aircraft that they cannot be seen.

I feel mild concern about the bailout light on the instrument panel and pray that Neeley does not have reason to turn it on. At this altitude I also feel a sense of insignificance and isolation; earthly concerns seem trivial. This flight is an epiphany, a life-altering experience.

I cannot detect air noise through the helmet of my pressure suit. I hear only my own breathing, the hum of avionics through my headset and, inexplicably, an occasional, shallow moan from the engine, as if it were gasping for air. Atmospheric pressure is only an inch of mercury, less than 4 percent of sea-level pressure. Air density and engine power are similarly low. The stratospheric wind is predictably light, from the southwest at 5 kt, and the outside air temperature is minus 61 degrees Celsius.

Neeley says that he has never experienced weather that could not be topped in a U-2, and I am reminded of the classic transmission made by John Glenn during Earth orbit in a Mercury space capsule: "Another thousand feet, and we'll be on top."

Although not required, we remain in contact with Oakland Center while in the Class E airspace that begins at Flight Level 600. The U-2's Mode C transponder, however, can indicate no higher than FL600. When other U-2s are in the area, pilots report their altitudes, and ATC keeps them separated by 5,000 feet and 10 miles.

Our high-flying living quarters are pressurized to 29,500 feet, but 100-percent oxygen supplied only to our faces lowers our physiological altitude to about 8,000 feet. A pressurization-system failure would cause our suits to instantly inflate to maintain a pressure altitude of 35,000 feet, and the flow of pure oxygen would provide a physiological altitude of 10,000 feet.

The forward and aft cockpits are configured almost identically. A significant difference is the down-looking periscope/driftmeter in the center of the forward instrument panel. It is used to precisely track over specific ground points during reconnaissance, something that otherwise would be impossible from high altitude. The forward cockpit also is equipped with a small side-view mirror extending into the air stream. It is used to determine if the U-2 is generating a telltale contrail when over hostile territory.

Considering its 103-foot wingspan and resultant roll dampening, the U-2 maneuvers surprisingly well at altitude; the controls are light and nicely harmonized. Control wheels (not sticks) are used, however, perhaps because aileron forces are heavy at low altitude. A yaw string (like those used on sailplanes) above each canopy silently admonishes those who allow the aircraft to slip or skid when maneuvering. The U-2 is very much a stick-and-rudder airplane, and I discover that slipping can be avoided by leading turn entry and recovery with slight rudder pressure.

When approaching its service ceiling, the U-2's maximum speed is little more than its minimum. This marginal difference between the onset of stall buffet and Mach buffet is known as coffin corner, an area warranting caution. A stall/spin sequence can cause control loss from which recovery might not be possible when so high, and an excessive Mach number can compromise structural integrity. Thankfully, an autopilot with Mach hold is provided.

The U-2 has a fuel capacity of 2,915 gallons of thermally stable jet fuel distributed among four wing tanks. It is unusual to discuss turbine fuel in gallons instead of pounds, but the 1950s-style fuel gauges in the U-2 indicate in gallons. Most of the other flight instruments seem equally antiquated.

## I TRAIN AT "THE RANCH"

Preparation for my high flight began the day before at Beale Air Force Base (a.k.a. The Ranch), which is north of Sacramento, California, and was where German prisoners of war were interned during World War II. It is home to the 9th Reconnaissance Wing, which is responsible for worldwide U-2 operations including those aircraft based in Cyprus, Italy, Saudi Arabia, and South Korea.

After passing a physical exam (whew!), I took a short, intensive course in high-altitude physiology and use of the pressure suit. The 27-pound Model S1034 "pilot's protective assembly" is manufactured by David Clark (the headset people) and is the same as the one used by astronauts during shuttle launch and reentry.

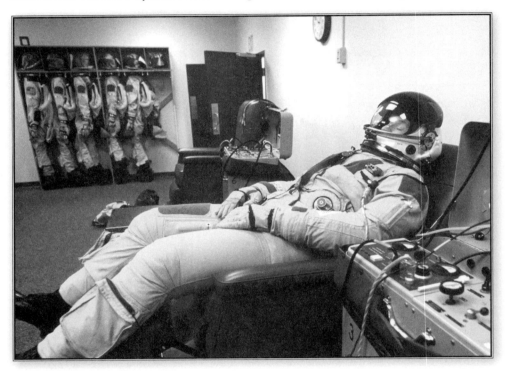

After being measured for my $150,000 spacesuit, I spent an hour in the egress trainer. It provided no comfort to learn that pulling up mightily on the handle between my legs would activate the ejection seat at any altitude or airspeed. When the handle is pulled, the control wheels go fully forward, explosives dispose of the canopy, cables attached to spurs on your boots pull your feet aft, and you are rocketed into space. You could then free fall in your inflated pressure suit for 54,000 feet or more. I was told that "the parachute opens automatically at 16,500 feet, or you get a refund."

I later donned a harness and virtual-reality goggles to practice steering a parachute to landing.

After lunch, a crew assisted me into a pressure suit in preparation for my visit to the altitude chamber. There I became reacquainted with the effects of hypoxia and was subjected to a sudden decompression that elevated the chamber to 73,000 feet. The pressure suit inflated as advertised and just as suddenly I became the Michelin man. I was told that it is possible to fly the U-2 while puffed up but that it is difficult.

A beaker of water in the chamber boiled furiously to demonstrate what would happen to my blood if I were exposed without protection to ambient pressure above 63,000 feet.

After a thorough preflight briefing the next morning, Neeley and I put on long johns and UCDs (urinary collection devices), were assisted into our pressure suits, performed a leak check (both kinds), and settled into a pair of reclining lounge chairs for an hour of breathing pure oxygen. This displaces nitrogen in the blood to prevent decompression sickness (the bends) that could occur during ascent.

During this "pre-breathing," I felt as though I were in a Ziploc bag-style cocoon and anticipated the possibility of claustrophobia. There was none, and I soon became comfortably acclimatized to my confinement.

We were in the aircraft an hour later. Preflight checks completed and engine started, we taxied to Beale's 12,000-foot-long runway. The single main landing gear is not steerable, differential braking is unavailable, and the dual tailwheels move only 6 degrees in each direction, so it takes a lot of concrete to maneuver on the ground. Turn radius is 189 feet, and I had to lead with full rudder in anticipation of all turns.

We taxied into position and came to a halt so that personnel could remove the safety pins from the outrigger wheels (called pogos) that prevent one wing tip or the other from scraping the ground. Lt. Col. Greg "Spanky" Barber, another U-2 pilot, circled the aircraft in a mobile command vehicle to give the aircraft a final exterior check.

I knew that the U-2 is overpowered at sea level. It has to be for its engine, normally aspirated like every other turbine engine, to have enough power remaining to climb above 70,000 feet. Also, we weighed only 24,000 pounds (maximum allowable is 41,000 pounds) and were departing into a brisk headwind. Such knowledge did not prepare me for what followed.

The throttle was fully advanced and would remain that way until the beginning of descent. The 17,000 pounds of thrust made it feel as though I had been shot from a cannon. Within two to three seconds and 400 feet of takeoff roll, the wings flexed, the pogos fell away, and we entered a nose-up attitude of almost 45 degrees at a best-angle-of-climb airspeed of 100 kt. Initial climb rate was 9,000 fpm.

We were still over the runway and through 10,000 feet less than 90 seconds from brake release. One need not worry about a flameout after takeoff in a U-2. There either is enough runway to land straight ahead or enough altitude (only 1,000 feet is needed) to circle the airport for a dead-stick approach and landing.

The bicycle landing gear creates little drag and has no limiting airspeed, so there was no rush to tuck away the wheels. (The landing gear is not retracted at all when in the traffic pattern shooting touch and go's.)

We passed through 30,000 feet five minutes after liftoff and climb rate steadily decreased until above 70,000 feet, when further climb occurred only as the result of fuel burn.

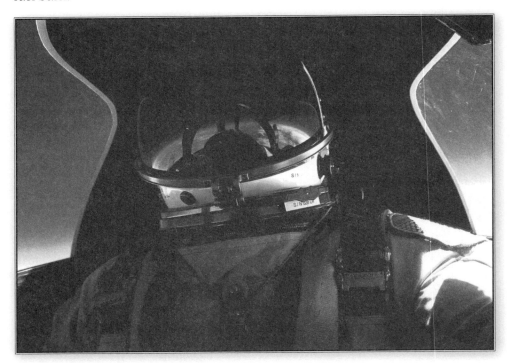

### ON FINAL APPROACH

Dragon Lady is still drifting toward the upper limits of the atmosphere at 100 to 200 fpm and will continue to do so until it is time to descend. It spends little of its life at a given altitude.

Descent begins by retarding the throttle to idle and lowering the landing gear. We raise the spoilers, deploy the speed brakes (one on each side of the aft fuselage), and engage the gust alleviation system. This raises both ailerons 7.5 degrees above their normal neutral point and deflects the wing flaps 6.5 degrees upward. This helps to unload the wings and protect the airframe during possible turbulence in the lower atmosphere.

Gust protection is needed because the Dragon Lady is like a China doll; she cannot withstand heavy gust and maneuvering loads. Strength would have required a heavier structure, and the U-2's designer, Clarence "Kelly" Johnson, shaved as much weight as possible — which is why there are only two landing gear legs instead of three. Every pound saved resulted in a 10-foot increase in ceiling.

With everything possible hanging and extended, the U-2 shows little desire to go down. It will take 40 minutes to descend to traffic pattern altitude but we needed only half that time climbing to altitude.

During this normal descent, the U-2 covers 37 nm for each 10,000 of altitude lost. When clean and at the best glide speed of 109 kt, it has a glide ratio of 28:1. It is difficult to imagine ever being beyond glide range of a suitable airport except when over large bodies of water or hostile territory.

Because there is only one fuel quantity gauge, and it shows only the total remaining, it is difficult to know whether fuel is distributed evenly, which is important when landing a U-2. A low-altitude stall is performed to determine which is the heavier wing, and some fuel is then transferred from it to the other.

We are on final approach with flaps at 35 degrees (maximum is 50 degrees) in a slightly nose-down attitude. The U-2 is flown with a heavy hand when slow, while

being careful not to overcontrol. Speed over the threshold is only 1.1 $V_{SO}$ (75 kt), very close to stall. More speed would result in excessive floating.

I peripherally see Barber accelerating the 140-mph, stock Chevrolet Camaro along the runway as he joins in tight formation with our landing aircraft. I hear him on the radio calling out our height (standard practice for all U-2 landings). The U-2 must be close to normal touchdown attitude at a height of one foot before the control wheel is brought firmly aft to stall the wings and plant the tailwheels on the concrete. The feet remain active on the pedals, during which time it is necessary to work diligently to keep the wings level. A roll spoiler on each wing lends a helping hand when its respective aileron is raised more than 13 degrees.

The aircraft comes to rest, a wing tip falls to the ground, and crewmen appear to reattach the pogos for taxiing.

Landing a U-2 is notoriously challenging, especially for those who have never flown taildraggers or sailplanes. It can be like dancing with a lady or wrestling a dragon, depending on wind and runway conditions. Maximum allowable crosswind is 15 kt.

The U-2 was first flown by Tony Levier in August 1955, at Groom Lake (Area 51), Nevada. The aircraft was then known as Article 341, an attempt by the Central Intelligence Agency to disguise the secret nature of its project. Current U-2s are 40 percent larger and much more powerful than the one in which Francis Gary Powers was downed by a missile over the Soviet Union on May 1, 1960.

The Soviets referred to the U-2 as the "Black Lady of Espionage" because of its spy missions and mystique. The age of its design, however, belies the sophistication of the sensing technology carried within. During U.S. involvement in Kosovo, for example, U-2s gathered and forwarded data via satellite to Intelligence at Beale AFB for instant analysis. The results were sent via satellite to battle commanders, who decided whether attack aircraft should be sent to the target. In one case, U-2 sensors detected enemy aircraft parked on a dirt road and camouflaged by thick, overhanging trees. Only a few minutes elapsed between detection and destruction. No other nation has this capability.

The U-2 long ago outlived predictions of its demise. It also survived its heir apparent, the Lockheed SR-71 Blackbird. The fleet of 37 aircraft is budgeted to operate for another 20 years, but this could be affected by the evolution and effectiveness of unmanned aircraft.

After returning to Earth (physically and emotionally), I am escorted to the Heritage Room where 20 U-2 pilots join to share in the spirited celebration of my high flight. Many of them are involved in general aviation and some have their own aircraft.

The walls of this watering hole are replete with fascinating memorabilia about U-2 operations and history. Several plaques proudly list all who have ever soloed Dragon Lady. This group of 670 forms an elite and unusually close-knit cadre of dedicated airmen.

*The author expresses his gratitude to Colonel Eric Stroberg, Lt. Colonel Greg Barber, Major Dean Neeley, and the men and women of the 9th Reconnaissance Wing for so graciously sharing their time and expertise.*

## Beech T-34 Mentor

| | |
|---|---|
| Engine | Continental O-470-13 |
| Power | 225 hp |
| Length | 25 ft 11 in |
| Height | 9 ft 7 in |
| Wingspan | 32 ft 10 in |
| Wing Loading | 16.3 lb/sq ft |
| Power Loading | 12.9 lb/hp |
| Maximum Takeoff Weight | 2,900 lb |
| Fuel Capacity | 50 gal |
| Rate of Climb (sea level) | 1,000 fpm |
| Normal Cruise Speed | 173 mph |
| Stall Speed | 58 mph |

# The Beech T-34 Mentor

*Deep in the heart of every private pilot lurks a fighter* pilot. There are very few of us who have not daydreamed his 150-horsepower Cessna into a mighty, fearsome attack plane zooming across the battle-scarred hills of some warring nation.

Close your eyes. Gently squeeze the trigger on the black, molded handle of the control stick. Eagle-eyed, watch the tracers stream from your wing-mounted cannons. Atta' boy! You scored! Now for a high-speed, low-altitude victory roll over those burning tanks.

But it is difficult to pretend you are in a P-51 Mustang when flying a Cessna 152. So perhaps you should buy an F-4U Corsair or a T-6 Texan. But first you should call your stockbroker and order a block of Mobil Oil. Those fuel guzzlers can quickly put you out of the flying business.

Fortunately, there is a more sensible approach for those who aspire to an airplane with the feel of a military fighter. The Beech T-34 Mentor not only satisfies the desire to fly a warbird under a sliding canopy, but it is relatively economical. Powered by a 225-hp Continental engine (original Mentors had only 185 hp), fuel consumption in cruise flight at 169 mph is only 11 gph. The aircraft is built like a Sherman tank. Mentor owners find that maintenance costs are about the same as those of its kissing cousin, the Beech Bonanza (although recent problems have developed with the integrity of the wing structure that will be resolved).

The T-34's resemblance to the Bonanza is apparent during a walk-around inspection. Wings and landing gear seem to have been lifted directly from the Bonanza's blueprints. The wings, of course, have been beefed up to accommodate aerobatic requirements. On the Navy version only, the T-34B, the landing gear has been strengthened up so that fledgling naval aviators can practice drop-'em-in, carrier-type landings.

Photos courtesy Beech Aircraft

The best way to tell an Air Force Mentor (T-34) from one enlisted in the Navy (T-34B) is to glance at the tail. The navy model has a large V-shaped notch under the rudder; the T-34 does not.

There are other subtle differences, too. For example, the fuel selector valve on the T-34 allows selection of either the left or right tank, whereas the selector on the –B model is strictly on or off.

Two small lights, one adjacent to each main landing-gear leg, illuminate when the respective gear leg on the T-34 is down and locked. This allows the tower to more easily spot a stuck gear leg during a low pass over the field.

The fuselage of the Mentor has borrowed some of the lines from the butterfly-tailed business plane from Wichita, but the similarity ends there. The individual cockpits are in tandem, housed under a military, greenhouse canopy. Cockpit visibility is unlimited in all quadrants.

There is only one fuel sump drain, but it is under the fuselage at the approximate intersection of the lateral and longitudinal axes and is tough to reach. The 25-gallon wing tanks do not have drains.

The two stainless-steel exhaust stacks at the bottom of the engine cowling are augmenters. Exhaust flowing through them creates a venturi effect in the tubes that helps to suck ambient air across the engine and into the stacks, which augments engine cooling.

Two small, flush-mounted doors are on the right side of the engine cowling forward of the external power-unit receptacle and are spring-loaded to the closed position. There are two theories about their purpose. Some say this is where a ground attendant shoves a fire extinguisher in case of an engine fire. Others say that the doors are sucked open by the evacuating effect of the augmenters, which enables ambient air from outside the cowling to enter the engine compartment and assist in cooling during slow flight at high power settings. Take your pick. The pilot's operating handbook fails to discuss them.

Another noteworthy preflight item is battery accessibility. Pop open a small door on the right side of the cowling, lift a securing rod, and pull on the handle. The 28-volt battery conveniently slides out for servicing or changing.

Solo flight is permitted only from the front seat to keep the center of gravity within limits.

Entering the cockpit is simple. Slide back the canopy, step over the sidewall, and sit down in the typically military cockpit. It has no fancy trim or decorations. The layout and appearance of the instruments and controls are strictly functional.

As the good book says, the first thing to do is "fasten yourself to the machine and with it become one." The shoulder harnesses are equipped with inertia reels that can be locked for inverted flight. Also, the pilot can adjust the fore-and-aft position of the rudder pedals with a crank (T-34B only) to accommodate variations in the length of human legs.

The main instrument panel has the look of a P-51. It is marked and placarded with luminescent printing against a black, non-glare background. The instruments have individual eyebrow lights.

The attitude and direction indicators need A.C. electrical power supplied by either of 2 inverters. During VFR flight, the inverter switch may be off. The gyros are inoperative, of course, but there is considerably less load on the electrical system. When gyros are needed, turn on one of the inverters. The instruments then perform their spastic and then stabilizing dance while spinning up. An inverter-failure light advises the pilot to select the other inverter.

I love the tachometer. The range of 0-to-1,000 rpm occupies the entire circumference of the gauge. As the tach needle begins its second revolution, a "1" pops up in a small window informing the pilot that engine rpm is between 1,000 and 2,000 rpm. The large needle then indicates engine speed to the nearest 2 or 3 rpm. Engine speed between 2,000 and 3,000 rpm is indicated similarly.

The left-hand console contains three trim wheels (pitch, roll, and yaw), the fuel selector, electric boost pump switch, flap handle, and a military-style power quadrant. The throttle is big, fitting nicely into the palm of the hand. It gives you the feeling that you in command of a Mustang or a Corsair. The constant-speed propeller and mixture controls can be adjusted with the fingertips as your hand rests on the throttle.

The rear cockpit is not as well equipped but has sufficient controls and instruments to enable an instructor to do his thing. There are a few switches that transfer command of certain controls from the student in front to the instructor in the rear.

Larry Hamovitz, who flew for Continental Airlines, checked me out in N363MD, an ex-Navy T-34B. He talked me through an engine start: battery on, fuel selector off, mixture rich, boost pump on (the pump does not energize until the fuel selector is turned on), throttle cracked, and starter switch depressed. As soon as the engine hints of life, open the fuel valve, which also energizes the boost pump. The pump is deactivated after engine start.

I nudged the Mentor out of its tie-down spot at Santa Monica Airport and turned onto the taxiway using differential braking. There is no direct control of the nosewheel. This is similar to the early A-model Bonanza, the Lake Amphibian, and more recently, the Cirrus SR-22.

It feels wonderful to taxi a Mentor. With the canopy open, arms resting on the sills, and left hand resting easily on the throttle while listening to the deep-throated song of power from the augmenters. The Mentor is not quiet, however. During flight you can hardly hear yourself think; noise-canceling headsets are a must.

At the run-up pad, Hamovitz instructed me to verify proper operation of the constant-speed propeller at 1,800 rpm. Magnetos and carburetor heat are checked at 2,000. The fuel pump is switched on, and rudder trim is set 6-degrees right to offset the Mentor's tendency to yaw left during takeoff rotation and initial climb.

The microphone button is on the throttle instead of the control stick as it is on civilian aircraft. The Mentor was a military trainer, and if military pilots got into the habit of pressing a button on the control stick every time they wanted to chat, the control tower would wind up being a missile target.

A major decision must be made immediately before takeoff. One of us must close his canopy, because only one may be open during flight. Hamovitz volunteers to close his and I will enjoy the air conditioning.

After takeoff power is applied, steering is accomplished easily with rudder only. The Mentor accelerates relatively well but the noise level makes it seem greater. The nose comes up at 55 knots and liftoff occurs at 60. The landing gear and flaps are retracted electrically, just like on a Bonanza.

According to the military flight handbook, climbs should be executed at full power, 2600 rpm and throttle to the firewall. But because civilian pilots have to pay hard-earned cash for engine maintenance and fuel, Hamovitz suggested 2500 rpm and 25 inches of manifold pressure.

The Mentor accelerated to the recommended climb speed of 100 knots and the vertical speed was disappointing, only 750 fpm. I later discovered that the T-34 climbs better at 80 or 90 knots but that cylinder-head temperatures begin to climb almost as rapidly. Engine cooling is a problem with the Mentor, and the aircraft could use a set of cowl flaps.

The T-34B is a joy to fly; it handles like a kiddy cart. Sitting on the centerline of the aircraft makes it equally easy to make steep turns to the right or left.

With either canopy open, the cockpits are surprisingly free of wind. Navigational charts can be opened and used without fear of them being sucked out and blown away.

The Mentor has a Bonanza wing, so you expect the stall characteristics to be similar, and they are. Approaching a stall induces a mild buffet, and a deep stall reveals no nasty habits. The Mentor stalls at 58 knots (clean) and 46 knots dirty. A full-power stall with the flaps even partially deployed, however, can roll you onto your back if you do not recover quickly and aggressively.

As far as aerobatics are concerned, the Mentor will take almost anything the average pilot is willing to give (between +6 and –3 Gs). If your seat-of-the-pants gauge is inoperative, an accelerometer (G meter) on the panel indicates when you have gone too far.

Inverted flight is limited to 15 seconds because the engine does not have an inverted oil system.

The military airspeed redline of the Mentor is 240 knots, but the FAA does not allow civilians to exceed 219 knots. Either way, the Mentor can accelerate to some impressive speeds if a rapid descent is desired or if a pilot fails to pull out of a split S with sufficient vigor.

Hamovitz and I had no difficulty spotting Dick Cole in his newly painted Mentor as we approached the prearranged rendezvous spot over the Pomona Vortac for some formation flying. Before long, Cole broke ranks. The chase was on, and the dogfight began. After each of us ultimately claimed victory, and both the sun and the fuel gauge began to ebb, we headed home.

At the optimum glide speed of 90 knots, the Mentor has a glide ratio of 7.0 to 1 (propeller set to low pitch). With the prop control pulled back to high pitch, however, glide ratio increases to an impressive 10.5 to 1.

Landing gear and flap speed is 109 knots. When both are extended and the propeller is set to low pitch, a power-off descent at 109 knots results in a steep dive in excess of 3,000 fpm.

Landing the Mentor is pleasantly easy. The long control stick provides lots of leverage, and the controls remain light and sensitive during the flare and touchdown.

A pilot becomes quickly addicted to the Mentor. This is a fun machine that provides the feel and thrill of a hot warbird at a wee fraction of the cost.

The Beech Model 45 Mentor (named after the trusted servant of Greek mythology) first flew as a prototype in late 1948. Production ended in 1958 after almost 2,000 had been built. Although the piston versions have long ago been retired from military service, the turboprop-powered version, the T-34C, is still on active duty with the Navy.

The T-34 was designed originally to simulate the feel of the Lockheed T-33 jet trainer (the Thunderbird), and the FAA felt that these control responses are too sensitive for civilians. As a result, FAA required that all civilian Mentors be equipped with a bungee-neutralizing control system to reduce sensitivity.

So if a pilot wants to pretend he is a Korean War ace and bore holes in the sky over Pasadena or Paducah, the Mentor is his best bet. It provides a wonderful opportunity to play fighter pilot without having to join the Air Force or the Navy (even though Uncle Sam would pay the bills).

## DeHavilland DHC-1 Chipmunk

| | |
|---|---|
| Engine | Rolls-Royce Gipsy Major |
| Power | 145 hp |
| Length | 25 ft 5 in |
| Height (3-point attitude) | 7 ft 0 in |
| Wingspan | 34 ft 4 in |
| Wing Loading | 12.8 lb/sq ft |
| Power Loading | 15.2 lb/hp |
| Maximum Takeoff Weight | 2,200 lb |
| Fuel Capacity (usable) | 22 gal |
| Rate of Climb (sea level) | 800 fpm |
| Normal Cruise Speed | 95 kt |
| Stall Speed | 43 kt |

# DeHavilland DHC-1 Chipmunk

## It is said that the DeHavilland DHC-1

Chipmunk looks the way an airplane should look. Designed as a military trainer, it has a tapered wing and a narrow, sleek fuselage that give the "Chippie" the appearance of a petite World War II fighter. It also has that distinctively shaped vertical fin, the signature of many DeHavilland designs (including the DH98 Mosquito fighter/bomber).

After World War II, DeHavilland Aircraft of Canada wanted to develop an airplane for use in the Canadian bush. The parent company in England preferred instead that their Canadian counterpart first develop a replacement for the Tiger Moth, an open-cockpit biplane that had been the mainstay of the Royal Air Force (RAF) and Royal Canadian Air Force (RCAF). The Moth had become too antiquated to continue as a basic trainer. (The parent company was preoccupied with the development of the Comet, the world's first jetliner.)

The prototype of the Chipmunk first flew in Canada on May 22, 1946. Production aircraft were subsequently built there and in England (with some also built in Portugal). There is no significant difference between the Canadian and British models except that the last of the Canadian aircraft have bubble canopies while all others have greenhouse canopies like those on the North American T-6 Texan.

The Chipmunk is all-metal except for the control surfaces and the rear two-thirds of the wings, which are fabric covered.

The DHC-1 designation indicates that the Chipmunk was the first original design of the Canadian firm, which eventually was allowed to develop its bush plane, the DHC-2 Beaver.

DeHavilland built 1,283 Chipmunks between 1946 and 1961, a 16-year production run, and the Chippie served the RAF longer than any other trainer. But time and technology caught up with the Chipmunk in 1971. The RAF began to replace its beloved trainer with British Aerospace Bulldogs, offsprings of the Beagle Pup.

There currently are 350 airworthy Chipmunks in civilian hands of which 100 are in the United States, and 138 are in the United Kingdom. The remaining aircraft are scattered worldwide.

The DHC-1 shown on these pages is the pride and joy of Robert "Chipmunk Bob" Hill, a web developer for Nordstrom. Hill grew up in aviation—his father was a naval aviator—and had always dreamed of owning an inexpensive, relatively simple warbird. He sought but could not find a Bulldog in good condition.

During his search, Hill obtained a taildragger endorsement in a Maule MX-7-180 and fell in love with that kind of flying. This redirected his search to include airplanes with tailwheels. The DeHavilland DHC-1 Chipmunk seemed to fit the bill perfectly. He found one on the Internet and bought it on his birthday, December 29, 1999, for $40,000.

Hill's Chipmunk, WK639 (a serial number provided the aircraft by the British Ministry of Defense) was manufactured in June, 1952 in Chester, England and was assigned to the RAF's University Air Squadrons, groups similar to the Reserve Officer's Training Corps (ROTC) in the United States. In 1971 it was assigned to active duty in the RAF to provide military students with the basic training needed to move up to a British Aircraft Corporation Jet Provost.

N6540C is based at Bremerton National Airport (PWT) in northwest Washington and is essentially the same as when it left the air force except for the addition of strobe lights and civilian avionics. The red, white, and blue roundel painted on the wings and fuselage is a post-war, Type D insignia used by the RAF.

Hill says that he has no problem with maintenance or finding parts, although fixed-pitch propellers for the Chipmunk are becoming scarce.

The Chippie is powered by a 145-hp version of the 1930s-vintage, 4-cylinder, inverted in-line Gipsy Major used in the trainer it was designed to replace, the DeHavilland Tiger Moth. Manufactured by DeHavilland, Bristol-Siddeley, and Rolls Royce, these engines have a TBO of 1,500 hours even though the military ran them to 2,250 hours without difficulty.

The Gipsy Major also is called the "Dripsy Major" because if it isn't dripping oil, something is terribly wrong. It typically burns 1.5 quarts per hour (most is blown out), and 2.5 quarts hour is maximum allowable. "The fuller the oil tank, the more oil gets blown out," says Hill. He operates with only a half-full oil tank for local flights.

The Chipmunk has a 30,000-hour airframe, and Hill's airplane has only 11,800 hours, but this has been raised to an effective 21,000 hours because of its aerobatic history.

The airplane does not have a baggage compartment per se, but a cubby hole behind the rear seat accommodates 40 pounds of personal items.

The brass, screw-in fuel cap for each of the two wing tanks looks more like something you would expect to find on a boat. A fuel gauge adjacent to each fuel cap can be read from the cockpit. Unfortunately, it is not illuminated, which restricts the Chipmunk from flying at night (but only in the United Kingdom). Each gauge has two scales, one for indicating fuel quantity on the ground with the tail down, and the other for indicating fuel remaining in level flight.

The Chipmunk does not have a primer in the cockpit like most airplanes do. This requires the pilot to undertake a quaint priming ritual before engine start. It involves either opening the left side of the cowling or accessing the priming controls through small circular ports cut out of the cowling. The index finger of the right hand is used to pull a ring that opens the carburetor, and the left index finger moves a lever up and down to manually pump fuel into the carburetor until fuel drips onto the ground from the overflow vent at the bottom of the engine. This done, the propeller is pulled through four compression strokes to suck fuel into each of the four cylinders.

Although there is no electric fuel pump, there are two engine-driven fuel pumps.

Hill and I are large pilots, but we are comfortable in the narrow cockpits, which has the fit and feel of a fighter. Both pilots are surrounded with controls and switches that fall easily to hand. You have no doubt that this is a military machine.

Although the seats are not adjustable, the rudder pedals are and move fore and aft to accommodate long- and short-legged pilots. Solo flight is allowed only from the forward cockpit.

A sliding knob on the floor near the base of the control stick that moves fore and aft is the "fuel cock." It opens and closes the valve supplying fuel from both wing tanks to the engine. Ahead of that (also on the floor) is the horizontally mounted, British-style compass that is so large that it looks as though it belongs on the bridge of an ocean liner.

Another interesting instrument is the "bat and ball," the British term for a turn-and-bank indicator. A spring-loaded push button on the left electrical panel is used to tap out Morse code via the yellow light on the Chippie's belly to communicate with others in your formation.

There are two magneto switches in each cockpit, and all four must be flipped up to start the engine. Only the front cockpit has a starter button.

Throttle cracked and mixture rich (meaning that the mixture control is fully aft, another British tradition), and you're ready to start.

Chipmunks in military service literally started with a bang and the smell of cordite from an exploding 12-bore shotgun shell (minus the lead shot), a part of the Coffman cartridge-type starter that uses rapidly expanding gases to turn the crankshaft. Most civilian aircraft have been converted with electric starters.

Hill's Chippie starts after only two blades. Power should not be applied for taxi, however, until the oil temperature reaches 40 degrees C.

The tailwheel is fully castoring and non-steerable, which means that differential braking is used to maneuver on the ground. But it is unlikely that you have ever used a brake system like the one in a Chipmunk.

You pull aft on a parking brake lever (similar to the parking brake handle on some cars) on the left side of the cockpit to engage a ratchet at the point where the disc brakes barely rub against the wheels. The ratchet then holds this slight amount of braking without your having to pull on the brake handle. After that, moving the rudder bar (pedals) determines the wheel to which the braking applies. In other words, move the right rudder pedal, and brake pressure is applied only to the right wheel, and so forth. When taxiing with a crosswind, add another notch of brake and apply downwind rudder to keep the Chippie tracking straight. A new Chipmunk pilot tends to overcontrol, but with a little practice, he discovers that the system is effective and can be operated without having to think about it.

On the right, a lever similar to the brake handle is used to operate the flaps. Lift it to the first notch for 15 degrees and to the second and final notch for 30 degrees (maximum).

Some S-turning is needed to see over the Spitfire-like nose.

The run-up is conventional, and there is a perceptible sense of excitement as you line up on the runway.

The rudder becomes effective almost as soon as the throttle reaches its forward limit, and the tail comes up shortly thereafter. Pilots new to a taildragger without a steerable tailwheel quickly learn that the airplane must be "flown" with the flight controls from the beginning of the takeoff roll until the aircraft comes to rest at the end of a flight.

The Chipmunk lifts off at 45 knots, and it is instinctive to pressure the right rudder pedal as the nose pitches skyward. Do not do that in this airplane. The nose of a Chipmunk yaws right, not left, because British engines turn the "wrong way" (counterclockwise when viewed from behind) and require left rudder to keep the airplane on an even keel during full-power climbs.

Surprisingly, the engine is canted 4 degrees right, which exacerbates the right-turning tendency. This was done in an effort to better prepare pilots for transition into high-horsepower fighters.

The tachometer has two hands, one to indicate thousands of rpm and the other hundreds. It is similar in appearance to the adjacent altimeter, which can be confusing. Retard the throttle as you level off after a climb, and you get a visual sensation that the airplane is losing altitude.

Maneuvering is the Chipmunk's strong suit. The controls are so exceptionally well balanced, light, responsive, and harmonized that the airplane could easily be the benchmark against which other lightplanes are measured. The DHC-1 is an absolute delight to fly, and you quickly feel as though you are at one with it. Some pilots, however, find the rudder to be too sensitive and learn to pressure a pedal instead of shoving a foot into it. The airplane does not tolerate a ham-fisted pilot. My friend, Brian Souter, says about DeHavilland trainers that, "they are easy to fly but difficult to fly well."

Aerobatics are allowed, but the engine will quickly burp and belch during negative-G maneuvers because it does not have an inverted fuel system. The Chippie is designed for +9 to −6 Gs.

There is no stall-warning indicator, but the strong pre-stall buffet serves the purpose. Although stalls can be sharp with power on and flaps extended, they are otherwise mild-mannered. (Wing camber increases from root to tip, and this helps to prevent the wing from dropping during a stall.)

A Chipmunk will not tolerate being taken for granted, though, and will drop a wing in protest to those who don't keep the slip-skid ball in its cage. Using ailerons to pick up a stalled wing can aggravate the roll. As a matter of fact, it is recommended that a pilot use opposite aileron to assist in spin entry.

Chipmunk pilots claim that it is as easy to avoid an inadvertent spin as it can be difficult to recover from one. A placard in the aircraft says that "Spin recovery [from a fully developed spin] may need full forward stick (emphasis mine) until rotation stops."

The Chipmunk's only serious shortcoming is endurance and range. With a total of only 22 gallons of avgas in the tanks, you are effectively limited to 2 hours and 200 nautical air miles (plus a 45-minute reserve).

Retard the throttle for descent and a pawl mechanically pulls back the adjacent mixture control into the rich position. This makes it impossible to make an approach and landing with a lean mixture.

The carburetor heater does not really heat the induction air. Instead, the carburetor uses ambient warm air from inside the cowling. The Royal Air Force wired this to the open position. Although this diminishes performance slightly, it helps to prevent students from learning about carburetor ice the hard way.

The canopy may be slid back to the first notch (a few inches) at any airspeed, but open it to the second notch (a few more inches) and the maximum-allowable airspeed is 90 knots. During approaches on warm, summer days, however, many pilots open the canopy all the way for a dose of delirious joy.

The Chipmunk glides best at 60 knots and is slowed to 55 over the threshold. Most pilots land with 15 degrees of flaps, but using 30 improves over-the-nose visibility. Slips are a joy because there is hardly any airframe buffeting and control forces are so light.

The Gipsy Major should be idled for a few minutes before shutdown to allow engine temperatures to stabilize. Then shut off the magnetos and advance the throttle fully forward to prevent backfiring and "dieseling."

As the propeller ticks to a stop, a new Chipmunk pilot usually just sits in the cockpit for a while wearing a gratifying smile that reveals his infatuation. The Chippie engenders that kind of affection from those lucky enough to fly one.

## Douglas DC-3

| | |
|---|---|
| Engines | 2 Wright Cyclone 1820-202A |
| Power | 1,200 hp ea |
| Length | 64 ft 5 in |
| Height (3-point attitude) | 16 ft 9 in |
| Wingspan | 95 ft 0 in |
| Wing Loading | 25.7 lb/sq ft |
| Power Loading | 10.5 lb/hp |
| Maximum Takeoff Weight | 25,200 lb |
| Fuel Capacity (usable) | 812 gal |
| Rate of Climb (sea level) | 1,140 fpm |
| Normal Cruise Speed | 157 kt |
| Stall Speed | 62 kt |

# The Douglas DC-3

## The first French town to be liberated during the

Invasion of Normandy on June 6, 1944 was Sainte-Mere-Eglise. In that small town is a museum that pays tribute to the 15,000 paratroopers who dropped behind German lines that day. In that museum is only one airplane. It is the airplane that General Dwight D. Eisenhower considered the most important in ensuring the Allied Victory of World War II. It is not a P-51 Mustang or a B-17 Flying Fortress. It is a C-47, the military version of the DC-3. Thousands of these aircraft flew across the English Channel on that day and on the bloody days that followed.

I have always had a strong desire to check out in a DC-3, a desire that almost became an obsession. Perhaps it was serendipity, perhaps fate. But when a DC-3 recently became available for training at my home airport, I knew that my dream was to become a reality.

The DC-3 based at Cloverfield Aviation at Santa Monica Municipal Airport was owned by the husband-and-wife team of Jan and Britt Aarvik. Jan was a pilot in the Norwegian Air Force and had amassed more than 17,000 hours (4,000 in DC-3s).

He had been using the aircraft to train pilots, haul skydivers, and fly in a variety of television and motion-picture productions.

A 7,000-hour pilot, Britt also was rated in the -3. So, too, was their son, Thomas, who also served as crew chief for the family airplane.

N7500A is powered by a pair of 1,200-hp, nine-cylinder, Wright Cyclone, radial engines. From the firewalls forward, these are the same supercharged engines used on the B-17 Flying Fortress. Many other DC-3s have 14-cylinder, Pratt & Whitney Twin Wasps that deliver the same power.

Oil drips anywhere within 50 yards of either engine and seems to have an affinity for expensive clothing. It is said that a pilot's experience in a DC-3 is measured more accurately by the number and value of shirts destroyed by oil stains than by the hours in his log.

Checking oil and fuel quantity during the preflight requires climbing atop the wings. The oil tanks have a capacity of 232 quarts of oil, which is more than the fuel capacity of many lightplanes.

The Plexiglas landing-light cover on the leading edge of each wing must be inspected to ensure that each is secured by a pair of crossed wires. These prevent the Plexiglas from blowing out due to strong pressure changes at large angles of attack.

The wing flaps are split, like those on a Cessna 310. On the -3, however, they span all the way from one aileron to the other (including under the fuselage). They increase lift by 35 percent and parasite drag by 300 percent. Slips are allowed with the flaps fully extended.

The DC-3 is an all-metal airplane except for the primary flight-control surfaces. These are fabric covered to save weight and facilitate field repair.

Climbing into the cockpit makes it obvious why a DC-3 pilot should not have to have a medical certificate. Climbing the long and steeply sloped cabin several times a day without passing out should be a sufficient testament of health.

The DC-3 was designed to seat 21 passengers plus the two required pilots. The record for the greatest number carried appears to be held by a China National Airways' DC-3 that evacuated 75 people from China to Burma during World War II. Among them was James H. "Jimmy" Doolittle who had recently completed his bombing raid over Tokyo.

Stirring an engine to life requires simultaneously engaging the starter and primer switches, waiting for the propeller to turn through four revolutions ("count 12 blades"), and then turning on the mags. With a little luck, the big radial will show some sign of life, which is the signal to enrich the mixture. The Wright Cyclone awakens one cylinder at a time, belching and coughing great swarms of smoke that is guaranteed to create IFR conditions for anyone standing behind.

When taxiing a DC-3, the aircraft moans and groans, and creaks and squeaks, as if it were a mechanized, prehistoric monster. Maintaining control of this oversized taildragger is not difficult as long as the tailwheel lock is engaged for the straight-aways, especially in a crosswind. Otherwise, the Gooney Bird seems to have a mind of its own and weathervanes into the slightest zephyr (even when there is none). One also must be mindful of the 95-foot wing span when taxiing in tight quarters. It is comforting to know that if the wing tips clear an obstacle while turning, so will the tail. Negotiating narrow taxiways and tight turns is made easier by visualizing that the main-gear wheels are directly behind the engines.

Over-the-nose visibility is excellent, better than in most small taildraggers.

When depressing the tops of the conventional rudder pedals, hydraulic pressure inflates a doughnut-shaped expander tube that has composition brake pads mounted on its outer perimeter. These press against the brake drum to slow the aircraft.

When retracted, the main-gear tires extend 11 inches below the nacelles. The wheels remain free to rotate so that normal braking is available during a gear-up landing (not that this would necessarily be needed).

Although you can crash a DC-3, it is said that you can never wear one out. Some have had so many parts replaced that the only original parts remaining are the registration plate and the airplane's shadow.

An example of the DC-3's adaptability occurred during the Summer of 1941. Another airplane operated by China National was on the ground at Suifu, China, when it was strafed by Japanese fighters. The right wing was destroyed, and there were more than 50 bullet holes in the rest of the airplane. The only available wing replacement came from a DC-2. Trouble is, this wing was 5 feet shorter and designed to carry much less weight than the wing of a DC-3.

The shorter wing was nevertheless installed. The "Dizzy Three" (also known as the DC-2½) looked lopsided but flew well despite all the aileron trim needed to keep the wings level.

The DC-3 is a very hydraulic airplane. In addition to hydraulic brakes and landing gear, hydraulic power also is used to operate the cowl flaps, autopilot, and—believe it or not—the windshield wipers.

The runup and preflight checks are conventional. After taxiing into position, lining up with the runway, and locking the tailwheel, the throttles are advanced to 25 inches of manifold pressure with the brakes locked. Each pilot then looks at the engine on his side to ensure that the cowlings are not shaking or vibrating. The brakes are then released and the throttles advanced for takeoff: 45.5 inches and 2,500 rpm.

The pilot must forcefully lower the nose to an approximately level attitude. During my first takeoff, this seemed excessive, and I had the distinct impression that I was going to shove the nose into the ground. It takes a whopping 12-degree attitude change to lift the tail 7 feet into the air and prevent the DC-3 from lifting off prematurely (below the 77-knot $V_{MC}$). Slight back pressure is applied to the yoke at $V_1$ and $V_2$ (both of which are fixed at 84 knots), and the DC-3 becomes a graceful creature of the sky.

The takeoff from Santa Monica was particularly nostalgic, a flight across the pages of history. This was the runway from which I made my first takeoff in 1952. It also is where this 31,000-hour airplane was born and made its maiden flight more than 50 years ago. Santa Monica was the home of the Douglas Aircraft Company and is where almost all of its piston-powered airliners were built.

The first DC-3 flew in 1935 (also from Santa Monica) and was so successful that by 1938 it carried 95 percent of all airline traffic in the U.S. A year later, 90 percent of the world's airline passengers flew on DC-3s, a record never likely to be broken.

Aarvik's airplane first flew on April 30, 1943, and was delivered to the U.S. Army Air Force, which used it to drop paratroopers and tow large gliders. Following a post-war career with Eastern and then Mercer Airlines, it was purchased in 1977 by actor John Travolta who sold it in 1983 to the Aarviks.

Douglas built 10,926 DC-3s, most of which were Navy R4Ds and Army C-47s. Despite their official designations, pilots affectionately refer to the DC-3 as a Gooney Bird, a king-sized, seagull-like bird found on some South-Pacific atolls.

Each cowling has a ring of 16 large cowl flaps that surround the big radials. They are wide open for takeoff but create so much drag that they should be closed to the trail position shortly after setting climb power (39.5 inches and 2,300 rpm). This eliminates enough drag to noticeably improve engine-out climb performance. Partially closing the cowl flaps also reduces airframe buffeting.

Leaning the mixture is a breeze. Use the auto-rich position for takeoff and climb, and the auto-lean position for cruise. Be careful, however, when richening the mixtures prior to landing a Wright-powered DC-3. The controls work backwards so that pushing them forward results in a very quiet and underpowered airplane.

In flight, the DC-3 is heavy on the controls and sluggish in roll and pitch. This airplane is not flown with the fingertips. A new pilot quickly learns that the trim tabs are his best friends. The airplane is so sensitive to movement of the center of gravity that some veteran airline pilots claim that they could tell the weight of a stewardess walking toward the cockpit with coffee.

Flying the airplane can be a workout and gives me great respect for airline pilots of yore who had to battle weather and turbulence a hundred hours a month.

The DC-3 cruises at 157 knots on 50 percent power and 94 gph. Some claim with tongue in cheek that the -3 consumes as much oil as it does fuel.

One would expect that the big, high-lift wings of a DC-3 would have docile stall characteristics. Don't bet on it. Stalls propagate from the wingtips and can result in strong rolling moments and substantial altitude loss. Recovery demands aggressive, albeit normal, manipulation of all primary flight controls.

On a nice day, either pilot can slide open his side window and rest his arm on the window sill as when driving a car. The shape of the front windshield creates a low-pressure zone near the side windows so that only a waft of air can be felt. Nor does the noise level increase with an open window. The din of a DC-3 assaults the ears equally well with the windows open or closed.

In those carefree days of ecological ignorance, airline pilots flying DC-3s used to revise their Jeppesen manuals while en route. Each obsolete page was lifted out of the binder on the pilot's lap. The reduced pressure outside the open window would remove the chart from between the pilot's fingertips and send it carelessly to oblivion. It is said that one could determine an airline's route structure simply by following the trail of discarded charts.

When the outside air is cold, a conventional Janitrol heater provides warm cabin air. On some older models, heat is provided by a steam boiler in the right engine nacelle.

The DC-3 has a reputation for leaky windshields on rainy days. This prompted more than one pilot to add the following to en route position reports: "Light rain outside; heavy rain inside."

Although one can make 3-point landings in a Gooney Bird, this is discouraged because dropping in such a heavy airplane can unduly strain the landing gear. Instead, wheel landings are the norm. Just pull off the power when about 10 feet above the ground. There is little or no tendency to drop as those big wings slice deeper into ground effect. There also is little tendency to bounce, which makes the DC-3 easier to land on the mains than many light airplanes.

Some experienced pilots claim that they can land shorter in a DC-3 with the tail up than down. The procedure involves simultaneously applying aggressive braking and enough back pressure on the yoke to prevent nosing over. According to Perry Shreffler, a retired captain who flew DC-3s for TWA, this combination of brake and elevator control is so effective that—with a little help from a headwind, a forward center of gravity, and a smidgeon of power—a competent pilot can come to a halt with the tail suspended in the air. (I did not have the courage to try this.)

A private-pilot's certificate is the only prerequisite for a DC-3 type rating. Aarvik advised that the training required (including the check ride) varies from 3-4 hours (for an experienced taildragger pilot with round-engine time who wants a VFR-only type rating) to about 10 hours for a private pilot with limited experience who wants a type rating with instrument privileges. These hours can be reduced, however, if the student first obtains some instruction in a small taildragger.

For me, learning to fly a DC-3 was a dream come true—even if it did empty my wallet.

## Martin 404

| | |
|---|---|
| Engines | 2 Pratt & Whitney R-2800 Double Wasp |
| Power | 2,400 hp ea |
| Length | 74 ft 7 in |
| Height | 28 ft 5 in |
| Wingspan | 93 ft 3 in |
| Wing Loading | 52.0 lb/sq ft |
| Power Loading | 9.4 lb/hp |
| Maximum Takeoff Weight | 44,900 lb |
| Fuel Capacity | 2,000 gal |
| Rate of Climb (sea level) | 1,905 fpm |
| Normal Cruise Speed | 240 kt |

# The Martin 404

## General aviation is replete with special-interest groups

There are pilots fascinated and involved with homebuilts, seaplanes, warbirds, and so forth. Only a few, however, are passionate about piston-powered airliners. One of them is Jeffrey "Jeff" Whitesell. He is dedicated to saving an example of as many such aircraft as possible before the cutting torch renders them extinct. His goal is to establish a flying museum, sort of a Confederate Air Force for the airliners of yesteryear.

Whitesell was raised in aviation. In 1961, his father, Capt. William C. Whitesell, medically retired from Eastern Airlines. He purchased and transformed a New Jersey farm into the popular Flying W Ranch, a unique fly-in resort with a Western motif. The elder Whitesell also ran a charter operation that at different times used five Martin 202s and 404s (originally designated as 2-0-2s and 4-0-4s). The last of Whitesell's Martins, N636X, had an executive interior that accommodated 16 passengers in luxurious comfort instead of 44 in airline configuration.

His customers included Muhammad Ali, Howard Cosell, Herman's Hermits, the Beach Boys, and film crews for Monday Night Football. Martins were popular in those days; Frank Sinatra, Ray Charles, and others owned them for personal transportation. This was the era in which young Whitesell's fascination and love for piston airliners began to grow.

Fast-forward 30 years. This is when Jeff Whitesell, now a captain for Delta Airlines, was saddened by the disappearance of piston-powered airliners. With the encouragement of his wife, Ginger, he attempted to do something about it. Perhaps, he thought, he could find a Douglas DC-3 or DC-4 that he could restore and operate. But when two such aircraft appeared on the auction block in Billings, Montana, in 1994, they sold for more than he could afford.

Depressed by his lack of progress and while still in Billings, he discovered an ex-Eastern Airlines Martin 404 parked in a remote corner of the local airport. The airplane had been used as a crop duster and was in deplorable condition. He climbed aboard the ancient hulk knowing that his father had flown this airplane; his father had flown all of Eastern's Martins. Jeff sat in the captain's seat, the very seat that his father had known and worn so well.

An old-timer soon climbed aboard, flipped over a rusty 5-gallon bucket, and sat where the first-officer's seat had been.

"Hey," the old man said with an impish grin, "bucket seats."

Both men were Martin aficionados and had little difficulty passing time by exchanging tales about these obsolescent aircraft. After awhile, the old man said, "Ya' know, there's another ol' Martin down in Pueblo. Got a real fancy interior."

Whitesell's eyes widened. "You wouldn't happen to know if it's 36X, would you?"

"Yup, that's the one," the old man said.

Whitesell arrived at the deserted, fog-shrouded ramp of Pueblo, Colorado's Memorial Airport at midnight. He discovered to his dismay that the once-beautiful Martin was only a decrepit reminder of its bygone glory days. There was no way, he thought, that he could possibly entertain the notion of restoring this aircraft, but he did not want to leave until taking a nostalgic look inside.

The next day, the owner of N636X lowered the aft airstairs, and Whitesell discovered with delight that the interior was still in great shape. Contrary to his initial reaction, he struck a deal to buy the derelict for $60,000 and subsequently poured a mountain of money into the airplane to make it airworthy. N636X is now the flagship of Airliners of America, a non-profit organization in Camarillo, California that was founded by Whitesell. It is made up of volunteers dedicated to the preservation of this fine airplane.

Whitesell's 404 is one of only three still flying in the United States. Two others earn their keep giving tourist rides over Angel Falls in Venezuela, and a few more are scattered around the world. This is all that remains of the 151 Martin 202s, 303s, and 404s that were built by the Glenn L. Martin Company between 1946 and 1953.

The Martin twins were designed as post-war replacements for the slower and smaller DC-3. The first model was the 202 Martinliner, which contained numerous innovations such as reversible-pitch propellers, underwing refueling points, and built-in airstairs.

The Martin 303 was a pressurized version of the 202, but only a few were built.

The 404 Skyliner was the final evolution of the Martin twins. It was an improved and somewhat larger version of its predecessors and was both pressurized and air-conditioned. It also had a combustion heater in each wing to provide wing and tail de-icing.

The Martin twins often are mistaken for the similar Convair 240, 340, and 440. (Some accused Convair of copying Martin's design.) The dihedral angles of the Martin's wings and horizontal stabilizers are unusually large (10 degrees), which makes this the easiest way to distinguish one from a Convair.

I had always wanted to fly a Martin 404 because of the affectionate manner in which TWA captains spoke about their experiences in the old airliner. This is when I was a newly hired first officer. I never thought that I would have such an opportunity until I heard that various levels of training—including type ratings—were available from Airliners of America. My decision to train for a rating was sealed when I learned that Whitesell's airplane had been in service with TWA as *Skyliner Peoria* from 1952 to 1959. (TWA did not allow N636X to be painted in TWA livery, which is why it displays the colors of Pacific Airlines, another 404 operator.)

The ground school that I attended at Camarillo Airport was filled with 14 enthusiastic students. Four were previously qualified pilots attending for the purpose of recurrent training. Five were qualifying in the Martin for the first time. Four were volunteer maintenance workers auditing the course to learn more about the airplane. FAA representative Gary Hunt also was there to ensure that the course met all FAA requirements.

Hunt need not have been concerned. The course was thorough albeit fast-paced. John Deakin, a captain for Japan Airlines, taught the first day's curriculum, and Whitesell taught the second. The intensity of the course reminded me of when I attended similar but longer initial-training courses at TWA. In those days, I was paid well to absorb the required knowledge. It somehow seemed incongruous (and perhaps a bit masochistic) that I was now paying to endure similar academic torture.

Pilots are attracted to the Martin 404 program for a number of reasons. Penny Wilson, a private pilot and co-pilot trainee, typified the feelings of many: "I am intrigued by the romance of that era and the sounds made by those big radial engines. They have so much more character and personality than screeching turbines. Best of all is associating with people who share the same enthusiasm."

Kerry Bean, a Boeing 757/767 captain for a major airline was there to sample the experiences of his predecessors. Randy Dettmer, a general aviation pilot and architect, met Whitesell at an airshow and "got hooked by his infectious enthusiasm. I also flew in these old piston airliners when I was a kid. I want to know what it is like to fly one."

After we completed ground school, Deakin taught us how to preflight the vintage airliner. Those wearing good clothes learned the hard way that the Martin spreads oil over itself almost as thoroughly as it consumes it. (Each engine has an oil capacity of 146 quarts.).

There are all sorts of access doors to open and a seemingly endless number of items to check. A thorough preflight inspection should take 30 minutes. If it takes less time, you've missed something.

The cockpit was designed before engineers knew much about ergonomics. Levers, controls, and instruments are distributed everywhere, seemingly without rhyme or reason. Some things simply went where they fit. The OFF position of a switch might be up, down, left, or right. But there is an ambiance to the Martin's flight deck that is inexplicably alluring.

Bringing a Pratt & Whitney twin-row, 18-cylinder, 2,400-hp, R-2800 Double Wasp engine to life requires both hands. One is on the throttle and the other reaches for the overhead panel and manipulates a series of switches like Van Cliburn playing the piano. Sequencing the starter selector, starter, primer, and magnetos at different times and with different fingers takes practice.

A starter is selected and engaged until 9 or 12 blades of the three-bladed propeller swing past any given point. This pre-start protocol proves that oil has not pooled in one of the bottom cylinders and formed a hydraulic lock. Attempting to start with this condition can result in engine damage such as a broken rod. The ignition is turned on and the primer is engaged, a procedure that is more art than science. If everything is done properly (and a silent prayer is answered), the prehistoric beast slowly awakens. It coughs, belches, and stirs to life one or two cylinders at a time, all the while spewing great clouds of exhaust (and, of course, oil).

Taxiing is conventional except that the nosewheel tiller operated by the captain's left hand is more sensitive than most aircraft so equipped. The 404 has a maximum-allowable gross weight of 44,900 pounds, but N636X is limited to 41,500 because the engines' anti-detonation-injection systems are deactivated. Empty weight for Whitesell's airplane is 32,570 pounds, which results in a useful load of 8,930 pounds.

TWA's runup checklist for the Martin 404 contained 44 items to be completed before takeoff, twice as many as was required on the DC-3. One important task is to operationally check and arm the autofeather system. This ensures that a propeller will automatically feather should the power of its engine drop below a specified level. This only occurs, however, if the power loss lasts for more than half-a-second. Otherwise, the propeller might feather at a time when the engine is only clearing its throat. If one propeller does feather automatically, the system is disabled so that the other propeller will not automatically feather for any reason.

After lining up with the runway, the throttles are advanced carefully so as not to exceed engine limits: 2700 rpm and 55 inches MAP. (Earplugs are recommended.) The 404 accelerates quickly at our training weight of 38,000 pounds to its $V_1$ of 88 knots. Shortly thereafter, the nose is rotated gingerly so that the aircraft lifts off at its $V_2$ of 100 knots. The gear is raised, and we accelerate at a shallow deck angle until reaching 120 knots. Power is reduced to 2,600 rpm and 48.5 inches (from 2,050 to 1,800 hp per engine).

We continue accelerating to 130 knots, and power is further pulled back to 2,400 rpm and 41 inches (1,400 hp). $V_Y$ with both engines operating is 140 knots and results in an initial climb rate of 1,905 fpm.

After completing the after-takeoff checklist, I begin to relax and enjoy the antiquated anachronism. Ghosts of TWA captains past seem to bark at me from every corner of the cockpit: "More rudder, dammit!" "Keep the ball centered!" "Watch those temps! Yer gonna' roast the heads!" "What's the name of that little town down there at three o'clock?" They never let up on a new co-pilot.

The Martin 404 cruises at 240 knots, 85 knots faster than the DC-3. Fuel consumption during the first hour of flight (including climb) is 300 gallons. Thereafter it burns 185-200 gph. Fuel capacity is 1,000 gallons in each of the two wing tanks.

The 404 has no bad habits and handles well as long as you don't expect it to change heading and attitude as sprightly as a smaller, lighter airplane.

It would be nice if a Martin crew included a flight engineer. The airplane is at least as complex and demanding of attention as many other aircraft that do have engineers. Oil and cylinder-head temperatures, for example, are critical, which means that the oil-cooler doors and cowl flaps have to be adjusted with almost every power and airspeed change.

After some stalls and engine-out drills, Whitesell directs me back to the airport. (Maximum landing weight is 40,200 pounds.)

While on a long final approach to Camarillo's Runway 26, I slow the Martin to below 165 knots and call for "gear down." Initial deployment of the slotted flaps is limited to 165 knots, and moving the handle to the second notch is allowed only below 130 knots. I expect a hefty pitch change when extending the flaps fully but was pleasantly surprised by only a mild pitching moment. This is the result of another Martin innovation. When the flaps are extended from the second to the third and final notch, the horizontal stabilizers automatically reposition to eliminate the large pitching moment that would otherwise occur. Also, a load-relief system prevents the extension of full flaps until below the maximum-allowable speed of 105 knots.

Airspeed "over the fence" should be 95 knots, and some power is maintained until the sink rate is arrested in the flare. The mains hopefully chirp, and the nosewheel is landed before commanding the propellers into reverse pitch. Maintaining airspeed between 95 and 105 knots on final approach can be challenging in a Martin

(especially when having to burn off excess altitude), but landing one is relatively easy.

After my first flight, I had more respect for the graybeards with whom I had flown early in my airline career. They operated a handful of airplane in the weather, not above it. This was when airmanship, instinct, and timing seemed to play larger roles than they do today. Flying a Martin 404 also makes one appreciate the increased reliability and relative simplicity of turbofan-powered airplanes.

Whitesell's goal is to collect, preserve, and keep flying as many piston airliners as possible. In the meantime, he is searching for a site that will accommodate the display of such aircraft, a place from which they also can be flown and maintained. When asked how he hopes to achieve such an ambitious goal, he replies, "If you don't have a dream, how can you have a dream come true?"

## Grumman G-44 Widgeon

| | |
|---|---|
| Engines | 2 Ranger 6-440-C5 |
| Power | 200 hp ea |
| Length | 31 ft 5 in |
| Height (on wheels) | 9 ft 7 in |
| Wingspan | 40 ft 0 in |
| Wing Loading | 18.5 lb/sq ft |
| Power Loading | 11.3 lb/hp |
| Maximum Takeoff Weight | 4,525 lb |
| Fuel Capacity | 108 gal |
| Rate of Climb (sea level) | 700 fpm |
| Normal Cruise Speed | 130 kt |
| Stall Speed | 57 kt |

# Grumman G-44 Widgeon

## A pilot inspecting a Grumman G-44 Widgeon

for the first time might think that a World War II tank manufacturer had built the airplane. The fuel caps weigh two pounds each, the landing gear assembly is so rugged that it can be extended safely at any airspeed, and the master switch is a hefty lever that when moved through its several inches of lateral travel goes "klunk" upon reaching its ON or OFF position. This clearly is an airplane designed and built to last.

This is why the Grumman Aircraft Engineering Corporation was known during its heyday as the Grumman Iron Works. There was nothing fragile about a Grumman-built airplane.

The Widgeon is the smallest of four amphibious flying boats built by Grumman. The first was the indestructible, 8-seat, G-21 Goose, which debuted in 1937. The popularity of the Goose created a demand for a smaller amphibian, which led to development of the Widgeon in 1940.

Except for size, the Widgeon and the Goose are similar in appearance. The most distinctive visual difference between the two aircraft is the powerplants. The diminutive Widgeon has 6-cylinder, inverted in-line engines (Ranger 6-440-C5, 200 hp each), while the larger Goose has 9-cylinder radial engines (Pratt & Whitney R-985 Wasp Junior, 450 hp each). A number of Widgeons, however, have been re-equipped with more powerful Avco Lycoming or Teledyne Continental engines and are called Super Widgeons.

Most Widgeons built before and during World War II were snapped up by the U.S. Coast Guard for use as submarine spotters (the J4F-1), the Navy (the J4F-2), the Army Air Corps (the OA-14), and the Portugese Navy. An improved civilian version of the Widgeon, the G-44A, was introduced in 1944. Production ended in 1949 after a total of 276 Widgeons had been built at Grumman's Bethpage, Long Island plant.

Grumman built two additional amphibious flying boats. One was the G-73 Mallard "air yacht" that seated 12 and had tricycle landing gear. The other was the 27,500-pound, twin-engine HU-16 Albatross that was used primarily by the military for air-sea rescue operations (although a few are now in private hands).

N1340V (Serial No. 1228) is a pristine example of a Grumman Widgeon that was kept by its owner, Merrill Wien, at Orcas Island Airport on Orcas Island, one of the San Juan Islands at the northern end of Puget Sound, Washington. This G-44 began life in 1941 when it was delivered to the Coast Guard. Wien purchased the airplane in 1981 for $40,000 and then, with the assistance of Pat Prociv and an investment of more than $250,000, totally rebuilt the airplane and finished it in its original Coast Guard colors. The most significant modification made to the airplane during the rebuilding process was exchanging the wooden, fixed-pitch, Sensenich propellers for constant-speed, full-feathering Hartzells.

"With fixed-pitch props," Wien says, "you could only get 2,060 static rpm at full throttle, which is only about 130-to-140 hp per engine. Performance is improved dramatically with constant-speed props because you can get maximum-allowable rpm (2,450) and a full 200 hp per engine from a standing start."

(Unfortunately, performance figures for a Widgeon with constant-speed propellers are unavailable; performance data in this chapter is for a G-44 with fixed-pitch props.)

Since it was rebuilt, Wien's airplane was never exposed to salt water operations and had an estimated value of $300,000 in the year 2000.

If the Wien name sounds familiar, it should. Merrill's father, Noel Wien, was the Alaskan bush pilot whose exploits and explorations are both legion and legendary. (Highly recommend is the book, *Noel Wien: Alaska Pioneer Bush Pilot*, by Ira Harkey.)

In this case, the apple did not fall far from the tree. Merrill Wien is a remarkably accomplished pilot in his own right. He soloed a Luscombe 8A in Seattle on his 16th birthday in 1946 and since then has accumulated more than 30,000, accident-free and adventurous hours doing what most of us can only dream about.

Wien's extremely diversified career included flying an assortment of piston and turbine airliners for Pan American Airlines, Air America, and Wien Alaska Airlines. He flew in the Air Force for five years and devoted another chunk of his life to bush flying in Alaska's hinterlands. The latter included glacier operations in a Cessna 185 skiplane, flying helicopters to tag polar bears on the ice shelf north of Point Barrow, and supplying scientific stations by flying a Douglas DC-4 in and out of ice islands near the North Pole. He also flew a Fairchild C-119 during covert operations to snag balloon-lifted surveillance cameras "somewhere" over Asia.

He has owned 10 aircraft (including a Lockheed P-38 and two North American B-25s) and is currently a command pilot with the Confederate Air Force flying such exotic military machines as the Boeing B-17 Flying Fortress, Consolidated B-24 Liberator, and Boeing B-29 Superfortress. And this just scratches the surface.

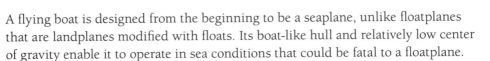

A flying boat is designed from the beginning to be a seaplane, unlike floatplanes that are landplanes modified with floats. Its boat-like hull and relatively low center of gravity enable it to operate in sea conditions that could be fatal to a floatplane.

Like almost all flying boats, the Widgeon has a high wing that places the engines as high as possible to reduce water spray that can damage propellers. The disadvantage becomes obvious during a preflight inspection. Without a tall ladder available, the pilot must climb forward along the top of the fuselage and onto the wings to check fuel and oil quantities, a decidedly unpleasant chore during harsh weather conditions. (The 108-gallon fuel supply is divided equally in two 54-gallon wing tanks.)

A single hull, however, is not as laterally stable as the wider stance of a floatplane. Wing-mounted floats are used on "boats" to prevent a wingtip from striking the water.

The original Widgeon was all-metal except that fabric covered the primary control surfaces, flaps, and that portion of each wing aft of the spar. (Fabric saves weight and reduces the likelihood of flutter.) During the rebuilding process, the flaps and aft wing sections of Wien's Widgeon were metalized. There is one trim tab on each elevator. The left tab is conventional, but the one on the right deflects only downward and automatically when the high-lift, slotted wing flaps are extended (to partially offset the nose-down pitching moment caused by flap deployment).

Aside from draining whatever water might have seeped into watertight compartments (which is normal during water operations) and verifying that no one has absconded with the stainless-steel anchor stored in the bow, the preflight inspection is routine.

Pilots and passengers enter the Widgeon through a single hatch on the left side of the fuselage immediately aft of the left wing, an initially challenging procedure for tall people.

The instrument panel spans only the left and center sections of the available space. This leaves a vacant area where the co-pilot's instruments would otherwise be. This open area allows someone to crawl forward and into the bow, open the top hatch compartment, and aid in anchoring or mooring at a buoy. It also is a great place from which to fish.

The arrangement and distribution of controls, switches, levers, and instruments takes getting used to. The upper control panel above the windshield contains the throttles, trim-tab controls, tailwheel lock, landing-gear lever and latches, flap control, ignition, and various other switches and instruments. The upper rear panel is on the ceiling aft of the upper control panel and contains fuel-system, mixture, and carburetor-heat controls. This also is where the oversized master switch is located. Because these controls are not logically or ergonomically placed, it behooves a new Widgeon pilot to spend ground time in the cockpit becoming familiar with the locations of critical controls.

The single vertical control column to which the control wheels are attached is between the pilots' seats. Before being modified, Wien's Widgeon had a single throw-over control wheel like many Bonanzas. Although the left-seat pilot is provided with rudder/brake pedals, the right-seat pilot has a rudder bar (like the steering handles of a snow sled) and no brakes.

The fully castering, retractable tailwheel is not steerable. Directional control is maintained using differential braking. There is no problem seeing over the low nose of this taildragger, and it is well-mannered on the ground. But if a pilot is concerned about the Widgeon expressing a directional will of its own while taxiing, taking off, or landing on land, he can engage the tailwheel lock using the lever on the overhead panel. Having to reach up to manipulate the throttles is different but is something to which a new "boat" pilot becomes quickly acclimatized.

Takeoffs and landings on land are unremarkable for a taildragger. It is when being operated on water that the Widgeon becomes challenging. Wien checked me out in water operations at 8-mile-long Lake Whatcom near Bellingham on the Washington mainland.

As the throttles are advanced for takeoff, the sprite little boat yaws left before the rudder has sufficient airspeed to arrest the turn. (Unlike floatplanes, the Widgeon does not have a water rudder; directional control while taxiing is maintained with differential thrust.) The same yawing moment is created by the engines of conventional twins but is largely negated by the nosewheel tire.

Taking off from water in a Widgeon requires advancing the left throttle ahead of the right to maintain a constant takeoff heading. An alternate method is to start the takeoff run at a heading that is 30 degrees right of the desired takeoff run. I found it preferable to use differential thrust while others prefer using an offset heading.

The only takeoff data available for a Widgeon in water is cited in the meager Pilot's Handbook as "25 seconds." With constant-speed propellers, this reportedly is reduced to 12 seconds.

When taking off with miles of water visible in the windshield, the notion of an engine failure immediately after liftoff is not as daunting as when flying a light twin from land. Simply land straight ahead and worry later about how difficult or impossible it can be to steer the boat on water with asymmetric thrust.

Once airborne, the Widgeon is just another light twin, but you still cannot escape the exciting notion that you are flying a boat that belongs as much on water as in the air. And although we went through the full regimen of aerial maneuvers, I was eager to return to the lake. One noteworthy observation is that the constant-speed, full-feathering propellers on Wien's Widgeon provide acceptable engine-out performance. The single-engine rate of climb and service ceiling with fixed-pitch propellers (that do not feather) are regarded as nil.

Also, the high thrust line of the engines causes a slight nose-down pitching moment when adding power and a nose-up moment when reducing power.

As we returned to Lake Whatcom, I went through the required mental litany over and over again. "This will be a water landing; the landing gear will not be extended."

Although each pilot has a small sliding-glass window that may be open in flight, I learned the wet way that they should be closed before landing. Otherwise, a bath towel should be included on the minimum-equipment list.

The 65-knot approach and 50-knot touchdown are relatively conventional. There are no surprises until the Widgeon is firmly on the water. This is when a new Widgeon pilot discovers that the most demanding aspect of operating a Widgeon on water is controlling its headstrong penchant for porpoising, especially during downwind step turns. It takes considerable practice and humility to learn the skills and develop the timing necessary to keep porpoising under control. If allowed to become sufficiently divergent, it is possible to lose the airplane. (One owner has understandably named his Widgeon *The Petulant Porpoise*.) Wien controls this tricky characteristic almost effortlessly; it is like watching a maestro at work.

The wing floats prevent pulling alongside a dock and parking without someone on the dock to grab a wingtip or float strut. Ramping is much easier. While very slowly approaching a ramp, lower the landing gear (hydraulically) and allow the wheels to contact the rising slope. As the aircraft comes to a stop, add substantial power to pull the machine out of the water and onto land, steering as necessary with differential power to remain on the ramp.

The rugged and hefty appearance of a Widgeon belies its delightful handling qualities and performance. It is a wonderful blend of amphibious utility and pure, unadulterated fun.

## Lake LA-4 Amphibian

| | |
|---|---:|
| Engine | Lycoming O-360A1A |
| Power | 180 hp |
| Length | 24 ft 11 in |
| Height (on wheels) | 9 ft 4 in |
| Wingspan | 38 ft 0 in |
| Wing Loading | 14.1 lb/sq ft |
| Power Loading | 13.3 lb/hp |
| Maximum Takeoff Weight | 2,400 lb |
| Fuel Capacity | 40 gal |
| Rate of Climb (sea level) | 800 fpm |
| Normal Cruise Speed | 131 mph |
| Stall Speed | 50 mph |

# Lake LA-4 Amphibian
## or "Lake Buccaneer"

*The sight of a boat with wings must have seemed* strange to the boating enthusiasts at Clear Lake in northern, California. As we maneuvered the Lake LA-4 amphibian on the water, a variety of powerboats made cautious passes to see what manner of craft was cruising the water so comfortably at 40 mph.

The Lake was designed to operate on the water at high speed, and I had no difficulty outperforming even the ablest of surface craft, except one. I noticed the twin inboard racer overtaking me from starboard. The driver meant to show that he was master of the lake.

The speedboat's occupants grinned with delight as they passed. With open water ahead and not to be outdone, I inched the throttle forward until we were indicating 50 mph and barely catching the mahogany racer. My opponent gave it all, and the twin screws churned the water mightily.

It was time. I asked my passenger to close the windows as I extended the flaps. The amphibian lifting out of the water and passing the racer at more than 100 mph was an embarrassing defeat for my opponent.

Earlier that day, my passengers and I arrived at Oakland Airport where Ron Timm, a Lake dealer, began my checkout in the LA-4. I then left my friends for the hour or so it would take Timm and me to fly to Lake Berryessa for the completion of my checkout.

During this checkout, Timm tossed around nautical terms such as port, starboard, bow, and so forth. His barnacles showed, though, when I referred to the tie-down ropes. "Seaplane pilots use lines, not ropes," he said smiling.

He then instructed me to remove the plugs from 6 watertight compartments to check for water leakage in the hull and wing floats. These are checked daily and after heavy water work. It is not unusual to find at least a cupful. "And don't forget to replace the plugs before operating on water," he stressed.

There are wide walkways along the top of the bow stressed to support as many people as can fit. These are excellent platforms from which to fish, dive, and sunbathe. I opened a small door on top of the bow to check for the anchor and 20 feet of line for mooring when a dock, ramp, or buoy is unavailable. An oar is stored between the left sidewall and the pilot's seat, just in case.

The 40-gallon fuel tank in the fuselage is refueled through a single filler. There are 2 fuel drains under the port wing root. Checking oil quantity requires standing on the walkway above the cockpit to reach the dipstick of the pylon-mounted pusher engine.

The split horizontal tail surfaces are unusual. The inboard halves of what look like elevators are indeed the elevators and operate conventionally. The outboard halves, though, are actually large trim tabs.

Tucked neatly into the bottom of the rudder is another, smaller rudder lowered from within the cockpit and used for steering on water during low-speed taxiing. It should be retracted at other times because it is not designed to take the hydrodynamic battering that occurs at high water speeds. Also the combination of aerodynamic and water rudders can cause overcontrolling.

After removing the tie-down "lines," we climbed into N1160L through the 2 hatches (not "doors") that when closed are the front windshields.

With the exception of the 4 engine controls, the cockpit appears normal in all respects. The throttle, propeller control, carburetor-heat control, and mixture control, however, are mounted on the ceiling between the pilots' seats. Most flying boats are similar because this simplifies connecting control cables to the engine. This initially confuses the transitioning pilot, and I was constantly reaching toward the instrument panel for the throttle.

Landing gear, flaps, and trim tabs are hydraulic and powered by an electric hydraulic pump. A small handle protruding from the instrument panel is a hand pump to be used if the electric pump fails. The handle is located where the throttle is on most single-engine landplanes, and every once in a while I reached for it out of habit.

After turning on the appropriate switches and energizing the starter, the 180-horsepower Lycoming 0-360A1A came to life.

Taxiing the small flying boat on land requires differential braking to move the nosewheel in the desired direction.

The run-up is similar to that of a typical landplane with one exception. Ensure that the water rudder is retracted so that it will not scrape the runway when the nose is rotated for takeoff. The flaps have only 2 positions, up and down; there is no intermediate setting. Full flaps are used for takeoffs and landings whether operating from water or land.

After a normal but noisy takeoff, I raised the gear and retracted the flaps at 75 mph. Best rate-of-climb airspeed is 85 mph.

En route to Lake Berryessa, Timm told me about the LA-4's structural integrity. "A novice was flying one over a lake and somehow managed to stall 75 feet above the surface. The aircraft nosed down into 40 feet of water, struck bottom nose first, and then bobbed to the surface. The pilot suffered only minor injuries. The windshields had to be replaced, but there was only minor damage to the bow and wing floats."

With the wings mounted aft of the cabin and the engine above the hull instead of on the nose, in-flight visibility is impressive.

Lake Berryessa appeared ahead and between a pair of peaks. Timm suggested that I maintain altitude for a unique demonstration. When over the lake, he asked me to reduce power to idle, extend the gear and flaps, and nudge the yoke forward until the amphibian was descending at a 35-degree, nose-down attitude. Airspeed held steady at 125 mph, and the vertical-speed indicator was pegged.

This airplane can descend like a rock without excessive airspeed. This was especially impressive because the Lake has the same glide ratio as a Cessna 172 when the gear and flaps are retracted.

Preparing for the water landing, Timm suggested that I lower flaps, and descend at 70 mph and 15 inches of manifold pressure. After trimming out the back pressure, the flying boat settled at only 200 feet per minute. Timm told me to "let the airplane touch down in this attitude. Don't touch a thing." This caused a little anxiety because my experience in floatplanes suggested that this was not the best way to land a seaplane, but Timm knew this flying boat intimately.

At 400 feet awl (above water level), Timm suggested also that I double-check to ensure that the landing gear is where it should be, up for water landings and down for landing on land, something about which all amphibian pilots must remain alert.

As the Lake approached the surface, I fought the temptation to flare. Before I knew it, the flying boat began skimming the water. I reached up, retarded the power, and held the control wheel aft. The airplane had not yet settled into the water when Timm surprised me by shoving the control wheel fully forward. We came to an abrupt halt.

"You can't do that in a floatplane," he said. "You'd probably bury a float and flip over."

Water taxiing is a snap. Lower the water rudder and steer with the rudder pedals. It handles just like a boat, which is no surprise. This amphibian is a boat, a boat with wings.

Timm next invited me to try step turns. The flaps stay down and the water rudder comes up. Full power is applied, and the Lake begins to plow through the water creating quite a spray pattern. At about 30 mph, back pressure is released and the

*Taxi down a ramp with the landing gear extended, but do not retract the wheels until the amphibian is floating on the surface.*

aircraft rises "over the hump" and onto the step. Power is reduced to about 20 inches of manifold pressure to prevent becoming airborne.

While zooming around the lake at 40 to 50 mph, you quickly forget that you are in an airplane. The Lake seems to handle as well as a conventional boat. We headed across the wake of another boat without as much as a nod from the amphibian.

Back over San Francisco Bay, it dawned on me that this airplane does not have the "automatic rough" commonly associated with single-engine landplanes flying over water. Happiness is flying over land or water without worrying about engine failure!

I picked up my friends at Oakland and loaded 40 pounds in the baggage compartment behind the rear seats. Minutes later we headed north for our weekend at Clear Lake, the largest lake wholly within California. Alcatraz Island slipped past our port wing.

While en route at 4,500 feet using 75-percent power, I noted an outside air temperature of 60 degrees F and an indicated airspeed of 115 mph. True airspeed was 124 mph. The Lake cruises at 131 mph at its optimum altitude of 6,000 feet.

As my experience with the Lake grew, I discovered that it does not tend to pitch up during a power decrease or pitch nose-down during a power increase, which is what

I had expected from an airplane with a thrust line so high above the longitudinal axis. I could detect only slight pitch changes when changing power radically, from full power to idle, and vice versa.

On short final approach to Clear Lake, I trimmed the airplane as I had done earlier that day to make a hands-off landing. The initial touchdown was smooth and barely discernable, making a better landing without my help than with it.

I kept the amphibian on the step and played motor boat during the rest of the to our lakeside destination, the Skylark Motel and Seaport near the town of Lakeport. My apologies go to the water skier who lost his balance and literally flipped at the sight of the Lake performing high-speed 360s in the water.

As we approached the Skylark's ramp, I retarded the throttle to idle. The amphibian gave up its speed and settled more deeply into the water. I had to be careful when maneuvering near the ramp because the approach was bracketed by a pair of docks. Seaplanes do not have brakes in the water, and the Lake does not have a reversible-pitch propeller as do some seaplanes. Closer to the ramp, I extended the landing gear, which further slowed the aircraft and were needed to taxi up the ramp and onto land.

The ramp was only 50 feet ahead and I slowed to a crawl. I made my final cockpit check; a green light on the panel confirmed that the landing gear was down and locked.

As the nosewheel touched and began to roll up the sloping ramp, I applied a fistful of power and raised the water rudder. The amphibian leaped out of the water and up the ramp. We parked on the motel's grass lawn.

After lunch, I preflighted the Lake, drained a little water from the hull, and prepared for recreation on the water. Before you could sing the first verse of *Anchors Aweigh*, we had taxied down the ramp and were moving toward open water. I raised the landing gear and completed a run-up.

Even with full power, the Lake accelerates slowly in the plowing phase of takeoff. The hull is still fully in the water, and the aircraft has insufficient speed to get onto the step. Once the aircraft began to rise from the water (about 35 mph), I released back pressure. The Lake rose smartly onto the step and picked up speed. We were soon airborne.

Minutes later, we flew over a remote cove, an ideal place to land and break out our picnic basket.

After landing, I approached the beach slowly, threw open the port hatch, and stuck the oar into the water until I felt it scraping bottom. I killed the engine with the mixture and allowed the aircraft to beach.

My friend and I jumped out of the aircraft and in the style of Sir Walter Raleigh carried our female companions ashore.

When needed for shelter, the Lake quickly converts to a sleeper for two. The rear seats are easily removable, and there is ample room to stretch your legs into the lengthy fuselage.

The next morning I stepped out of my second-story motel room and onto the veranda. I looked down and saw that the Lake was surrounded by curious and envious onlookers. Not many of those who had checked into the Skylark on the street of the motel expected to see an airplane parked on the lakeside lawn.

*An oar comes in handy if the engine fails before reaching shore.*

We spent the rest of the morning and much of the afternoon exploring, sunbathing, swimming, and fishing from the hull of the amphibian in a beautiful, sheltered, and, I might add, romantic cove.

We could have legally and safely water skied behind the LA-4 if it had been equipped with suitable quick release mechanism for the ski rope.

The time came too soon for the last leg of our flying vacation and the inevitable return to reality.

## Sikorsky S-38 Amphibion

| | |
|---|---|
| Engines | 2 Pratt & Whitney R-1340 |
| Power | 420 hp ea |
| Length | 40 ft 3 in |
| Height (3-point attitude) | 13 ft 10 in |
| Wingspan | 71 ft 8 in |
| Wing Loading | 14.5 lb/sq ft |
| Power Loading | 12.5 lb/hp |
| Maximum Takeoff Weight | 10,480 lb |
| Fuel Capacity (usable) | 340 gal |
| Rate of Climb (sea level) | 750 fpm |
| Normal Cruise Speed | 95 mph |
| Stall Speed | 55 mph |

# Sikorsky Amphibion S-38

## We called McCarran Approach Control for

permission to enter the Class B airspace surrounding Las Vegas, Nevada.

"Sikorsky Two Eight Victor, you're cleared into Class Bravo airspace. Descend to 2,700 feet."

I replied by saying that 500 feet over the city seems a bit low.

"You're a helicopter, right?"

"Negative. We're a flying boat."

The pregnant silence was followed by instructions to maintain present altitude.

One cannot blame the controller for believing us to be a helicopter. There are very few Sikorsky airplanes in the air these days, but there was a time when the Sikorsky was Queen of the Sky.

The legendary designer, Igor Sikorsky, was born in 1889 and emigrated from Russia at the onset of the Bolshevik Revolution. He arrived in the United States in 1919 and developed the world's first practical helicopter a few years later.

Because there were so few airports and is so much water, he focused his great intuition and engineering genius on seaplanes, airplanes that "could take their airports with them." His first certified airplane was the Sikorsky S-38 Amphibion, a spelling preferred by Mr. Sikorsky.

The airplane was developed primarily for Pan American Airways. The fledgling airline used the 8-passenger Sikorsky to expand its route structure from 90 miles (Key West, Florida to Havana, Cuba) to a 13,000-mile network that included more of the Caribbean as well as Central and South America. Pan Am was so pleased with the 7-hour range that it purchased 38 of the amphibians. Its expanding operations eventually evolved into the halcyon era of the China Clipper.

Charles Lindbergh flew an S-38 for Pan Am on proving flights between Miami, Panama, and Rio de Janeiro. Hawaiian Island Air Services used Amphibions to provide inter-island service, and Western Air Express used them to serve Avalon, a tourist resort on Santa Catalina Island off the coast of southern California. The Sikorsky amphibians proved to be rugged and reliable in what were occasionally difficult operating circumstances.

Larger and faster seaplanes followed in the wake of the S-38. The final Sikorsky seaplane was the long-range, 4-engine VS-44A flying boat (not an amphibian) that provided the fastest (183 knots) military passenger service across the Atlantic to Europe during World War II. The Great Seaplane Era ended soon after the war, and Igor Sikorsky shifted his attention to helicopters.

The S-38 made its maiden flight from the Sikorsky Manufacturing Corporation in College Point on Long Island, New York on June 25, 1928. The amphibian caught the attention of Martin and Osa Johnson, a husband-and-wife team of explorers, naturalists, authors, and motion-picture producers.

The Johnsons had spent years in Kenya, the Congo, British North Borneo, and the South Pacific taking more than 10,000 photographs of animals, people, and places that had never before been seen through a lens. They also produced nine full-length motion pictures and 17 shorter films (using hand-crank cameras) that captured the public's imagination with these first views of the customs, cultures, and civilizations found in remote regions of the world. The Johnsons wrote 18 books, one of the most popular being *I Married Adventure* (1940), a best-seller written by Osa.

Perhaps the best way to put the Johnsons into perspective is to say that they were during the 1920s and 1930s what Jacques Cousteau was during later years.

The Johnsons painted their Amphibion to resemble a zebra and called it *Osa's Ark*. It was used to make their first flying foray into "darkest Africa." They also purchased a smaller, single-engine Sikorsky S-39 (NC-52V) to serve as a companion aircraft.

It was painted with the reticulated pattern of a giraffe and was called the *Spirit of Africa*. Their pilots on this journey were Boris Sergievsky and Vern Carstens. (Carstens taught the Johnsons to fly and eventually became manager of flight test engineering and chief test pilot for Beech Aircraft.)

Flying in Africa in 1933 and 1934 was as primitive as the lands over which they flew. Airports were scarce, and inaccurate maps provided misleading guidance. The Johnsons were the first to photograph Tanzania's Mt. Kilimanjaro from above.

Coincidentally, another Johnson used a Sikorsky Amphibion for a 15,500-mile expedition to South America. S.C. Johnson was in search of carnauba, a vegetable wax exuded by the leaves of the Brazilian carnauba palm. SC Johnson & Sons is perhaps best known for Johnson Wax.

Of the 111 S-38s manufactured, none survived. Wanting to take his two sons on a recreation of his father's 1935 expedition to Brazil during the Great Depression, Samuel Johnson, commissioned Born Again Restorations of Owatonna, Minnesota to build an S-38 from scratch using plans that thankfully were still available. The flight was made in 1998, and the *Carnauba* now resides in the Johnson Museum in Racine, Wisconsin.

R.W. "Buzz" Kaplan, Born Again Restorations' owner, and his friend, Tom Schrade, a real estate investor and developer, were enamored by the aircraft and decided to build a second S-38, a restoration of *Osa's Ark* that is the subject of this chapter. It is considered a restoration because it includes the wings and tail booms of an original Amphibion. The project required an investment of 2.5 years, 40,000 man-hours, and more than $2 million. Gary Underland was the artisan and primary builder of both S-38s.

Schrade and Kaplan had planned to fly their aircraft to Africa until Kaplan perished in his 1917 Curtiss JN-4 Jenny in July, 2002.

(Richard "Dick" Jackson of Rochester, New Hampshire rebuilt a single-engine S-39 that is emblazoned with the giraffe-like markings of the *Spirit of Africa*. N50V, which is the original N-number, is the oldest Sikorsky airplane in the world and is the only airworthy S-39.)

The Sikorsky S-38 Amphibion is one of the all-time great airplanes from aviation's Golden Era. One of its most distinguishing features and a Sikorsky trademark are the twin booms that keep the tail high above the water and in line with the propeller slipstreams (to enhance the effectiveness of the elevator and twin rudders). The airplane is a labyrinthine maze of struts, braces, supports, and wires that provides a rigid structure for the parasol wing, lower wing, tail booms, and the fuselage, which also is the hull and is divided into 6 watertight compartments.

Lateral stability on the water is provided by a pontoon (float) under each of the lower wings.

The S-38 is a large airplane with a 72-foot wingspan, about the same as a Ford Tri-Motor, but do not call it a biplane. Because the lower wing area is less than half that of the upper wing, the S-38 is more accurately described as a sesquiplane.

Schrade's airplane, NC-28V, is pristine, apparently better than when it originally left the factory, but there have been a few significant upgrades. A tailskid would not be conducive to operating from hard-surface runways and taxiways, so it was replaced with a robust, fully-castoring tailwheel borrowed from under the nose of a Cessna 182. A pair of supercharged Pratt & Whitney R-985, 450-hp Wasp engines (sans cowlings) replace the 420-hp versions. The Johnsons would no doubt have paid a king's ransom for the pair of Garmin global positioning systems, moving-map displays, and other modern avionics on the instrument panel. The Johnsons wrote that "it was not unusual to get lost flying over Africa [during the early 1930s]."

The cabin has an "air-yacht" configuration almost identical to that of the original *Osa's Ark*. It has the appearance of a stateroom on a luxurious, turn-of-the-century seafaring yacht. There are curtains to keep the sun out, thank you, two bolted-down wicker chairs on the right, a divan that seats three on the left (a total of 5 passengers), and beautiful mahogany paneling and trim. A storage cabinet contains the elements needed for libation as well as a pullout table upon which to place the glasses. (Osa used the table for writing.) The rear of the cabin has room for a toilet and baggage.

A delightful feature is the hatch on top of the rear fuselage. It allows a passenger (or two) to stand and stick his head and shoulders out for a magnificent panoramic view in any direction. The vista is especially exciting when standing there during flight.

One of the Johnson's movies, *Baboona*, includes a scene that shows *Osa's Ark* surrounded by a pride of lions. Osa opens the S-38's hatch and quickly closes it as lions try to jump in.

Schrade keeps his airplane at the North Las Vegas Airport, which is where I was checked out in the S-38 by his friend and instructor, Waldo Anderson. Anderson retired as chief pilot for the University of Minnesota in 1997. There he ran the flight school and transported State personnel in a Beech King Air and a Baron. He met Schrade in 1975, instructed him for most of his ratings (including a flight instructor certificate that Schrade uses as a hobby). At 68, Anderson spends much of his time with Schrade flying the Sikorsky amphibian to air shows all over the country.

You enter the cockpit by stepping on a tire and climbing through the side and overhead windows. Passengers gain access by climbing through a hatch on the aft left side of the cabin. Agility is required in either case. Unfortunately, you cannot go back and forth between the cabin and the cockpit.

Starting the engines is unremarkable except for the wonderful sound of radial engines that always takes me back to a bygone era. Taxiing without a steerable tailwheel is not difficult using differential power and brakes.

Rotation is not needed for takeoff. When allowed, the airplane simply levitates in 3-point attitude at 45 knots. Lower the nose a wee bit to 65 knots, pull the go knobs back to 30 inches and 2,000 rpm, and climb rates settle at 500-800 fpm, depending on load.

The original S-38 required manually pumping up the landing gear one leg one at a time. Schrade's airplane has an electric hydraulic pump that results in a quaint ritual involving selector handles, locking valves, and pump switches. Although this requires less physical effort, the legs still come up very slowly and one at a time.

Raising the landing gear does not reduce drag. It simply raises the wheels and places them flush with the bottoms of the lower wings to get them out of the way for water operations. For land operations only, performance does not suffer if the wheels are left down, but the purist raises them anyway because he knows that the airplane looks better that way.

Schrade thankfully provides pilots with Telex noise-canceling headsets. Otherwise, the noise and vibration of the Amphibion would be fatiguing. I cannot begin to imagine how Martin and Osa Johnson endured such lengthy journeys in an S-38 without hearing protection. One can only wonder how the Johnsons avoided becoming stone deaf, like the rabbits that dwell between the runways at Los Angeles International Airport.

At 27 inches and 1,900 rpm at 6,000 feet, the S-38 cruises at 90 knots while consuming 46 gallons per hour. Total fuel capacity of the four tanks (all in the upper wing) is 340 gallons. Maximum-allowable gross weight is 10,480 pounds.

The airplane is heavily damped in roll, has poor roll response, requires effort to maneuver, and is a handful in turbulence. It also has neutral lateral stability, which means that you cannot pick up a wing with rudder. One can only imagine the physical effort required to fly an S-38 through and near the intertropical convergence zone of central Africa. The airplane is undoubtedly challenging during takeoffs and landings in gusty crosswinds.

Conversely, pitch forces are relatively light. The nose hunts noticeably about the yaw axis even during mild turbulence, a characteristic probably caused by the long bow. Coping with an engine failure is a no-brainer because the engines are so close to the aircraft centerline. Very little rudder is required to keep the Sikorsky on an even keel even during low-speed climbs with the "good" engine developing maximum power. Engine-out climb performance at heavy weights, however, is virtually nil, even with a feathered propeller.

The S-38 has benign stall characteristics even during a power-on stall with an engine shut down. Although there is very little stall warning—only a mild buffet a few knots before the break—it does not seem to matter because the airplane is so well mannered.

An advantage of the North Las Vegas Airport is its proximity to sprawling Lake Mead, a paradise for boating and seaplane enthusiasts.

Touchdown attitude for a water landing is about the same as when making a 3-point landing on a runway. The S-38 seemingly has no bad habits in the water and makes consistently smooth landings without a noticeable tendency to porpoise. The airplane has limited elevator authority with a forward center of gravity, however, so power is helpful in establishing the nose-high touchdown attitude.

Like other multi-engine seaplanes, the S-38 does not have a water rudder, but it turns easily using differential power. If necessary, you can lower one landing gear leg to add water drag that helps to turn more sharply in that direction.

During the plowing phase of a water takeoff, forward visibility all but disappears behind the heavy spray across the windshield, but this clears away rapidly as the airplane comes over the hump and onto the step. After that, it is a simple matter of establishing and holding the right attitude (finding the "sweet spot") and allowing the Sikorsky to accelerate and fly itself off the water.

Overall, the Sikorsky S-38 is an advanced, well-behaved airplane considering that it was designed only a year after Lindbergh's historic flight and 25 years after the Wright Brothers' first successful effort.

Those interested in the adventurous exploits of Martin and Osa Johnson are encouraged to visit the Martin and Osa Johnson Safari Museum's web site: www.safarimuseum.com

You are also invited to visit the museum in Chanute, Kansas. The city was named after aviation pioneer Octave Chanute and is the birthplace of Osa Johnson. Not coincidentally, Chanute is served by the Martin Johnson Airport.

## Piper Comanche 600

| | |
|---|---|
| Engine | AiResearch TPE-331 |
| Power | 605 eshp (flat-rated to 450 shp) |
| Length | 25 ft 9 in |
| Height | 7 ft 3 in |
| Wingspan | 36 ft 0 in |
| Wing Loading | 20.9 lb/sq ft |
| Power Loading | 8.0 lb/shp |
| Maximum Takeoff Weight | 3,600 lb |
| Fuel Capacity | 100 gal |
| Rate of Climb (sea level) | 2,475 fpm |
| Normal Cruise Speed | 250 mph |
| Stall Speed | 61 mph |

# Piper Comanche 600

*My son and I were soaking up heritage at an aviation* museum. Brian studied each archaic device with awe, wondering how pilots of bygone days had the courage to fly such ill-equipped and seemingly fragile-machines.

Soon we reached an area displaying engines of the past. The center of attention was an engine that triggered fond memories.

"Dad," he asked, "Did you really use these weird-looking engines?"

I nodded and realized just how far we had come since aviation's dawn at Kitty Hawk.

"But Dad," he continued, now more bewildered than before, "How did this thing work?"

"Well," I began, "There's a half-dozen coffee-can-shaped thingamabobs moving back and forth in holes inside that big iron block." I continued with verbal diagrams of valves, spark plugs, cam shafts, and other complicated aspects of the obsolete, reciprocating, piston engine.

This reverie describes what I really thought it would be like to someday take my son to an aviation museum. After my first exposure to a turboprop engine in a small, single-engine airplane, I had thought that the future of the reciprocating engine was doomed. But it was not to be so. The piston engine thrives and survives. Despite the advantages of turbine engines, the cost of manufacturing, maintaining, and operating them will have to improve dramatically if they are to displace piston engines in small, general aviation airplanes.

My first experience with a turboprop-powered single was in 1968. This is when I was invited by the Garrett/AiResearch Corporation to fly their experimental Piper Comanche 600, a Comanche 400 modified with their TPE-331 turboprop engine.

AiResearch told me that the unmodified Comanche fuselage was chosen as an early test bed for its turboprop engine because of the Comanche's relatively high redline airspeed of 250 mph. This choice had nothing to do with the Piper Aircraft Company and did not mean that Piper intended to produce a turbine-powered Comanche.

The one-of-a-kind aircraft, N8401P, and its veteran test pilot, Jack Womack, achieved public recognition on May 15, 1968 when they established a new world altitude record of 41,320 feet for that class of turboprop aircraft. The previous record of 34,173 feet had been held by Pierre Bonneau of France in a SIPA (French) aircraft.

The TPE-331 is a lightweight, single-shaft, production engine available in power ratings of 575 to 715 shp (shaft horsepower). The one in the Comanche had 575 shp but could put out 605 eshp (effective shp) during flight.

Even though AiResearch's Turbine Comanche 600 and the stock Comanche 400 had identical fuselages, it would be unfair to compare their performance. The engines were worlds apart, eliminating the significance of any visual similarity between the two airplanes. The 8-cylinder, 400-hp Lycoming engine weighed 597 pounds (dry) while the TPE-331 turbine weighed a little more than 300 pounds and produced 50 percent more power. In other words, the Lycoming engine produced only 0.67 horsepower per pound of engine weight while the turboprop engine enjoyed a 2.0 hp/lb ratio. Pound for pound, therefore, the turbine was almost 3 times as powerful as the 8-cylinder engine.

Although the turboprop engine does amazing things to an otherwise fine aircraft, AiResearch insisted that the Comanche fuselage was not designed or modified to accommodate a turbine engine. If an aircraft of the Comanche class were designed from the get-go to utilize turboprop power, the performance would compare to the Comanche 600 as a tiger does to an anemic house cat.

The Comanche 600 was based at AiResearch's Phoenix Division. It looked like any other Comanche except for its unique nose section. The cowling had been redesigned to house the smaller powerplant. Because the turboprop weighed considerably less than the piston engine, the propeller was extended 9 inches forward to preserve the original center of gravity. A large, stainless-steel exhaust stack was molded to each side of the cowling and directed the spent gases beneath each wing so as not to interfere with normal airflow about the wing roots. If the exhaust were to flow through a single-channel exhaust stack, an additional 30 hp of jet thrust could have been realized. The propeller was an 82-inch, 3-bladed Hartzell and was both reversible and featherable. The longer blades placed the propeller tips closer to the ground, requiring caution while taxiing on gravel.

After a quick look at this unusual aircraft, I was introduced to Womack who knew most about the project. He had been with AiResearch since 1948 and involved with the development of the turboprop engine since its first flight in a Martin B-26 Marauder test bed in February, 1964. He was the original test pilot of the Comanche 600 beginning with its maiden flight on July 16, 1965.

I asked Womack, "Because AiResearch is so deeply involved in turboprop development, why is the company equally aggressive in marketing turbochargers? It would seem that turbochargers and turboprop engines compete with one another."

Standing under the Arizona sun, Womack folded his tanned arms across his chest and said, "By selling turbochargers, more people will be exposed to the advantages of flying in the middle altitudes—between 12,000 and 20,000 feet—a regime where the turboprop engine is truly master. This will help to create a demand for pressurized aircraft. When these finally become available, we'll have aircraft properly designed for turboprop engines."

Womack showed me how to preflight the engine for internal damage. If the propeller can be rotated effortlessly and freely without binding or unusual noises from the engine, then everything is normal. He suggested also that I look into the air inlet duct while turning the propeller to check the compressor blades for damage. A small sensor located within the duct also was inspected. This probe sent inlet-air temperature and pressure signals to the fuel controller, which metered the proper amount of fuel to the engine, depending on the position of the power lever in the cockpit.

The tanks were filled with 130 gallons of jet fuel (kerosene). Although the engine holds 8 quarts of turbine oil, it was almost ludicrous to check quantity before every flight. The TPE-331 may require a quart every month or so, but the engine can almost always be flown from oil change to oil change without adding any.

Satisfied with the preflight, Womack motioned me into the left seat.

Having many hours in a Comanche, I felt comfortable although some changes had been made to the instrument panel. Instead of the manifold pressure gauge and tachometer were an engine torque meter redlined at 44 psi, a small exhaust-gas temperature gauge, an equally small tachometer that indicated turbine rpm in percent (redlined at 105 percent).

An engine control pedestal mounted at the center of the instrument panel contained a robust, stainless-steel power lever, one that a pilot could really get a grip on.

The other, smaller one was a condition lever that controlled propeller pitch.

Starting the engine was dirt simple: 1) Turn on the master and inverter switches; 2) Turn on the fuel and ignition switch (this armed the circuits for activation later in the start process); and 3) Tap the spring-loaded start switch and release. That is all there was to it. The remainder of the start process was automatic.

The engine began to whine and within a few seconds, engine rpm reached 10 percent. This activated the circuits that caused the fuel valve to open and the 2 spark plugs to spray high voltage into the engine's burner section. EGT rose rapidly, peaking at about 700 degrees C with the engine accelerating through 30 percent rpm. The whine became more intense and the propeller, rotating in flat pitch, began to make a neat whooshing sound.

We watched EGT carefully; if it continued climbing rapidly to 780 degrees or above, a hot start would have occurred (probably due to low battery voltage and weak engine cranking power). We would have had to shut down the engine. Instead, the engine continued to wind up. At 55 percent rpm, the starter disengaged and the ignition turned off automatically. (Once combustion had begun with a steady flow of fuel, ignition was no longer required.) The engine stabilized at 65 percent with the EGT at 350 degrees.

One hundred percent rpm is equivalent to 41,730 engine rpm and 2,000 propeller rpm. The propeller is geared down 20.9 to 1.

One of many early problems faced by AiResearch was providing 24 volts to the starter while the rest of the aircraft needed 12 volts. The solution was simple. Two 12-volt batteries were installed in the Comanche. When the engine was not running, the batteries were in series producing 24 volts for the starter. But at 55 percent rpm—when the starter disconnected—a relay operated to place the batteries in parallel and produce 12 volts for flight.

Without further ado, we were ready for takeoff. The propeller (condition) lever was left in the aft or low rpm position for ground operations. Womack pointed out that the condition lever should be kept in the ground-idle position while taxiing. Pulling back on the big T-shaped throttle, the propeller went into reverse pitch, which was used to save wearing out the brakes or to back up, literally.

Womack had me push the condition lever forward, out of the ground-idle detent and into the flight-idle position. He also cautioned me not to retard the throttle into reverse pitch when airborne because of possible tail buffeting that could result from the use of reverse thrust in the air. He emphasized that the Comanche was not designed to operate in this configuration. The Pilatus Porter, though, was designed to accommodate airborne reversing to enhance its unusual maneuvering requirements.

As we taxied to Runway 26R, I was shown how an engine fire (outside the engine but under the cowling) activated the fire-warning system and which button to push to spray fire-extinguisher agent into the engine area.

Propeller feathering was accomplished by a pulling a red vernier-type knob that allows oil to drain from the propeller dome. A flick of the unfeathering switch pumps oil back into the dome should the pilot want to windmill the propeller in preparation for an airborne start.

There were no engine checks to make at the runup pad. Nor did the turbine engine need to be warmed up.

The rpm (condition) lever was advanced to the flight idle, high-rpm position.

As we waited in position on the runway for takeoff clearance, Womack pointed out that the engine was canted 3 degrees right to compensate for left-turning tendencies. This correction was obvious when looking over the Comanche 600's long nose.

Although the engine can put out 605 eshp under standard conditions at sea level, power demanded from N8401P's turbine was limited to less than 450 shp. Womack explained that the aircraft structure was not designed to accept the stress and strain of so much power. The application of full throttle could have caused structural twisting and failure aft of the firewall. "But," Womack said, "All 450 shp is available up to 18,000 feet. At higher altitudes, available power decreases."

The clearance to go crackled through the cabin speaker and by advancing the power lever, I commanded the fuel controller to pump 45 gph into the fiery pits of the engine's burner section (engine torque was about 44 psi). The large propeller took huge bites out of the desert air and hurled the Comanche forward. Acceleration was incredible. The strong and steady pull of the turboprop engine was smooth, and we used much less runway than I had anticipated.

I rotated the nose at 80 mph. After raising the gear, I asked Womack about reducing to climb power. "Forget it," he stated flatly. "The power has already been reduced (from 605 to 450 eshp). Hold the airspeed at 140 mph and let's see what happens."

The climb angle was steep and the vertical-speed indicator showed more than 2,000 fpm on the way up to 5,000 feet. "She'll climb even better at 120 mph," Womack said, "but the steep attitude makes some pilots uncomfortable."

It was a hot day, and we still climbed to 20,000 feet in only 17 minutes. Thirty thousand feet, I was told, usually requires only 26 minutes. Once at 30,000 feet on a standard day, climb rate is still a respectable 1,000 fpm.

At 20,000 feet, N8401P cruised at 250 mph while burning 30 gph. At economy cruise, the Comanche 600 flew at 215 mph with a consumption of 21.5 gph. This was less fuel per mile than was possible with the piston engine. The range under these conditions (allowing for taxi, takeoff, climb, descent, and a 10 percent fuel reserve) was an impressive 1,225 sm.

Cavorting about the Arizona skies in this marvelous machine gave me a privileged feeling, as though I was flying a futuristic airplane, and I suppose that was true. The airplane had a heavy, solid feel, and the sound of the engine was exciting. It exuded strength and capability; it did not scream or vibrate to attract my attention. If the turbine could talk, it might have said, "Watch what I can do in my own quiet way; ignore the bellowing roar of lesser engines."

An irritating characteristic, however, was the need to change elevator trim with even the slightest power change.

Upon entering the pattern for a few touch and go's, I retarded the power lever to idle, but the Comanche showed little inclination to slow down. This was because even when idling, the engine still produced 80 hp.

A gear-warning-horn cutout button on the power console preserved my sanity while the lengthy slow-down process took place.

I lowered the flaps and landing gear at placarded speeds, stabilized the Comanche in a normal approach slot, and added sufficient power to maintain 90 mph.

The flare and landing were routine. As soon as the wheels touched, I depressed two small buttons under the grip of the power lever. This unlocked the lever and allowed me to pull it aft and into reverse pitch. The aircraft stopped smartly without having to use the conventional toe brakes.

I was impressed, and Womack knew it. He said that "if the airframe could take it, the use of all available horsepower would result in a sea-level cruise speed of at least 300 mph. A 3,000 fpm climb rate also could be expected. Now imagine how an airplane designed for high-speed flight would perform with this engine. We would expect a cruise speed of 350 mph."

After taxiing back to the AiResearch hangar, I gave considerable thought to this brief glimpse into the future and realized that this was the way flying would be someday. No other conclusion was possible.

## Anderson-Greenwood AG-14

| | |
|---|---|
| Engine | Continental C-90-12FP |
| Power | 90 hp |
| Length | 22 ft 0 in |
| Height | 6 ft 5 in |
| Wingspan | 34 ft 0 in |
| Wing Loading | 11.7 lb/sq ft |
| Power Loading | 15.6 lb/hp |
| Maximum Takeoff Weight | 1,400 lb |
| Fuel Capacity (usable) | 24 gal |
| Rate of Climb (sea level) | 630 fpm |
| Normal Cruise Speed | 110 mph |
| Stall Speed | 57 mph |

# Anderson-Greenwood AG-14

When World War II ended in 1945, a number

of existing and emerging airframe manufacturers developed new aircraft hoping to capitalize on the widely anticipated postwar boom in general aviation. After all, everyone believed, returning military pilots with a passion for flight would help to fill the skies with light airplanes.

Sadly, this sales surge never materialized, and a number of new aircraft died aborning. These included the Douglas Cloudster, Lockheed's Little Dipper, the Taylorcraft Foursome, and the Thorp Skyscooter. Another was the innovative Anderson Greenwood AG-14.

Following wartime stints at Boeing, Ben Anderson and his brother-in-law, Marvin Greenwood, opened shop at the Sam Houston Airport in Houston, Texas to develop a general aviation airplane using their own resources. (Greenwood had been assistant chief engineer during development of the B-29 Superfortress.)

The result was the AG-14, which first flew on October 1, 1947. After a few years of redesigning and tweaking, the aircraft earned its type certificate on June 1, 1950. It sold for $4,200, about the same as a new Cadillac of that era. Such a price, Anderson and Greenwood hoped, would help to make the popular dream of an "airplane in every garage" come true.

The AG-14 is an attractive, 2-place monoplane with an egg-shaped fuselage containing a rear-mounted engine and a pusher prop. The tail booms have rectangular cross-sections and lead aft to an H-tail reminiscent of the Lockheed P-38 Lightning (although the comparison ends there).

The narrow-chord, rectangular wings have an unusually large 9.6-to-1 aspect ratio. The left wing root contains the single-point refueling receptacle, and 24-gallons of avgas flow from there to a center tank between the cabin and the engine.

Mechanics were delighted with engine accessibility. You simply raise the "hood" as you would that of an automobile. Engine cooling was initially a problem solved by installing an NACA duct under the "armpit" of each wing.

Cockpit entry is effortless and automobile-like through a single door on the right. Neither the left nor the right window can be opened for ground ventilation, so the cockpit gets toasty on warm days. You can hold the door open while taxiing, but there is no propwash from ahead to provide cooling.

The cockpit is roomy and comfortable; the baggage compartment behind the bench-type seats can hold 250 pounds but is inaccessible in flight.

There are four pedals on the floor ahead of the pilot instead of the customary two. Two of them control the single rudder, which is attached to the left vertical stabilizer. These pedals, however, are not used for nosewheel steering. Like the Ercoupe, the nosewheel is operated with the control wheel.

The third pedal (to the right of the rudder pedals) operates the right and left hydraulic brakes simultaneously, another attempt to make the AG-14 as much like an automobile as possible. Differential braking is not possible.

The fourth and smallest pedal is in front of (aft) of the right rudder pedal and is really a large, foot-operated button used to engage the electric starter and is similar to starter pedals found in many automobiles of the 1940s.

You do not have to worry about someone walking into the propeller disk when starting the 90-hp Continental engine because there is no propeller on the front end of the airplane. On the other hand, you cannot see behind and between the booms to determine if someone might have crawled in there. So it is important to yell "clear" loudly and pray that someone standing behind can hear you. (It is nice that you do not have to look through a propeller disc when operating the AG-14 as when operating conventional singles.)

Directional control during the takeoff and landing ground roll obviously is maintained with the control wheel.

If a wing goes down during a crosswind takeoff, do not try to pick it up with opposite aileron. This would cock the nosewheel into the wind, turn the aircraft unexpectedly, and cause the low wing to go down farther. The idea is to steer the airplane with the control wheel and apply rudder in the direction of the high wing. The rudder, however, is so small that it has little effect at low speed. It absolutely, positively cannot be used to maintain directional control during the takeoff or landing roll.

The ailerons are unusual. When you raise the right aileron about 20 degrees, for example, the left one goes down about 10 degrees. Continue moving it up to about 45 degrees, and the left aileron returns to neutral. Finally, when you raise the right aileron to its maximum limit of 60 degrees, the left aileron goes up about 10 degrees.

This explanation given for this odd arrangement has to do with coupling the nosewheel to the control wheel. To prevent the nosewheel from moving too much for a given movement of the control wheel and thereby being too sensitive, the linkage was adjusted so that the ailerons move farther than necessary to get optimum nosewheel movement for ground handling.

When rotating for takeoff, there is a tendency to raise the bottom of the windshield to the horizon because there is no engine cowling that can be used to establish climb attitude as is done in conventional tractor airplanes. This results in an excessively steep attitude, too low an airspeed, and a reduction in climb performance.

Without an engine to block the view, though, forward visibility is unobscured, and with the wings behind the cockpit, visibility to the side is equally outstanding, much like that of a helicopter.

Performance is similar to early model Cessna 150s. The AG-14 climbs at 630 fpm and cruises at 110 mph. With the approved substitute of a 100-hp Continental O-200-B, climb performance is sprightlier.

The ailerons produce little adverse yaw, and the slip-skid ball stays in its cage whether using coordinated rudder input or not. After a while, I simply took my feet off the pedals and rested them flat on the floor.

A delightful characteristic of the cute little airplane is that very little trim is required during power and airspeed changes. But when needed, the overhead elevator trim handle is rotated in a horizontal plane like on many postwar Piper aircraft. Most pilots need a little time to learn which way to turn the trim to obtain the desired result. When uncertain, just trim in either direction. If elevator pressure increases instead of decreases, just turn it the other way.

The vertical stabilizers are small and there is no vertical surface area that would be contributed by a conventional fuselage. Consequently, the aircraft has weak yaw stability. It is not so bad, however, that you cannot fly with your feet on the floor (as was intended), but the nose does hunt a bit. One quickly gets used to mild fishtailing in turbulence like those who fly Beech Bonanzas.

Wing dihedral outboard of the booms is a steep 7 degrees, and lateral stability is outstanding. Combine this with the small rudder, and you can understand why only shallow slipping is possible.

Elevator movement is limited as it is on the Ercoupe. This makes both aircraft stall- and spin-resistant. Intentional spins, it appears, are virtually impossible. Aerobatics are not approved.

The airplane was introduced before stall-warning indicators were required, but such a warning would be redundant. During an attempt to stall the AG-14, the entire airplane buffets in a way that warns immediately and effectively of an excessive angle of attack. A slight release of back pressure restores normal flight.

If you ignore the buffeting and pull the control wheel fully aft, the nose drops to about 10 degrees above the horizon, and the aircraft continues to fly along merrily in this mushing manner. While locked in such a stall, the aircraft exhibits a high sink rate and better-than-expected roll control.

Landings offer a surprise to those who simply approach at the best glide speed of 65 mph and then attempt to arrest the sink rate and flare. At this speed there is insufficient elevator effectiveness to prevent plopping onto the ground no matter how much or how quickly you pull back on the wheel. The best way to land an AG-14 is to glide at 65 mph for most of the approach and then increase to about 80 mph when still a few hundred feet above the ground. This extra speed provides the elevator effectiveness needed to flare and make a normal landing.

During one's first landing, though, there is a tendency to flare too high because of how close to the ground you sit. After that first landing, all that follow are a snap. You do need to fly the nosewheel onto the ground, however. If you hold it off until falling on its own, it will hit with a bang.

When landing, do not forget that there is insufficient rudder to maintain directional control. Use the control wheel for ground steering.

When making a crosswind landing, do not land in a crab as you would with an Ercoupe. Instead, straighten the airplane just before touchdown, and be certain that the control wheel is neutral before allowing the nosewheel to touch down.

Landing with one wing low can create a problem for the unwary. By holding left aileron during touchdown on the left main landing gear with a left crosswind, for example, remember that this also cocks the nosewheel to the left. So be certain not to lower the nosewheel onto the ground until first neutralizing the ailerons and the nosewheel. Otherwise, you might go for a swerving ride you do not expect.

Limited elevator effectiveness makes it difficult to flare for a landing with two people on board and when using full flaps. Landings are much easier using only half flap.

Only 5 AG-14s were built, and the airplane used in this chapter (serial number 3) is one of possibly two surviving examples.

Unfortunately, the AG-14 was introduced at the beginning of the Korean War when building materials came under tight control. As a result of this and the failure of the postwar boom to materialize (especially for 2-place airplanes), the petite fork-tailed pusher did not have an opportunity to evolve into something better. Instead, Anderson, Greenwood & Company directed its attention toward military research. It is now a major manufacturer of pressure-relief valves, manifolds, and other components.

## Beriev Be-103

| | |
|---|---|
| Engines | 2 Continental IO-360-ES4 |
| Power | 210 hp ea |
| Length | 34 ft 11 in |
| Height | 12 ft 4 in |
| Wingspan | 41 ft 9 in |
| Wing Loading | 18.5 lb/sq ft |
| Power Loading | 11.9 lb/hp |
| Maximum Takeoff Weight | 5,011 lb |
| Fuel Capacity (usable) | 90 gal |
| Rate of Climb (sea level) | 984 fpm |
| Normal Cruise Speed | 127 kt |
| Stall Speed | 60 kt |

# The Beriev Be-103

*Seaplane pilots looking at the Beriev Be-103 light*
amphibian for the first time express skepticism about its unusual low- to mid-wing configuration and are curious to know how such an airplane performs on water. After all, other seaplanes have wings intended to be kept well clear of the water. These pilots usually are surprised to learn that the Be-103 performs and handles extraordinarily well on water.

The airplane was developed by the Beriev Design Bureau in western Russia, a company that has been designing seaplanes for more than 70 years and seems to have unrivaled expertise. (Beriev recently introduced the Be-200, a 90,000-pound, twin-jet amphibian used as a water-drop firefighter.)

The airplane is manufactured by KnAAPO (you don't want to know what Russian words these letters represent) in Komsomolsk-on-Amur in eastern Russia. KnAAPO also builds the Sukhoi Su-27 Flanker, an impressive twin-jet fighter.

Enter Kent Linn, owner of the publicly used Sky Manor Airport (N40) in Pittstown, New Jersey. Seventy-one years young, Linn learned to fly in Alaska where he became enamored with seaplanes. Now a retired flight-test engineer for Douglas Aircraft at Edwards Air Force Base, he read about the history of the Beriev Design Bureau and the Be-103 in the year-2000 *Water Flying* annual. The airplane so intrigued him that he ultimately become its North American distributor. He accepted delivery of 3 aircraft when they were disgorged from a mammoth Antonov AN-124 during EAA AirVenture 2003.

Linn explains that the wing displaces water to help keep the amphibian afloat and contributes to superior seaworthiness.

The low-set wing also takes maximum advantage of ground effect during takeoff and landing. No other airplane operates with its wings so close to the water. Because of this, the Be-103 does not need flaps and can skim the water on its trailing edges.

The aircraft has slightly inverted gull wings so that the inboard sections prevent the airplane from rolling when on water. Gone is the weight and drag caused by wingtip floats common to other flying boats. Gone also is the undesirable yaw that can occur when a float digs into the water during a wing-low water landing.

The wing is swept 22 degrees and from certain viewing angles gives the illusion of being a delta or bat wing.

The 210-hp Continental IO-360-ES4 engines are mounted high to prevent the German MTV-12, 3-bladed composite, reversible-pitch propellers from being damaged by water spray. Checking oil requires climbing on the wing, unfastening and lifting the upper half of a nacelle with one hand, and pouring oil with the other. (There are no oil-access doors; in Russia, airplanes are serviced only by ground personnel; the pilot just flies.)

The fuel system consists of 4 tanks, 2 in the wings and 2 gravity-feed header tanks in the engine pylons. Refueling consists of filling the wing tanks, turning on transfer pumps to fill the pylons, and then refilling the wing tanks as necessary. During flight, the header tanks are automatically kept full as long as there is fuel in the wings.

The airframe is primarily lithium-aluminum, an alloy reportedly lighter, stronger, and more corrosion-resistant than conventional aluminum. Stress areas utilize titanium while the wingtips and nacelles are fiberglass.

The airplane appears overbuilt, reminiscent of Grumman-built seaplanes. Jerry Inella, a United Airlines' captain who checked me out in the Beriev, says that "a seaplane really takes a pounding on the water. I want it built like a battleship, and this airplane fits the bill perfectly."

The workmanship is not always pretty, but it appears durable. There is nothing flimsy or fragile about a Be-103.

Circuit breakers are accessible only when on the ground through an exterior hatch on the right side of the bow. They are inaccessible during flight because Beriev does not want popped breakers to be reset in the air.

The Be-103 is the first Russian design to be FAA-certified in the Normal category and marketed in the United States. The Russians, however, do not seem to have a firm grasp of general aviation operations, probably because there is so little of it in their homeland.

Instead, they build small airplanes as if intended for the airlines or military, which explains some of the Be-103s oddities.

The original 3 aircraft were delivered, for example, with only one control stick. The Russians consider the right front seat to be for a passenger, and passengers in Russia are not allowed access to the controls. (Second sets of controls have since been installed in all 3 aircraft.)

The Russians favor a stick over a wheel perhaps because a stick does not interfere with a pilot's view of the instrument panel. I prefer a stick to a wheel and found the flight controls nicely balanced and harmonized. The ailerons and stabilator are operated with pushrods; the rudder is cable controlled.

The stick contains the pitch-trim and push-to-talk switches. The rudder trim tab also is operated through an electric actuator.

Solo flight requires that ballast be placed near the right front seat to keep the center of gravity within limits.

Because of the builder's airline and military mentality, the airplane has sophistication rarely seen in light twins. This includes a 30-parameter, 5-hour flight-data recorder, an angle-of-attack system, engine fire-detection systems, a second attitude indictor (in addition to a turn-and-bank indicator), a second altimeter, a radome, an ice detector, and so forth.

This partially explains the heavy empty weight. The aircraft I flew, N29KL, has an empty weight of 3,810 pounds. Linn is hoping to have KnAAPO remove some of the unnecessary equipment to increase useful load, which in the test aircraft is 1,201 pounds.

Linn also would prefer the airplanes to be delivered green so that a sexier paint scheme can be applied stateside.

A ladder stowed in the wing root is used to climb into the cabin through the left gull-wing door. An identical starboard door is for emergency egress. The cabin is capacious and comfortable for all 6 occupants. The rudder pedals adjust fore and aft to accommodate the tall and the short. This is the only light airplane I can recall having flown in which I could not reach the pedals with my seat fully aft.

The airplane is functionally beautiful but not aesthetically so. All placards and instrument labeling are in English, but the lettering is distinctively Russian.

There is a life jacket under each seat, and sea equipment (titanium anchor, grapple hook, waterproof gloves, etc.) is stowed in sidewall compartments next to each pilot.

The brakes and landing gear have their own hydraulic systems. One must not forget to turn on the electric brake pump before taxiing. I can attest that this is a mistake you make only once. Differential braking steers the castoring nosewheel.

During flight the Be-103 tends to hunt slightly in turbulence, not unusual for a flying boat, and is due to the destabilizing effect of a long bow.

With the wing behind the pilot, cockpit visibility is excellent.

The wing-in-water concept precludes the possibility of flaps, so there are none. An 11-foot-long fixed slat on the outboard leading edge of each wing enhances slow flight (and costs only 1 knot of cruise speed). The resultant high-lift wing has benign stall characteristics, but the stall-warning indicator sounds like a ringing telephone. You might be more likely to respond by saying "hello?" than lowering the nose.

The large, tall vertical stabilizer combined with closely coupled engines makes handling an engine failure relatively easy. Little rudder pressure is required to keep the aircraft on an even keel.

If an engine-driven fuel pump fails, an electric boost pump automatically takes over and delivers the correct amount of fuel pressure as dictated by throttle position.

If the pilot should respond to an engine failure by pulling the incorrect mixture control to idle cutoff (before identifying and confirming the dead engine by retarding the throttle), the boost pump will automatically activate and keep the good engine running, a wonderful safety feature. It is difficult to shut down the operating engine by mistake.

Water landings are easy, but landing in a significant crosswind with such a low wing could be problematical. The good news is that seaplane pilots almost always land directly into the wind.

Attitude remains stable and flat in step turns from downwind to upwind, a time when conventional seaplanes tend to tip outboard.

The propellers are moved into reverse pitch by pulling the throttles aft of idle. There is no independent water rudder, but the air rudder partially extends into the water and has the effect of a water rudder.

Docking is not quite as easy with a Be-103 as with high-wing airplanes. Instead of pulling alongside a dock, you must maneuver the airplane to a corner of a dock so that one edge is alongside the forward fuselage and the other is near the wing. It is not ideal, but it works.

Water takeoffs are initiated with the stick held fully forward or aft. Elevator input matters not. The wing in the water forces the airplane to assume the proper attitude and rise onto the step unassisted. With the wing roots riding the water, the airplane has remarkable roll stability.

On the step, the forward portions of the wings are out of but extremely close to the water, which maximizes the influence of ground effect and minimizes induced drag. Nose-down elevator is needed to optimize acceleration on the step.

One measure of how well a seaplane is built is the amount of water drained from the hull's watertight compartments after extensive water operations. After my water work at New York State's Greenwood Lake, I found surprisingly little water in any compartment.

The trailing-link main landing gear makes every pilot seem like a pro when touching down on land. The gear legs retract forward into watertight wells.

The nice thing about an amphibian is that malfunctioning landing gear is not as serious as when flying landplanes. If the gear cannot be made to extend, just land on water, and vice versa.

The pilot's operating handbook reflects the builder's airline and military mentality. On the plus side, it is one of the most complete and elaborate handbooks I have ever encountered for a light airplane.

On the negative side are a host of illogical limitations that clearly need to be removed for general aviation operations. For example, it is unreasonable to ban water takeoffs and landings at night, to limit operating altitude to 10,000 feet msl, to restrict land operations to a minimum runway length of 3,900 feet, to limit takeoffs and landings to elevations below 3,000 feet, and so on.

The Russians also include the weight of a 176-pound pilot in the empty weight, further reflecting their airline mentality.

The Beriev 103 is a lot of airplane (5,011 pounds) to be pulled by only a pair of 210-hp engines. The twin could use more muscle, and the factory is being encouraged to increase power to 250 or 300 horsepower per side on future models.

One nice thing about KnAAPO's attitude toward general aviation is that in Russia, ground crews are sent in advance to a pilot's destination. Upon his arrival, they tie down the aircraft, service it, and clean the windshields. I could handle that.

## Curtiss Wright Junior

| | |
|---|---|
| Engine | Salmson Aero Engine AD-9 |
| Power | 40 hp |
| Length | 21 ft 3 in |
| Height (3-point attitude) | 7 ft 4 in |
| Wingspan | 39 ft 6 in |
| Wing Loading | 5.54 lb/sq ft |
| Power Loading | 18.1 lb/hp |
| Maximum Takeoff Weight | 975 lb |
| Fuel Capacity (usable) | 9.2 gal |
| Rate of Climb (sea level) | 580 fpm |
| Normal Cruise Speed | 65 mph |
| Stall Speed | 30 mph |

# The Curtiss-Wright CW-1 Junior

## The silhouette of a Curtiss-Wright CW-1 Junior

is distinctive and unmistakable. It has a petite radial engine perched atop a parasol wing that shades a fuselage resembling the hull of an amphibious flying boat.

The 2-place, open-cockpit landplane also looks like a powered glider. The pilot sits way out in front. Without an engine cowling in the way, he enjoys the same superlative visibility as those who fly sailplanes, and the pusher engine behind him precludes the possibility of his being sprayed with oil.

The Junior was significant because it represented an effort by Curtiss-Wright to produce an affordable, personal aircraft that would appeal to the average citizen. It was the beginning of the industry-wide attempt to produce an "airplane for every garage."

The airplane made its first flight on December 10, 1930 and had a price tag of $1,490. Orders poured into the St. Louis plant at rates that were unprecedented in the fledgling aircraft industry. For a while during 1931, the factory produced 21 Juniors per week, outselling its three main competitors combined. (The junior competed primarily against the Aeronca C-2, American Eagle's Eaglet, and the Buhl Pup.)

But the CW-1's production line came to a screeching halt in early 1932 after 270 aircraft had been built. A victim of the Great Depression, the Junior was Curtiss-Wright's last attempt to build light airplanes for the "sportsman."

The airplane shown on these pages belongs to Paul T. Cullman, a retired rancher, and is based at Meadowmist, a residential airpark at Ferndale, Washington (between Bellingham and Abbotsford, British Columbia).

An actively flying octogenarian, Cullman soloed in a Piper J-3 Cub on skis in 1942, has accumulated more than 5,000 hours, and has had an uninterrupted AOPA membership since 1943. He has owned numerous aircraft over the years and presently has a Stinson L-5B Sentinel, which I flew as the camera platform for these photos, an American Eagle Eaglet (into which I could not fit), a Mooney MSE modified with a glass cockpit, and his pride and joy, NC11832, a Curtiss-Wright Junior.

He purchased the airplane in 1985 for $3,500, but it needed quite a bit of work. He built new wings and ailerons, and fabricated a mount for the petite, French-made, 187-cubic inch, 9-cylinder, 40-hp Salmson AD-9 radial engine that was built in 1929.

The Junior originally had a cantankerous, temperamental, 3-cylinder, 45-hp Szekely (pronounced Say-kay) SR-3 radial engine made in Holland, Michigan. This relic ran rough and had a nasty habit of throwing cylinders. A steel restraining cable had to be attached to each cylinder head to prevent it from being blown into the pusher propeller.

Cullman's airplane, serial number 1206, rolled out of the factory on June 19, 1931. He estimates that it currently is worth more than $40,000 but would not sell it.

Fuel and oil tanks are combined in a single, compartmentalized aluminum tank above the wing and ahead of the engine. The forward and largest part of the tank holds 9.2 gallons of avgas (the red vented filler cap), and the smaller aft section holds 6 quarts of oil (the yellow cap) that the engine sprays, drips, and spits almost as quickly as you can refill the tank.

Cullman's Junior has no electrical system and is certified only for daytime, VFR flight. Aerobatics are prohibited.

NC11832 has an empty weight of 570 pounds and a maximum-allowable takeoff weight of 975 pounds. It qualifies, therefore, as a light-sport airplane. Like many other aircraft of that era, it has a chrome-molybdenum, tubular-steel frame covered in fabric, and the wing has a solid spruce spar.

There is no baggage compartment, but "cargo" may be stored on the rear seat during solo flight, which is allowed only from the front seat. Strangely, baggage is limited to 14 pounds, much less than the weight of the passenger or instructor who otherwise could be sitting there.

The Junior cannot be trimmed during flight but does have a ground-adjustable stabilizer that is positioned during preflight preparation according to the anticipated load distribution. (Given my not inconsiderable mass, the stabilizer was set to full nose-down trim prior to my solo flight.)

Starting the engine involves first turning on the fuel by rotating the valve handle (on the leading edge of the wing) and leaving it on until the carburetor begins to drip fuel. You then turn off the fuel and turn on the oil using a small in-line valve below the oil tank. Starting is accomplished the old-fashioned way, by hand-propping the engine. You have about 30 seconds to turn the fuel back on before the engine quits.

The airplane has a 2-leaf, spring-steel tailskid and no brakes, so be sure that the airplane is headed in the right direction before advancing the throttle to taxi. The Junior does have a relatively large rudder, so taxiing turns are made easily by blasting propwash across the tail. Tighter turns are made by applying full rudder in the direction of turn and pushing the stick forward to lower the elevator and take some weight off the tailskid. It is surprisingly easy and almost as effective as a steerable tailwheel. (An optional tailwheel was available from the factory for $10.)

The nose-high attitude of most taildraggers is a result of the need to provide adequate propeller clearance above the ground. This is unnecessary in the case of a Junior, so the landing gear was made short. This results in less weight, less drag, and a nose-low taxi attitude. S-turning to avoid obstacles is unnecessary.

There is not much to the runup because there is none. Without brakes to restrain the aircraft at high rpm and with only one magneto, the ignition check consists simply of verifying that the engine is running smoothly. Turning off the magneto, of course, would shut down the engine. Cullman has the carburetor heater wired open because of the carburetor's propensity for icing. Finally, there are no flaps to deploy or trim to adjust.

With such a high thrust line, adding power for takeoff helps to raise the tail and poise the Junior for flight. Liftoff from the downhill, 2,000-foot grass strip at Meadowmist took only about 200 feet.

A pleasant surprise is that there is hardly a breeze in the open cockpit; goggles are unnecessary. Cullman reports, however, that it is windy in the back seat and much noisier. (The rear cockpit contains a control stick, rudder pedals, a throttle, and nothing else.)

Because the wing is behind the pilot and the nose is short and blunt, visibility from the front seat is incredible. This made the Junior popular as a photo platform and aerial scenes for some of Hollywood's epic films were shot from there. Because a hunter sitting in front had clear shots from so many angles, the airplane also was used to hunt coyotes (as well as for patrolling pipelines and power-lines).

Frise ailerons reportedly eliminate some of the significant adverse yaw effect typical of older designs, but the Junior is still very much a stick-and-rudder airplane and is intolerant of sloppy flying. Although there is no slip-skid ball on the panel, uncoordinated flight is easily sensed through the seat of one's trousers.

The Junior also has a low wing loading and bounces around easily in turbulence. It is one of those airplanes that are easy to fly but not easy to fly well.

It is even difficult to accurately maintain a given altitude. Firstly, there is no part of the airframe ahead of the pilot to position with respect to the horizon. Secondly, the non-sensitive altimeter is of little help. The single altimeter hand makes one rotation every 20,000 feet—it moves only 2 degrees during a 100-foot altitude change, which is difficult to detect. You can use the wings to maintain the desired attitude but only by looking somewhat aft.

There is no pilot's operating handbook for the Junior. During the formative years of aviation, pilots learned about an airplane by flying it.

Critical airspeeds? There aren't any. The airplane does not even have an airspeed indicator. A Curtiss-Wright instructor probably would tell you to "raise the nose for $V_Y$, and pull back a little more for $V_X$." According to original advertising literature, the Junior cruises at 65 mph.

The airplane is equipped, however, with a safety meter designed by a Curtiss-Wright engineer named Walter Beech. It consists of a small metal plate that projects into the relative wind ahead of the front windshield. Wind pressure on the plate pushes against a coiled spring and causes a pointer to move up and down in a slot on the indicator plate on the instrument panel.

The plate is marked with a lower red band (too fast), a white band (normal range) and an upper red band (too slow). The idea is to keep the pointer "in the white."

When asked how the beginning of the high-speed (lower) red band was established, the Junior's designer, Karl White, said, "We dived the Junior until we figured she was going about as fast as she ought to and made a mark on the plate." The beginning of the other red band is where the airplane begins to stall.

The cost of manufacturing this sophisticated instrumentation in 1931 was 35 cents. (Wouldn't it be fun to have a Beech Safety Meter in a Bonanza?)

Stalls are unremarkable unless you suffer from acrophobia. As the open-cockpit pitched down and with no aircraft structure in front of me, I had the uneasy feeling that I could have been thrown out of my seat and into Puget Sound.

Fuel consumption averages 3.5 gph and provides a safe endurance of 2 hours. Cullman says that he tries not to fly more than 100 miles at a time. Curtiss-Wright borrowed the fuel gauge from a Model A Ford but is at the front of the tank and behind the pilot. A mirror is needed to see it during flight, but everything shakes too much to get an indication.

The approach to landing is made with the indicator of the safety meter near the top of the white band. Although the controls are light, reducing power helps to flare for landing because the high thrust line changes to a high drag line, which raises the nose somewhat.

The Junior has rigid landing gear; there are no shock absorbers. The balloon tires, however, are filled with only 10 pounds of air pressure and do an adequate job of smoothing the touchdown and rollout. A hinged mud guard behind each main-gear tire prevents debris from being flung into the propeller disk, an especially important feature when operating from unimproved surfaces. (The airplane can operate on hard-surface runways, but the tailskid will wear out rapidly.)

Minimal braking after touchdown is available by holding the control stick fully aft and forcing the tailskid to press harder against the turf. Otherwise, allow enough room to coast to a stop.

There is large lettering on the back of the front seat that is clearly visible to the rear-seat passenger. It warns him to walk forward after deplaning to avoid the "whirling propeller."

The Curtiss-Wright Junior is a cute, loveable little airplane that engenders great affection and would be a joyful companion for frolicking on a warm, summer afternoon. As Joseph P. Juptner, author of the U.S. Civil Aircraft Series, says, "Flying a Junior is hard to describe. It waddles and sputters its way into your heart and offers a continuous panorama of pleasure."

## Aeromot AMT-200S Ximango

| | |
|---|---:|
| Engine | Bombardier-Rotax 912-S4A |
| Power | 100 hp |
| Length | 26 ft 6 in |
| Height (3-point attitude) | 6 ft 4 in |
| Wingspan | 58 ft 0 in |
| Wing Loading | 9.3 lb/sq ft |
| Power Loading | 18.7 lb/hp |
| Maximum Takeoff Weight | 1,874 lb |
| Fuel Capacity (usable) | 23.2 gal |
| Rate of Climb (sea level) | 557 fpm |
| Normal Cruise Speed | 97 kt |
| Stall Speed | 42 kt |

# Aeromot AMT-200S Super Ximango

## It is not often that a pilot takes off in a single-engine

airplane with the intention of shutting down the engine once underway, but that is exactly what you can do when flying an Aeromot AMT-200S Super Ximango, which means falcon in Portuguese. (*Xi* is pronounced like the French pronunciation of *Gi* in *Gigi*.)

Okay, so the Brazilian-made aircraft is not really an airplane, although it can be used like one. The Ximango is a self-launching sailplane, a touring glider that can take off without a towplane and fly hither and yon in search of thermals and other forms of atmospheric lift, something that power pilots typically prefer to avoid. Moreover, the motorglider pilot is not concerned about the possibility of an off-field landing when soaring conditions diminish.

The Ximango was designed by famed French designer Rene Fornier whose name became familiar in this country with the introduction of his Volkswagen-powered Fornier motorgliders in the 1960s. (Mira Slovak flew one from West Germany to California.)

The Brazilian Super Ximango competed against an offering from Diamond Aircraft of Canada. After evaluation tests were performed by test pilots from Edwards Air Force Base, the Ximango was chosen to replace the Air Force Academy's aging fleet of Schweizer TG-7s. The last of 14 Ximangos (TG-14As) were delivered to the academy last July, and 35 others have thus far been sold to civilian customers in the United States.

The airframe is an all-composite structure made from Ciba-Geigy resins and fibers and is finished in polyurethane. This, along with the tightly cowled engine, contributes to the aircraft's sleek appearance. The spar caps are carbon-fiber.

The 58-foot-long wings fold like those found on carrier-based Naval aircraft. This results in a reduced span of only 33.4 feet that allows the Ximango to fit in a small T hangar. One person can fold or unfold the wings in about 5 minutes, but it is easier with a helper. The wings lock into place by moving a sturdy lever aft until it snaps into position. Wing fairings are then placed over the mechanisms but cannot be attached unless the wing-locking lever is properly positioned, thus ensuring that the wings are secure. The system is simple and foolproof.

Most power pilots need a little time to get used to the semi-supine seats and typically tend to lean forward when taxiing. Just lie back and relax, and you will find them to be extraordinarily comfortable. Although the seats are not adjustable, the rudder pedals can be moved fore and aft, thus accommodating tall pilots. The Ximango's body, however, is not wide enough to comfortably accommodate a pair of wide bodies without some shoulder rubbing.

Firing up the engine is as easy as starting an automobile. Touch the starter button and the 100-hp Bombardier-Rotax engine springs to life. (A choke is used during cold starts.)

Lower the Swiss-made canopy and secure it with a lever-lock on each side rail. The canopy is claimed to be optically perfect, and I could detect no distortion to disprove that claim.

The Ximango has a steerable tailwheel, but some differential toe braking is needed to make moderately tight turns. Such long wings require that you use caution when taxiing in tight quarters. Yes, you may taxi with the wings folded, but trying to take off that way is a no-no. Over-the-nose visibility is excellent; there is no need to S-turn this taildragger.

There is nothing unusual about the preflight runup except for checking the Hoffman 3-position propeller. It is changed from minimum pitch for takeoff to climb/cruise pitch to feather by pulling a spring-loaded lever from under the instrument panel and then allowing it to return to the stowed position after implementing the desired pitch change. Also, be certain that the Schempp-Hirth spoilers are stowed.

The takeoff roll is routine for a taildragger, but keep the tailwheel on the ground during the early part of the takeoff roll to facilitate directional control and prevent those long wings from developing a yawing mind of their own.

Do not be alarmed by the 5,800-rpm indication on the tachometer. This is engine rpm, not propeller rpm. With a gear ratio of 2.43:1, the 67-inch propeller is spinning at less than 2,400 rpm, which results in a relatively low noise signature.

After liftoff and when climbing comfortably at $V_X$ (52 KIAS) or $V_Y$ (59 KIAS), reach for the handle in the center console between the seats, lift it from its stowed position, and push forward to raise the main landing gear. Pulling aft lowers and locks the wheels into position. The Ximango does not have flaps.

Climb at 5,500 rpm, cruise at 5,000, and do not be surprised when overtaking Cessna 152s and 172s.

When the mood strikes and conditions are conducive for soaring, you can shut down the engine and dramatically increase specific range (miles per gallon). I had the feeling that a summertime flight from Los Angeles across the Mojave Desert to Las Vegas can be made using little more than the few cupfuls of avgas required to takeoff and climb to altitude.

The Ximango's engine does not have a mixture control (or carburetor heat or alternate air source). Shutting down involves retarding the throttle and turning off the dual electronic ignition systems. Then turn off the alternator, turn off the fuel-selector valve, feather the propeller, and tap the starter button, if necessary, to move the propeller to a horizontal position (to minimize drag).

Do not forget to move the 3-position master switch to the Soaring position. This turns off all unnecessary electrical loads, such as engine gauges, electric gyros, and so forth. Forgetting this can result in a low battery and a difficult engine restart. If the transponder and transceiver are not required, turn the master switch completely off.

Finally, close the cowl flap to further minimize drag and reduce airspeed to a best glide speed of 58 KIAS or a minimum-sink (189 fpm) speed of 52 KIAS.

Then just settle back, enjoy hearing only a whisper of air passing by the canopy, and employ your soaring skills to maintain or gain altitude.

The Ximango has a glide (lift-to-drag) ratio of 31:1, which is outstanding for a motorglider and is due to the laminar-flow wing, clean design, retractable landing gear, and full-feathering propeller. (Optional winglets provide increased glide performance.)

Aircraft with long wings typically exhibit low roll rates (because of roll damping). This seems largely overcome in the Ximango, which rolls into and out of turns crisply. Nor is top aileron pressure required to prevent overbanking during steep turns. The flight controls are effective, well balanced, and nicely harmonized. There is an abundance of adverse yaw effect, however, which is typical of sailplanes.

When operating in the silent world of soaring flight, it is easy to become a victim of complacency and allow the sailplane to descend unobtrusively below some minimum safe altitude. Always have a restart altitude in mind and abide by it.

Relighting the fire and making the metamorphosis from sailplane to "airplane" is quick and easy: select one of two wing tanks with the fuel selector; pull out the choke if the engine is cold; close the throttle; turn on the master switch; turn on the fuel pump; and position the propeller to minimum pitch (takeoff position). You then can either tap the starter button or enter a gentle dive to get the propeller windmilling. In either case, the engine abruptly returns to life. All that remains is to turn on the alternator and turn off the fuel pump.

Need to go down in a hurry? The spoilers are deployed by pulling back on the blue handle in the center console. Pull back a little or a lot, but be careful with a lot. The spoilers are powerful, add substantial drag, and necessitate a significant nose-down attitude to maintain a given airspeed.

When in the traffic pattern, use some spoiler deployment for descent to the runway. Otherwise, a substantially extended traffic pattern will be required, something that those flying in trail will not appreciate. (With a glide ratio of 31:1, losing 1,000 feet requires more than 5 nm.)

A typical approach is made with the engine throttled (or shut down!) and the spoilers deployed partially to approximate the glide ratio of a typical single-engine airplane (about 9:1). If at any time the Ximango seems high, add a bit more spoiler; if low, retract the spoilers somewhat. Modulating the spoilers and glide path in this manner is like using an engine to make glide path adjustments. Spoilers can be used to vary the glide path anywhere between 31:1 and 5:1. With a little practice, you will find it easier to make a spot landing in a glider than in an airplane. It is nice to know, however, that this is one sailplane in which you have the option of executing a missed approach.

A horn and a flashing red light are not-so-subtle reminders to lower the landing gear. These warnings are tied to spoiler activation and not throttle position because landings can be made safely with the engine shut down.

Wheel landings are not difficult in the Ximango and high-speed directional control after touchdown is enhanced by the very effective rudder and wide-stance landing gear (the mains are 9 feet apart).

The Super Ximango has been certified under the European JAR-22 standards and by the FAA in the Utility category, but intentional spins are not allowed.

Don't have a medical certificate? No problem. Pilots exercising the privileges of a glider rating are not required to have one (even when carrying a passenger) even though a motorglider can be operated like an airplane. The Ximango, however, is certified only for day, VFR operations, and spins are not permitted.

Because it is a glider and not an airplane, the minimum age for soloing a Ximango is only 14 (compared to 16 for airplanes) even when flown with power. A teenager can obtain a private pilot certificate with a glider rating at 16 (compared to 17 for an airplane rating).

This is a fun machine for the sportsman-pilot in search of a recreational aircraft that can be flown as high and as far as conditions allow. The sky is the limit, literally.

## STPA Minijet

| | |
|---|---|
| Engine | Turbomeca Palas Turbojet |
| Power | 330 lb thrust |
| Length | 17 ft 1 in |
| Height | 5 ft 10 in |
| Wingspan | 26 ft 3 in |
| Wing Loading | 18.2 lb/sq ft |
| Power Loading | 5.7 lb/lb thrust |
| Maximum Takeoff Weight | 1,874 lb |
| Fuel Capacity (usable) | 55.5 gal |
| Rate of Climb (sea level) | 1,140 fpm |
| Normal Cruise Speed | 205 kt |
| Stall Speed | 50 kt |

# SIPA S-200 Minijet

## The French SIPA S-200 Minijet was the world's

first civilian turbojet airplane to enter production. With its twin booms, the diminutive aircraft bears a striking resemblance to the DeHavilland DH.115 Vampire built in England after World War II.

SIPA (Société Industrielle Pour L'Aéronautique) introduced the Minijet at the Paris Air Show in 1951, but the maiden flight did not occur until January 14, 1952.

The S-200 was designed by Yves Gardan, a respected designer of several European-built general aviation airplanes such as the Socata GY-80 Horizon.

Unfortunately, the petite jet made its debut as general aviation was experiencing a significant economic recession that did not show signs of ending until the late 1950s. Anticipated interest in the Minijet never materialized, and only 7 were built.

In 1993, Asher Ward, an aircraft broker in Van Nuys, California who specializes in unique aircraft, discovered the Minijet in Florida in 1993. N917WJ was owned by Don Whittington, a vintage aircraft collector. (Whittington had found the airplane in Argentina during the mid-1980s where it was painted solid black and reportedly used for clandestine operations.) Ward purchased the aircraft from Whittington and had it trucked to Van Nuys. The aircraft was equipped with its original engine, a Turboméca Palas turbojet that delivered only 330 pounds of thrust. This resulted in a low thrust-to-weight ratio and relatively anemic performance (as reflected in the specifications accompanying this chapter).

Unsatisfied, Ward modified the Minijet by replacing the French engine with a General Electric T58, the same engine used in the Bell UH-1 Huey. The T58 develops 1,350 shaft horsepower in the legendary helicopter, but produces 800 pounds of thrust when used as a turbojet instead of a turboprop. This 142-percent increase in thrust produces impressive performance.

The more powerful engine also is heavier and keeps the empty center of gravity relatively far aft. Ballast must be placed in the cabin to prevent the airplane from resting on its tailskid instead of its nosewheel. Ward uses a pair of heavy automotive batteries that are removed as soon as one person climbs aboard.

An air intake in each wing root leads to the engine, which is aft of the firewall behind the pilots.

Installation of the more powerful engine created an endurance problem, too. Fuel capacity is 55 gallons. This was acceptable for the smaller engine, but the G.E. powerplant is much thirstier. Endurance is now only 30-45 minutes, which means that a flight should not be planned for much more than 15 or 20 minutes. This explains why the air-to-air photography on these pages had to begin almost immediately after liftoff, and we were forced to accept whatever background happened to slip beneath our wings.

Ward, however, has a pair of original 15-gallon tip tanks that he plans to install. Thankfully, the plumbing needed for this is already in the wings. This will increase safe endurance to almost two hours.

The refueling receptacle is in the rear of the pod-shaped fuselage. This feeds 2 small fuel tanks in each wing that in turn feed a central sump tank so that fuel management requires nothing more than an on-off selector valve.

The preflight inspection is typical of a small, general aviation airplane. One does notice, however, that the rudders seem unusually small, probably because they are seldom required when flying a Minijet except during crosswind takeoffs and landings.

Entering the cabin is made through a large gull-wing door on each side of the cabin.

There are very few engine instruments on the panel because very few are needed. In addition to the oil temperature and pressure gauges, there is only an exhaust temperature gauge and a tachometer that indicates percentage of maximum-allowable rpm.

There also are two red warning lights. One warns of metal chips in the oil (land as soon as possible) and another warns of an engine fire. The only thing you can do about the latter is to shut down the engine; the aircraft is not equipped with bottles of extinguishing agent.

The large General Electric engine requires more electrical power to start than was required by the original, smaller engine, so the electrical system in the Minijet is not quite as substantial as it should be. Consequently, a pilot should be careful not to attempt a start unless the 28-volt battery is fully charged. Otherwise, he runs the risk of slow engine acceleration during the start sequence and the possibility of a hot start, which, of course, requires an immediate shutdown. My check pilot on this flight, Matt Jackson, told me that a fully charged battery is good for three start attempts, although he has found that the T58 in this Minijet almost always starts the first time (especially if the aircraft is headed into the wind during engine start).

Add fuel and ignition at 20-percent rpm by moving the start lever forward while maintaining an ever-vigilant eye on exhaust temperature.

Considering that the big T58 engine produces substantial idle thrust, it is not surprising that the Minijet wants to accelerate and takeoff while taxiing with the thrust lever fully retarded. After all, the airplane has a maximum-allowable gross weight of 1,874 pounds, only 204 pounds more than a Cessna 152.

Ground steering is accomplished with differential braking and toe brakes are conventional.

Extending the double-slotted Fowler flaps to 12 degrees for takeoff provides a new Minijet pilot his first opportunity to experience the unique H-style selector lever on the console between the pilots.

This lever resembles the 4-speed stick shift ("four on the floor") found on many automobiles with manually operated transmissions and is colloquially referred to as the gear-shift lever.

With the electric hydraulic pump turned on, you move the lever to the lower right position (where fourth gear would normally be found in a car) until the flaps reach the desired position. The lever is then moved to neutral and left there.

During flight, the lever is moved to "first gear" to raise the landing gear, "third gear" to raise the flaps, "fourth gear" to extend the flaps, and finally "second gear" to lower the landing gear.

This might seem a bit complicated at first, but becomes intuitive and easy to use after a little practice.

The thrust and elevator-trim levers are immediately aft of the "gear-shift" lever. A second throttle on the left sidewall allows each pilot to operate his control stick with his right hand and a throttle with his left in the tradition of military trainers and fighters. (SIPA had hoped to sell the Minijet as a military trainer and liaison aircraft as well as to the civilian market.)

Takeoff is simple enough. Accelerate the engine to 100-percent rpm and hang on. The modified Minijet rockets to rotation speed in less time than it takes to shift your attention to the airspeed indicator. After liftoff, pull the nose up sharply so as not to exceed the landing gear limit speed of 120 knots and continue holding it high so that you do not violate the red-line airspeed of 250 knots.

Unless power is reduced, the S-200 with a Huey engine climbs at approximately 8,000 fpm. (With the original French engine, it had a maximum climb rate of only 1,140 fpm.)

One cannot, of course, climb this way very long because of limited fuel. In reality, you should begin to think about landing as soon as the landing gear is retracted. Consequently, my investigation of handling qualities, performance, and stall characteristics was necessarily and severely curtailed.

The good news is that the controls are delightful. The Minijet is an easy to maneuver airplane with a brisk roll rate and fingertip control forces. It also has a 9-G limit load factor and is approved for aerobatics (except snap maneuvers). Inverted flight is limited to 20 seconds. Sadly, I did not have the fuel needed to explore this corner of the envelope either.

After posing the aircraft briefly for the camera, it was time to land. (It is time to land almost as soon as you leave the ground, and you always keep the airport in sight and within glide range.)

I flicked on the electric hydraulic pump, shifted to "second gear" to extend the landing gear and then shifted into "fourth gear" a second or so at a time to ramp the flaps down to a maximum of 35 degrees. The lever is then placed in neutral.

There is not much to landing the Minijet except that you should not begin flaring until you feel as though the seat of your trousers is about to scrape the runway. You are seated that low. (The tailskid below the tailpipe of the engine ensures that a tail strike does not damage the engine.)

N917WJ is truly fun to fly as long as you do not try to fly it for very long. It is perfect for someone who does not need to go far. (Range with the tip tanks, however, would not be quite so bad as long as power is reduced immediately after takeoff and low-power settings are used thereafter.)

## Lockheed 12A Electra Junior

| | |
|---|---|
| Engines | 2 Pratt & Whitney R-985 |
| Power | 450 hp ea |
| Length | 36 ft 4 in |
| Height (3-point attitude) | 9 ft 9 in |
| Wingspan | 49 ft 6 in |
| Wing Loading | 26.1 lb/sq ft |
| Power Loading | 10.2 lb/hp |
| Maximum Takeoff Weight | 9,200 lb |
| Fuel Capacity (usable) | 200 gal |
| Rate of Climb (sea level) | 1,470 fpm |
| Normal Cruise Speed | 212 mph |
| Stall Speed | 64 mph |

# Lockheed 12A Electra Junior

## This is more than an account of an airplane.

It is also a love story.

It begins when Ruth Richter Holden was a child. Her father, Paul Richter, Jr., was executive vice-president of Trans World Airlines and one of its three founders. She grew up in Kansas City, Missouri, TWA's hometown, as an "airline brat" surrounded by TWA people and their airplanes.

Holden was enthralled by flight and became a TWA "hostess" in 1955 working the round-engine airliners of that era. She married in 1958. At that time, though, management did not permit flight attendants to be married. She was forced to resign but eventually returned to the sky as a pilot and now has 1,500 hours, an instrument rating, and a Piper Warrior.

Wanting to honor her legendary father, who died at 53 when she was a teenager, Holden created a web site, www.PaulRichterTWALegend.com, detailing his involvement with TWA.

This web site caught the attention of Ed and Connie Bowlin who wanted to sell their Lockheed 12A Electra Junior. The airplane had once been owned by TWA, and the couple had hoped that Holden could provide historical information that would help them to sell the airplane.

NC18137 was built in 1937 at Lockheed Aircraft's Burbank, California factory and delivered new to Continental Airlines for use on its short, lean routes. Continental sold the airplane to Transcontinental and Western Air (later called Trans World Airlines) in 1940. The Electra Junior was operated by TWA from 1940-1945 as an executive transport and as an airborne research laboratory. It was used, for example, to develop static discharge wicks. At the end of the war, TWA sold the Electra to the Texas Oil Company (Texaco).

Holden knew that TWA had owned only one Model 12A (TWA aircraft #240), and the Bolins' email sent her scurrying to her father's stack of logbooks. There she verified that her father had taken her at the age of 10 on a flight from Kansas City to Washington, DC in that same airplane. That was on July 16, 1944. She also recalls having been flown in it two years earlier by TWA President, Jack Frye.

During a subsequent telephone conversation with Connie Bowlin, Holden said matter-of-factly, "I don't know why I should help you to sell this airplane. I should be the one to buy it."

She recalls thinking that she could not afford the airplane but simply had to have it. "You don't go looking for love; it finds you."

Holden adds, "I purchased the airplane sight unseen in June, 2005 even if it might mean having to mortgage my home, sell my firstborn, and letting the county bury me in a pauper's graveyard. I placed my faith in the ancient aviators who will help me to find a way to keep and fly Ellie [so named by Holden from the initials of the Lockheed Electra]."

Holden had no buyer's remorse even though she had no idea how she would get it from Griffin, Georgia to her home in San Luis Obispo, California. She had neither a taildragger endorsement nor a multiengine rating. Fortunately, she was able to "sweet-talk" her close friend, Curt "Rocky" Walters, a captain for American Eagle, into going to Georgia with her and getting checked out in the airplane.

Walters flew the airplane to California with Holden riding shotgun and grinning all the way. He, too, fell in love with the airplane and became Holden's partner. They immediately began the process of restoring "old number 240" to its original condition and TWA livery.

The untrained eye often mistakes the Lockheed Electra Junior for the venerable Model 18 Twin Beech. They are very similar in appearance, and there are so many more Twin Beeches than there are Electras. Lockheed had built only 130 Juniors when World War II began, necessitating a shift in the factory's focus from civil to military aircraft. Less than a dozen are still flying worldwide.

The fuselage tapers to distinctive and petite vertical fins, a trademark of its legendary designer, Kelly Johnson. The landing gear was designed by Lloyd Stearman.

With a maximum cruise speed of 225 mph, it was the fastest transport airplane of its day.

The Electra Junior was the airplane in which Victor Laszlo and his wife, Ilsa Lund, escaped from Morocco in the classic 1942 film, Casablanca, starring Humphrey Bogart and Ingrid Bergman.

Paraphrasing author Bob Grimstead, "the Electra Junior is reminiscent of an elegant era when style was an integral part of all great designs." Lockheed's next airliner, the curvaceous Constellation (colloquially called Connie), was arguably the most stylish of all.

The airplane has two cargo compartments, one in the nose and another aft of the cabin. They carry a maximum of 450 pounds, 250 up front and 200 in the rear. The center-of-gravity limits reportedly cannot be violated as long as neither cargo compartment is overloaded.

Cabin entry is made through a passenger door behind the left wing. You then climb up the inclined cabin, over the wing spar, and into the cockpit.

Walters invited me to sit in the hallowed left seat, the same seat that decades ago had been occupied by famed TWA aviators such as Frye, Richter, Daniel "Tommy" Tomlinson, and the most famous of all, Howard Hughes. (Although Hughes flew many of TWA's airplanes wherever and whenever he wanted, he never flew one in passenger service.) It almost felt as though I were walking on a grave.

Cockpit ambiance reeks of aviation's Golden Age. Even the smell is from a bygone era. I slowly and reverently allowed my fingers to wander and lightly touch and become familiar with the old controls, levers, knobs, switches, and instruments.

I pulled out the large, square knob that is the master switch, completed the Before-Start Checklist, and began the busy, 2-handed sequence of steps needed to awaken the supercharged, 450-hp, Pratt & Whitney engines. The procedure is more art than science. Like other radial engines, it comes to life one or two cylinders at a time, belching and coughing great swarms of smoke guaranteed to create instrument conditions for anyone standing behind.

Before taxiing, Walters told me that I was the only one with access to the toe brakes. "The bad news is that the airplane has poor brakes," he cautioned. He then added with a smile that "the good news is that it has poor brakes." I understood; although we would not be able to stop in a short distance, the ineffective brakes made it less likely that I would ground loop or cause their beloved taildragger to nose over during a botched landing.

Over-the-nose visibility is not great. Shallow S-turning is helpful during taxi to ensure that it is clear ahead.

After a conventional runup, I taxied onto the runway, lined up with the centerline, and engaged the tailwheel lock to tame the taildragger during its takeoff roll. Flaps are not used for takeoff.

I advanced the throttles leading slightly with the left to help keep Junior tracking true. The tail comes up by itself at about 40 mph, but some forward pressure is required with a cabin full of passengers. Ellie shows that she is ready to fly by serenely levitating without any help from the pilot, thank you.

The engines are limited to 450 hp for 1 minute. Maximum continuous is 400 hp.

Surprisingly, there are no cowl flaps, and as expected, high oil temperatures can be a problem.

In-flight visibility from the cockpit is fair to poor because of the small windscreens and huge engine cowlings acting like a pair of blinders.

Did I mention that the cockpit is noisy? It is. There are two reasons to keep the power low, to preserve fuel and hearing. Noise level in the cabin, though, is pleasantly acceptable.

The airplane flies nicely about all axes at all speeds, except that the ailerons are a bit heavy and create considerable adverse yaw effect without appropriate rudder assistance.

Many of the V-speeds and performance information to which modern pilots usually have access are not available to Electra pilots. Niceties such as landing distance, $V_X$ (best angle-of-climb speed), and $V_{YSE}$ (best rate-of-climb speed with an engine out), for example, can only be estimated.

The fuel system consists of 4 tanks, a forward and an aft tank in each wing, that hold a total of 200 gallons. Either engine can be supplied by any tank. A safety feature usually found only on larger airplanes is that the forward fuel tanks can be dumped to improve engine-out performance at heavy gross weights.

Each engine has a vacuum pump to spin the gyros, but you must select which one you want to use. The other serves as a standby pump.

The landing gear is extended electrically between 120 and 140 mph. At more than 140 mph, the motor has difficulty pushing the legs down and forward against the relative wind and into the locked position. At less than 120 mph, the gear clunks hard against the forward stops.

The main landing gear legs are physically interconnected, so if one comes down, you know that the other is down, too. The tailwheel, however, is welded down.

Once the main gear has been extended you can accelerate to the redline airspeed of 275 mph (if desired).

There are no wheel-well doors. When the gear is retracted, half of each wheel protrudes from the bottom of its nacelle and would help to protect the airframe in the event of a wheels-up landing.

The Electra Junior is strictly an electric airplane. Hydraulics is used only to operate the disc brakes.

With a 2-foot chord, the electrically operated split flaps are large and effective, but they move slowly, requiring 22 seconds to go all the way down. As the flaps extend, the ailerons droop about 10 degrees providing the effect of full-span flaps.

Both the landing gear and the flaps can be raised or lowered using a hand crank in case of an electrical malfunction.

I retired from TWA in 1998, and my airline ceased to exist when American Airlines acquired TWA in 2001 and immediately stripped away the historic logo from wherever it existed. The sense of déjà vu was almost overwhelming when I heard the voice of San Luis Obispo Tower coming through the headphones after I reported downwind. "TWA One Three Seven, you're cleared to land."

The cockpit seemed filled with ghosts. I could almost hear a TWA graybeard with four gold stripes warning me as I turned onto final approach. "Don't screw up the landing, kid. We're watching."

I came over the fence at 85 mph and touched down with a wheel landing at 65 mph. The long-legged Lockheed rolls on effortlessly making even a mediocre pilot look good. The elevator is so effective that forward pressure on the control yoke keeps the tail off the ground until slowing to almost taxi speed.

The Lockheed Electra Junior first flew on June 27, 1936, six months before the Twin Beech, and was an advanced airplane for its time. It was a slim, scaled-down version of the Model 10E Electra, the larger airplane in which Amelia Earhart attempted to fly around the world in 1937. With the same engines and much less weight and drag than the 10E, the Junior has superior performance leading some to speculate that Earhart might have succeeded had she used the more efficient 12A. (Only 2 Model 12Bs built. These were identical to the 12As but had less-powerful, 420-hp Wright Whirlwind engines.) The "Baby Electra" carried 8 passengers in airline configuration but only 4 or 6 as a corporate aircraft.

Only 6 Electra Juniors were purchased by the airlines; the rest were sold as corporate, private, and military aircraft. The airplane was so well designed and built that it is one of very few never to have had an airworthiness directive issued against it.

Thanks to Holden, Walters, and The Spirit of TWA (the official name they have given to their airplane), the memory of TWA is alive and well.

Holden and Walters do not consider themselves owners of the Electra Junior. They instead regard themselves as guardians of a living, flying legacy. They insist that the airplane belongs to the public in general and to the TWA community in particular. They use it to bring joy and inspiration to all who experience it.

The airplane touches your soul.

## North American P-51 Mustang

| | |
|---|---|
| Engine | Rolls-Royce Merlin |
| Power | 1,490 hp |
| Length | 32 ft 2 in |
| Height (3-point attitude) | 13 ft 8 in |
| Wingspan | 37 ft 0 in |
| Wing Loading (@ 10,500 pounds) | 44.7 lb/sq in |
| Power Loading (@ 10,500 pounds) | 6.6 lb/hp |
| Maximum Takeoff Weight | 13,000 lb |
| Fuel Capacity (usable) | 184 gal |
| Rate of Climb (sea level) | 3,200 fpm |
| Normal Cruise Speed | 361 mph |
| Stall Speed (@ 9,000 lb) | 94 mph |

# The P-51 Mustang

## There is nothing that can be written about the North

American Aviation P-51D Mustang that hasn't already been said. It is the ultimate single-engine, propeller-driven airplane, a sculpture of aerodynamic eroticism that stirs a pilot's heart. The distinctive snarl of its liquid-cooled, V-12 engine turns heads wherever and whenever it is heard.

Can there be a pilot who has not wanted to fly one?

The clearance crackled through my headphones, "Mustang One Five One Delta Papa, cleared for takeoff."

This was the moment of which dreams are realized and memories are made.

I pushed forward on the control stick to unlock the Mustang's full-swiveling tailwheel for the turn onto Camarillo's Runway 26. Pulling the stick back limits tailwheel swivel to 6 degrees left or right, enough to make wide-radius taxiing turns.

I held in position to collect my thoughts, to ensure that I was ready for what lay ahead. The idling Merlin engine made that distinctive popping sound. I nudged the throttle to 1,500 rpm for a final check of the gauges.

At 69 I was about to solo a Mustang for the first time and felt as much anxiety as when I had made my first solo flight 53 years ago. I dried my hands on my pant legs.

I couldn't help thinking about the Mustang's reputation for being difficult to control during the takeoff roll. An unsettling rumor says that more P-51s were lost during training than in combat, although Bob Hoover doesn't agree with that. It was comforting, though, to know that the typical World War II pilot stepping into the single-place fighter for the first time had only 200 hours of flight time. I had a wee bit more.

The long nose seemed to slope up and away for as far as the eye could see but is thankfully slender. Although I could not see directly ahead, I could see a considerable length of the runway edges. More of the runway is visible than when flying many airplanes equipped with wide radial engines that block more of the view. The 11-foot propeller made humongous, blurred slices across the sky.

I rechecked rudder trim: 6-degrees right. The canopy was locked, engine-coolant temperature was in the green, boost pump was on, and the mighty Merlin was feeding from the left tank.

Toe brakes firmly applied, I advanced the throttle to 2,300 rpm and 30 inches of manifold pressure. The Mustang trembled slightly as if champing at the bit, impatient to be cut loose.

Brakes released, we began to accelerate, and I kept my feet dancing to arrest directional transgressions. As airflow increased across the rudder, I advanced the throttle to 3,000 rpm and 40 inches. (The geared propeller turns at only 1,437 rpm.) I held the stick fully aft to keep the tailwheel on the ground and assist with tracking. I had been taught that the best way to maintain directional control is to increase power in steps as control effectiveness increases.

At 50 knots I slowly but forcefully pushed the stick forward. The end of the runway came into view, and I increased power to 55 inches (120 gallons per hour of fuel flow). I began to appreciate why the British (for whom the P-51 was developed) called this airplane a Mustang, a wild stallion of the American prairie. The unbridled acceleration, energy, and noise level are startling and impressive.

Although 61 inches of manifold pressure are available for takeoff, I was not ready for the combination of twisting and turning forces that accompany 1,490 horsepower slinging that huge propeller. (Torque alone is impressive and causes the left tire to wear much faster than the right.) A takeoff using maximum power could wait until I had more experience.

Besides, a lightly loaded Mustang inspired by 55 inches of manifold pressure performs better than a wartime edition loaded with armament and drop tanks using 61 inches. During emergencies, combat pilots could pull 67 inches (1,720 horsepower), and modified Mustangs racing at Reno develop as much as 155 inches.

I raised the nose at 100 knots and the Mustang was immediately unlike any other piston-powered single I had ever flown. With landing gear retracted, the climb at takeoff power is exhilarating, almost 4,000 fpm.

I was relieved to discover that it takes less right-rudder pressure during initial climb than a Cessna 210. The immediate goal, though, was to accelerate to the best glide speed of 150 knots, just in case.

If you have to make an off-airport landing, I was admonished, be certain that the gear is up. If the Mustang flips onto its back when landing on an unimproved surface, the top of the canopy could wind up pressing against the ground. Getting out would be impossible. Also, don't ditch; the P-51 wants to dive for the bottom.

Although the Mustang can be trimmed easily, it is almost a constant process when maneuvering. Rudder and elevator trim are needed with even the slightest changes in power or airspeed.

In-flight visibility is unlimited in all directions. Maximum speed for opening the canopy is 130 knots. The down-sloping cowling initially gives the impression that the nose is too low during cruise. As advertised, control pressures increase and stiffen with airspeed but are not heavy.

## THE CHALLENGE BEGINS

Wanting to solo a Mustang and doing it are obviously two different things. I was fortunate to have a friend who owns one. I had known David Price for years but never had the courage to ask if I could fly his pride and joy, *Cottonmouth*.

Price is a 5,500-hour Navy pilot who has owned a wide variety of warbirds. These include a Messerschmitt Me-109, a Mitsubishi Zero, a Hawker Hurricane, and a pair of Spitfires. He has flown 40 types of warbirds and 8 unlimited races at Reno in his highly modified P-51, Dago Red. He owns the Supermarine jet center at Santa Monica Airport and is the founder and president of American Airports, an organization dedicated to the management of airports.

Recognizing that I was not getting any younger, I kiddingly but on the square asked Price when he was going to let me fly his cherished Mustang. Surprisingly and without hesitation, he said, "Whenever you'd like."

"You're kidding, right?"

"No, I'm not. Just get some back-seat time in a T-6 to prepare for the Mustang."

Needing no further encouragement, I joined the Southern California Wing of the Commemorative Air Force. After two hours of touch-and-go landings from both seats of the T-6, CAF instructor, Steve Barber, who was also an experienced warbird pilot, felt that I could handle the Mustang. He said that the T-6 is actually more difficult to fly than a Mustang. Sure, I thought skeptically.

I called Price and announced my readiness. His insurance company, however, had other ideas. The underwriter said that I could fly *Cottonmouth* but only after obtaining an endorsement to solo a Mustang from a P-51 instructor.

Stallion 51 in Kissimmee, Florida is the only place in the world to obtain formal, FAA-approved Mustang training. The school has two magnificent TF-51s, Crazy Horse and Crazy Horse 2. These are P-51Ds that have been highly modified with a second, fully-equipped cockpit.

Although many P-51s have a jump seat replacing the 85-gallon fuel tank installed behind the pilot in wartime editions, these seats have no access to controls or instruments.

Stallion 51's curriculum is not a quick-and-dirty checkout; it is a full-blown program that is as professional and comprehensive as the transition courses I had taken at TWA. Instructors there take their responsibilities seriously.

My instructor was Lee Lauderback, who I am tempted to call Mr. Mustang. He has more than 7,000 hours in P-51s and might know more about flying the airplane than any man alive. His modesty, however, defers that honor to Bob Hoover.

Lauderback began his aviation career as a youngster soloing at 16 and worked his way up the ladder to eventually become Arnold Palmer's chief pilot. In 1987 he and a partner, Doug Schultz, purchased a P-51 under the terms of a contract they had with the Navy's test pilot school. The pair eventually recognized that there was no formal way for pilots to learn to fly a Mustang. This led to the organization of Stallion 51. Lauderback's younger twin brothers, Peter and Richard, were Air Force mechanics and are responsible for preening, primping and maintaining the two Mustangs as well as other warbirds that Stallion 51 maintains.

On my first and subsequent days at Stallion 51, Lauderback provided numerous hours of one-on-one ground school for each hour spent in the air. I had no idea that there was so much to learn about the airplane. My classroom notes include these interesting items:

- The liquid-cooling system is an engineering marvel. Air enters the inlet on the belly, travels through radiators, and exhausts in a way that produces as much thrust as there is cooling drag, a phenomenon known as the Meredith Effect.

- The coolant-temperature gauge is arguably the Mustang's most important instrument. An overheating engine requires immediate action such as fully opening the cooling door, reducing power, and possibly making an emergency landing. (The cooling system is reportedly very reliable and normally operates automatically.)

- The laminar-flow wing delays until Mach 0.77 the development of supersonic shock waves and the drag rise associated with them.

- Be careful about inadvertently moving the landing-gear handle on the ground. There are no switches or downlocks to prevent retraction. In flight, the wheels freefall into position in case of hydraulic failure.

Flight lessons ran the gamut of Mustang maneuvering and nibbled at the edges of the performance envelope. Emphasis was placed on emergencies, stall characteristics in all configurations, and a variety of takeoffs and landings. More than an instructor, Lauderback is an effective, enthusiastic teacher who enjoys passing along his love and lore of Mustangs. He is thoroughly dedicated to the safe operation of these thoroughbred aircraft.

Although the full-blown course is expensive, those wanting to sample a Mustang can obtain dual instruction during one or more orientation flights. You will leave with precious memories, a video of your experience, and some appreciation of what it takes to fly the airplane.

## FINAL APPROACH

The Mustang is so aerodynamically clean that it glides more efficiently than most general aviation airplanes but only when the propeller is set to high pitch. Blade pitch affects glide ratio so much that it can be modulated during descent to vary glide performance as necessary during an engine-out approach. (The P-51 loses about 2,000 feet per 360-degree turn.)

You probably have seen fighter aircraft make high-speed overhead approaches. This enables pilots to make a dead-stick landing on the runway irrespective of where an engine failure might occur during such an approach. This is not true about a conventional traffic pattern, especially when extended downwind legs are required.

I reminded myself on final approach not to overreact to a botched or bounced landing by jamming in full throttle. It is possible at low airspeed for the Merlin to torque the Mustang into an uncontrollable half-roll into the ground. A go-around can be made safely with only 46 inches of manageable manifold pressure.

The entire runway is visible over the nose when on final. The goal is to be in landing configuration with the flaps at 50 degrees and indicating 100-110 knots when a quarter-mile from the runway. You then very slowly reduce power and airspeed for the wheel landing. If you begin to hear the crackling pops of the idling, backfiring Merlin at the same time that you touch on the stiff mains, you will know that you have done it properly properly. Maintain directional control by working the rudders and positively lowering the tail to get the tailwheel on the ground.

(When making a short-field landing, move the mixture control to idle-cutoff after touchdown. This eliminates the thrust produced by an idling Merlin. Propeller inertia and windmilling prevent the monstrous "flywheel" from stopping quickly. As the Mustang slows and you begin to see individual blades, return the mixture to auto-rich. The engine restarts nicely and in time to taxi.)

It is axiomatic that an airplane that looks good flies well. That certainly is true of the Mustang. It is not a difficult airplane to fly, easier in some ways than a T-6, but it demands respect and adherence to procedure.

More than anything, the Mustang is addictive and intoxicating. The more you fly it, the more you want to fly it.

When asked what it is really like to fly a Mustang, I am reminded of a cell phone call from my wife, Dorie, immediately after my first flight in Crazy Horse. Lauderback had put me through the wringer, and I told her that I was "tired, hot, sweaty and breathless."

"You sound like someone who has just had sex," she said.

I couldn't have put it better.

Courtesy Jim Thompson

## Ryan PT-22 Recruit (ST-3KR)

| | |
|---|---:|
| Engine | Kinner R-55 radial |
| Power | 160 hp |
| Length | 22 ft 8 in |
| Height (3-point attitude) | 7 ft 2 in |
| Wingspan | 30 ft 1 in |
| Wing Loading | 13.9 lb/sq ft |
| Power Loading | 11.6 lb/hp |
| Maximum Takeoff Weight | 1,860 lb |
| Fuel Capacity (usable) | 24 gal |
| Rate of Climb (sea level) | 860 fpm |
| Normal Cruise Speed | 110 mph |
| Stall Speed | 62 mph |

# Ryan PT-22 Recruit

## More than 300,000 young, patriotic Americans

volunteered to become military pilots during World War II. Most of them received their primary training in that beloved biplane, the Stearman Kaydet (the "yellow peril"). The rest were trained in the Fairchild Cornell and the Ryan STA-3KR Recruit, the PT-22.

Although the Ryan was not as successful (in terms of numbers built) or as well known as its competitors, proponents of the PT-22 claim that it was the superior trainer because it was more demanding and less forgiving. The Stearman and the Fairchild, they claim, were pussy cats by comparison.

The PT-22 shown on these pages, NC53178 (serial number 1859), was built along with all of its sister ships by the Ryan Aeronautical Company at Lindbergh Field in San Diego, California. It made its maiden flight on February 5, 1942 and was drafted for military service at Visalia (California) Army Air Field.

The PT-22 was retired from the military and began its civilian career at the end of World War II.

Subsequent years took their toll on NC53178, and the airplane eventually became a basket case. In 1992 Greg Heckman came to its rescue and purchased the derelict aircraft for $11,000.

Heckman, a research-and-design engineer in Illinois had been assisting in the restoration of warbirds for Pride Aircraft in Rockford, Illinois. He had always had a fascination for these historic aircraft and wanted to restore one for himself. Unable to afford a World War II fighter, he opted instead to restore a trainer. Because of his fascination with the *Spirit of St. Louis*, he had always been fond of Ryan airplanes, and this led to his selection of a PT-22.

Heckman obtained a copy of the Recruit's design and manufacturing plans from the Smithsonian National Air & Space Museum. He then devoted 4.5 years and 2,300 hours of painstaking, hands-on work (excluding time spent on research and tracking down parts) to the effort while paying strict and meticulous attention to detail.

This Recruit made its second maiden flight on May 6, 1998. This was in time for Heckman to enter the competition at EAA AirVenture 1998 at Oshkosh, where he was justly rewarded. The judges decreed that NC53178 was the Grand Champion Antique. It has been described as "the finest PT-22 ever built by Ryan or anyone else."

This magnificent machine caught the eye of Terry Ballas at Oshkosh during AirVenture 2002. He fell in love with the trainer and eventually bought it from Heckman.

Ballas discovered, however, that a stock 1942 airplane has unacceptable limitations when operating in and out of controlled airports in major metropolitan areas during the 21st century. To the dismay of purists, he made certain modifications that included

- Replacing the non-sensitive altimeter, which had a single hand, with a sensitive altimeter;
- Modifying the instrument panel to accommodate the addition of avionics;
- Replacing the canvas baggage nook with an aluminum compartment so that items couldn't fall through and interfere with flight control cables lying below;
- Adding an electrical system that included a wind-driven alternator and starter because it was impossible at times to find people at en route airports who are willing to hand-prop the engine;
- Modifying the valves and valve seats to accommodate 100LL avgas. The engine was designed for 80 octane fuel; 100LL can burn stock valves;

- Adding external grease fittings so that the rocker covers didn't have to be removed to grease the rocker arms, a frequent ritual with the Kinner R-55 engine.

The result is what in the automobile industry is called a "resto/mod," a restoration modified to take advantage of technological improvements. Some claim that this contaminates the original design and reduces its value.

Ballas' Recruit is likely the most beautiful airplane I have ever flown. Its bright yellow wings are mated to a slim, polished-aluminum fuselage. Overall it has a sexy, sassy, inviting appearance.

Immediately ahead of the front cockpit on top of the nose is a turn-over mast designed to act like a roll bar and protect the occupants should the airplane wind up inverted on the ground, although I question its effectiveness (especially on sod).

Ahead of the mast is a glass tube, a sight gauge with a float that reliably indicates fuel remaining in the 24-gallon nose tank.

The baggage compartment is accessed through a small door on the left side of the fuselage behind the rear cockpit and is placarded for a maximum capacity of 6 pounds. The handbook, however, says that 53 pounds may be carried there when the front cockpit is empty.

The Kinner radial is a dry-sump engine, and its oil tank is between the engine and the fuel tank. Oil supply on this PT-22 normally is turned off if the airplane is not going to be flown for a while. This prevents oil from seeping into the lower cylinders and creating a hydraulic lock. A panel on the left side of the cowling is removed to ensure that the in-line supply valve is open prior to engine start. This also is where the primer is located, so give it a few squirts before starting.

Heckman's masterpiece is so immaculate that it is difficult to climb aboard for fear of soiling or scratching something. (One cannot find as much as a fingerprint on the shiny aluminum fuselage.) But I forced myself to overcome this fear and happily lowered myself into the rear cockpit. Solo flight is not allowed from the front although there are sufficient controls and instruments there for an instructor.

The seats adjust vertically and the rudder pedals can be adjusted fore and aft like most military airplanes.

Some PT-22s had direct drive starters. Someone standing behind the propeller rotated a hand crank that turned the engine and, hence, the propeller. NC53178 does not have such a starter nor is hand-propping required. Simply depress the starter button, spin the propeller 2-3 revolutions, and turn on the mags.

The Kinner crackles and pops, and the sound is somewhat magical, strangely and inexplicably satisfying, reminiscent of another time. As expected, S-turning is required to see ahead while taxiing and downwind rudder is applied to prevent weathervaning into a crosswind.

There is nothing unusual about the flaps-up takeoff other than the gathering sense of impending adventure as speed increases and the outside air begins to curl around your head and take you gently into its womb. There is no joy like that of an open cockpit.

The Kinner radial normally feels a little rough during flight, as if running on 4 cylinders instead of 5, and has a distinctive sound: *pockety, pockety, pockety.* It seemed strange that the engine sounds differently when leaning one's head to the left than when leaning right, but I soon discovered why. Exhaust from the two cylinders on one side exits loudly from two short stacks, while exhaust from the two cylinders on the other side flow through a carburetor-heat muff and exit that through a single stack. So you hear the barking of a Kinner on one side and a somewhat muffled sound on the other.

The engine turns a long, 91-inch propeller, and engine speed is limited to 1,850 rpm, although 2,128 rpm is briefly allowed when diving. Cruise rpm is between 1,560 (economy cruise) and 1,680 (maximum continuous) resulting in cruise speeds of 110–120 mph.

As expected, in-flight visibility is wonderful, much better than an open-cockpit biplane flown from the rear (especially a Stearman).

Ryan made extensive use of ball bearings to help make the flight controls smooth, light and sensitive. Stalls and recovering from them are honest and straightforward, and there is ample pre-stall buffeting to warn of an impending stall. An observant pilot will notice, too, that the upper left flying wires begin shaking shortly before buffeting begins.

Be careful, though, not to let the ball out of its cage at large angles of attack. The Recruit is intolerant of sloppy footwork, not unlike many aircraft of that era, and rewards the errant pilot with a spin. The PT-22 *loves* to spin and will do so enthusiastically and with little incentive. It spins rapidly and at a relatively steep nose-down attitude, which must have unnerved students training to be military pilots.

Standard spin-recovery techniques are effective but one must be careful not to be ham-fisted and induce a secondary stall during the pull-up or to hold opposite rudder too long during recovery lest ye wind up spinning in the opposite direction.

Applying bottom rudder during a tight, slow turn from base to final can lead to a spin without any warning whatsoever. Some attribute the PT-22's spirited willingness to spin to the 4-degree wing sweep of the leading edges, but I have been unable to confirm this.

The PT-22 reputedly tends to spin flat with a rear center of gravity (when the front seat is empty), although I did not notice such a tendency. The airplane is limited to 3-turn spins, so perhaps flattening develops if the spin is held much longer.

With limit load factors of +7.6 and –3.5 Gs, you can perform almost any aerobatic maneuver for which you have the skill and desire. Snap rolls, however, are the PT-22s forte and are a joy to perform. An entry speed of 90 mph seems best although a little less airspeed reduces entry loads. The airplane flicks around quickly and can be arrested with ease.

Gliding flight, however, is not one of the airplane's fortes. Power off at the best glide speed of 85 mph, it comes down more steeply than one would expect from a trainer. It is best to approach with plenty of altitude or carry power during shallow approaches.

The flaps can be ratcheted down (using a handle near the floor to the left of the seat) as much as 30 degrees for landing, but I cannot imagine why anyone would do this. They reduce stall speed by only 2 mph (from 64 to 62 mph) and increase sink rate dramatically. They probably were intended to train pilots in the use of flaps for when graduating to basic and advanced trainers in such aircraft as the BT-13 Valiant (the "Vultee Vibrator") and the venerable AT-6 Texan.

Landing the airplane is unexpectedly easy. The trunion (knee-action) landing gear incorporates long-stroke Aerol (air-oil) oleo struts that soak up any tendency to bounce. It is difficult to make a hard landing in the Recruit. It simply squishes onto the ground during either 3-point or wheel landings.

Do not, however, allow this to lead to overconfidence and complacency. The PT-22 is one of those airplanes that helped to give taildraggers a bad reputation. Although the touchdown is easy, hang on. This is when the fun begins. Inattentiveness to or overcontrol of the rudder during the ground roll can lead to a wicked ground loop, especially if you are flying alone and the CG is aft. If your feet are not busily and adroitly dancing on the pedals, then you're probably doing it wrong. PT-22s have steerable, full-swiveling tailwheels.

No sooner had I shut down the engine when the airplane was pounced upon by John Montalvo whose job it was to clean up oil streaks and polish away any marks that I might have left on the airplane. He took great pride in preserving the airplane's pristine appearance.

Ryan Aeronautical entered the trainer market in 1934 with the Ryan ST (sport-trainer), progenitor of the PT-22. T. Claude Ryan had always favored monoplanes over biplanes, a design element of Lindbergh's flying fuel tank.

The ST was a sleek and sexy machine partly because its narrow, inverted, in-line, 95-hp Menasco engine fit into a slender cowling that melted gracefully into the long, shiny-aluminum fuselage. The result looked as much like a sculpture as it did an airplane.

The airplane became the Ryan STA Super Sport when horsepower was increased to 125; the Ryan STA Special had a 159-hp, supercharged Menasco engine.

A Ryan STA was sent to the U.S. Army Air Corps in 1939 and was called the XPT-16, the first monoplane acquired by the AAC. Fifteen more were requested and called YPT-16s. Thirty more were delivered as PT-20s.

General Henry "Hap" Arnold, however, was displeased with the Menasco engine's reliability and suggested that it be replaced with the more robust Kinner engine even though the 5-cylinder radial disturbed the beautiful lines of previous models. Ryan delivered 100 of these PT-21s.

During 1941 and 1942 the Army Air Corps (and Army Air Forces) ordered 1,023 of Ryan's wire-braced monoplanes with improved Kinner engines and without landing-gear fairings (for ease of maintenance). The result was the Ryan PT-22 ST-3KR. The Navy also ordered 100 of them (designated as NR-1s).

Although not as pretty as previous STs, the PT-22 made up in strength and reliability what it might have lost in sex appeal.

Although the PT-22 and the STA are closely related, the Recruit is not an STA with a radial bolted on the nose. The PT-22 was designed as a military airplane. Its fuselage, for example, has a circular cross-section to accommodate larger pilots while the STA has a shapelier, oval fuselage.

*For further information about Ryan aircraft, contact the International Ryan Club at http://www.ryanclub.org/.*

# Special Treats

# Boeing 707-331BA

| | |
|---|---|
| Engines | 4 Pratt & Whitney JT3D-3 |
| Power | 18,000 lb thrust each |
| Length | 152 ft 11 in |
| Height | 42 ft 5 in |
| Wingspan | 145 ft 9 in |
| Wing Loading | 111.6 lb/sq ft |
| Power Loading | 4.7 lb/lb of thrust |
| Maximum Takeoff Weight | 336,000 lb |
| Maximum Landing Weight | 207,000 lb |
| Fuel Capacity | 159,800 lb |
| Range | 5,357 nm |
| Cruise Speed | Mach 0.85 |
| Stall Speed (flaps down, 207,000 lb) | 100 knots |
| Maximum operating altitude | 42,000 feet |

# Around the World in a Boeing 707

## The world is smaller for pilots than other people

make it out to be. When I flew for TWA, I made numerous trips around the world during the early 1970s. I saw places that only a relatively few pilots see and had experiences that do not occur on a cross-country flight between Denver and Dubuque.

The farther afield we fly, the more fascinating becomes the topography that slides beneath our wings, wings that slice through the same air and obey the same laws whether attached to a Cessna 182, a Cirrus SR-22, or a Boeing 707.

So if you are inclined to wander, I would like to share with you notes taken during one of those round robin flights, a circumnavigation of the world from Los Angeles to Los Angeles in a Boeing 707-331B. Remember that this is a verbal snapshot taken decades ago. Much has changed in the interim, but I think that you will enjoy this historical perspective of international airline operations.

We are within VHF range of Ocean Station November, a weather ship positioned midway between California and Hawaii. After giving a position report, we ask for a radar fix, although none is needed. We've been cruising along Route Bravo below the contrails of a 747 equipped with inertial navigation. This visual reference offers guidance as reliable as a railroad track. The jumbos are rarely more than a mile off course.

It is almost impossible to get lost when flying the other way, from Honolulu to Los Angeles. North America is simply too big to miss. Upon reaching the coast, all a pilot need do if lost is to look at the mountains. If they are green or white, he is too far north. If they are parched and brown, he is too far south.

The ocean station confirms our position and asks if we have time to copy a few messages to be mailed for the ship's crew when we land. It is difficult to understand how these sailors can trust the addresses of their wives and girl friends to the dozens of lecherous pilots within VHF earshot, all of whom know that the men on November will not be home for several weeks.

The crew on Ocean Station Charlie (situated in mid-Atlantic) is savvier. They hold a "Miss Ocean Station Charlie" contest, collecting the names and addresses of willing flight attendants from overflying jetliners. At the end of a 40-day cruise, the winner is selected from a hat and receives a bouquet of flowers. We wonder what happens to the remaining names and addresses.

We reach the equi-time point, signifying that from here it would take as long to return the mainland as it would to continue in the event of an engine failure or other emergency. Several hundred miles later we pass the point of no return, an event more dramatic in fiction than in reality. Because Hawaii's main airports have never been closed simultaneously, there is no reason why a pilot would want return to California after passing the equi-time point.

Our next stop, Guam, is a dot, a minute oasis floating on the Pacific vastness, the end of a 3,800-mile-long line drawn on the chart. The South Kauai VOR points an electronic finger toward this distant fleck of land, but the deviation indicators soon relax and we are without guide.

We used to be led across oceans by navigators using sextants to shoot the stars in the mystical manner of ancient mariners. Today, we use Doppler navigation (an electronic form of dead-reckoning) updated with fixes provided by Loran A (predecessor to Loran C).

The puffy clouds below are like sheep grazing on a boundless, emerald meadow, but ahead the cumulus grows tempestuously taller, confirming that our route partially coincides with the intertropical convergence zone, a cauldron of thunderstorms brewed by mixing the northeast and southeast trade winds.

It seems inconceivable that more than 50,000 thunderstorms occur daily above the Earth until you have flown the South Pacific. At times, all 50,000 of them seem to be in your way, challenging your right to the sky and necessitating the most devious, serpentine flight path imaginable.

One transceiver is tuned to 121.5, waiting patiently for a voice of desperation to break the silence. Once, while en route from Shannon to New York, I heard that voice. It belonged to the pilot of a Beech Baron flying from Narssarssuaq, Greenland to Goose Bay, Labrador. He was hopelessly lost, low on fuel, and his ETA had become history. His call for help was answered by so many well-intentioned airline pilots that the emergency frequency became temporarily jammed.

The pilot's position was eventually determined, and he was directed toward a sub-Arctic settlement where a helicopter later plucked him from the tundra after his fuel ran out.

The electronic pulses wriggle across the Loran scope like topless dancers across a stage, curving and twisting irregularly. Soon, one is superimposed upon another to provide a line of position and confirm that ground speed has decreased drastically during the last hour, adding to the deceiving effect of slow motion at high altitude. We are suspended in a wispy, ethereal blackness where nothing seems to move except the fuel gauges.

A patch of turbulence, a change in outside temperature, an increase in groundspeed. The jet stream has tired of pushing against us and has veered north to perpetrate its folly elsewhere. It is cold outside, –97°F, dangerously close to the fuel-freeze point of –100°F. A lower, warmer altitude is requested, and we discuss with renewed amazement the incongruity that the coldest temperatures in the atmosphere occur above the Tropics.

The Doppler system announces that Sunday night has suddenly become Monday night. The International Date Line, drawn to meet man's need for order and definition, has been crossed. A passenger sends a note to the cockpit, complaining with mock disappointment that he has been cheated out of his birthday. We respond unsympathetically advising that he should have flown in the opposite direction and celebrated his birthday twice.

Parenthetically, if America and the Allies had been defeated by Hitler and the Nazis, the date line would not be where it is today. *Der Fuehrer* declared that Berlin was the center of the world and planned to exercise his egomaniacal power by moving the Prime Meridian from Greenwich, England to Berlin, thereby shifting all meridians 13 degrees east. He even had maps printed to reflect this change.

Our shadow streaks south of wishbone-shaped Wake Island, a 4.5-mile-long atoll that was put to use in 1935 as a seaplane base for Pan American Airlines' Clippers. Today the island is governed by the FAA, and those learning to fly there are not required to make cross-country flights. The closest airport is on Eniwetok, 600 miles south.

The small cumulus below drift behind with metronomic regularity, casting shadows on the water that look like small islands. An island or an atoll usually can be distinguished from a shadow by a green ring of shallow water surrounding it, but not always, causing me to wonder if any flight-weary pilot ever let down to a shadow thinking that it was an island.

The Pacific immensity is monotonous. More clouds, more water, more sky. Once in a while when the passengers are asleep and the pilots would like to be, some comic on a nearby flight breaks the boredom by transmitting risqué jokes on 121.5. Occasionally, someone sings or even plays the harmonica. Such diversions, scorned but undetectable by the authorities, is stimulating and rarely lasts more than a few minutes. Each pilot then returns to his personal thoughts and a bout with the "Pacific blues," a fatiguing form of long-range boredom.

Those in the cabin also do strange things to break the monotony. Yemenites have been known to start campfires in the aisle to cook a meal. Passengers accustomed only to train travel have attempted to climb into overhead baggage compartments for a nap, and there are the inevitable honeymooners unable to wait.

The weather at Guam is reported CAVOK (ceiling and visibility okay), which is comforting because there is not a suitable airport close enough to Guam to be used as an alternate.

While soaking up the South Pacific sun on a coral-covered beach on Guam, it occurs to me that we are spending our layover on the summit of what may be the world's tallest mountain. Guam's foundation rises from the Marianas Trench, the deepest part of the Pacific basin, 35,640 feet below sea level.

The dispatcher hands me a weather folder containing the familiar prognostic charts and weather reports. Included also is a list of the speed, course, and last-known position of every large surface vessel steaming in the vicinity of our route to Hong Kong.

When I ask if he thinks that we'll really need this information, he responds by adding a mimeographed sheet to the maze of preflight paperwork work scattered before me. It is entitled, *Recommended Ditch Headings for Western Pacific Weather Zones.*

Our flight to Hong Kong will be via Typhoon Alley, a nickname given to this region when Pacific hurricanes are on the rampage. It can be a severe weather area, but neither it nor any other region I have visited is as rough as Tornado Alley in the Midwestern U.S.

Once while en route from Guam to Okinawa, we tangled with a seemingly innocuous precipitation cell barely large enough to show on radar. It lifted the crew meal from my lap and slammed the tray against the instrument panel. Ever try to read your gauges in severe turbulence through a gooey film of *coq au vin*?

On the way to Hong Kong, I review the approach plate for Taipei, an en route stop, and am amused at the precision with which the Chinese expect us to make a visual approach: "After passing the TP radiobeacon at 140 knots, turn to heading 140 degrees at 4.2 degrees per second, fly straight for 6,382 feet, execute a 10-second, 45-degree turn while covering a ground distance of 2,364 feet, fly the downwind leg 6,360 feet from the runway," and so forth.

A rumor—something you start if you do not hear one by noon—claims that intrepid and cunning aviators from the People's Republic of China stole onto Taipei Airport one night and relieved the Nationalist Chinese Air Force of several aircraft. This partially explains why the Formosans are such sticklers for detail. You get the feeling while on the airport that permission is required to sneeze.

While taxiing for takeoff at Taipei, a red light warns us to stop so that a guard can verify that our N-number coincides with the one on the flight plan. If the two do not match, we will be escorted back to the ramp. The guard's machine gun and several anti-aircraft batteries surrounding the airport convince us that this is one red light we cannot afford to run.

The guard salutes respectfully and shines a green light. We trundle to the runway.

We are soaring through placid valleys of white cotton candy, banking gently to follow the contours of an aerial fantasy land. Our wings are outstretched arms and slice through soft cumulus castles. This exhilarating sense of speed and freedom is what flying is all about.

A glance at the chart, however, returns us abruptly to the stark reality of the world below. We have passed over Makung, a small island in the Formosa Strait, and are paralleling a buffer zone intended to immunize the Chinese mainland against trespass by aircraft of the Free World. One notation on the chart informs us to be on the alert for transmissions from unlisted radio aids within Red China that could be hazardous and misleading. Another notation states matter-of-factly "that any aircraft infringing upon the territorial rights of China may be fired upon without notice."

Nearing Hong Kong's Kai-Tak Airport, we receive a descent clearance, and prepare for what might be the world's most unusual instrument approach. At first glance, the approach plate looks confusingly similar to an Aresti aerobatic diagram.

*Kai-Tak's Runway 13 points to Hong Kong's Victoria Harbor.*

Upon reaching the Cheung Chau Radiobeacon, we descend through thick globs of nimbostratus to 1,000 feet msl while flying a series of graceful figure eights using the "Charlie Charlie" Beacon as a pivot point. Inbound from the beacon, we break out of the dripping overcast and peer through an onslaught of heavy rain. We now fly visually for 15 miles at only 750 feet above the sea. Visibility is one mile, but 12 miles ahead the Stonecutters Radiobeacon encourages us to continue. We pass abeam the tip of Hong Kong Island and enter Victoria Harbor, our screaming turbines seemingly unnoticed by those aboard the dozens of Chinese junks below that plod and heel through windswept waters.

Crossing Kowloon Beach, we begin a gentle right turn, our eyes straining, searching for the visual aiming point, an orange-and-white checkerboard on the side of a 300-foot-high hill near the approach end of Kai-Tak's Runway 13.

Tall buildings below stretch for the sky, probing for our belly. The illuminated checkerboard appears straight ahead, and we bend the Boeing right to avoid the hill, simultaneously descending toward concrete canyons and torrents of turbulence that conspire against us. Wings level at 200 feet, we are at last aligned with the 8,350-foot-long concrete ribbon projecting into the harbor from Kowloon's east shore.

Hong Kong, a sweet-and-sour mixture of Chinese antiquity and modern British colonialism, a place where you can go broke saving money and where you can eat bird's nest soup, a glutinous compound made by stewing bird saliva from their nests.

After fulfilling the dictates of my shopping list, I tend to an essential chore in Hong Kong, buying a survival kit. No, I do not expect an en route emergency. This survival kit consists of canned groceries to obviate my having to eat anything in Bombay, our next layover point. Eating the local food there can incapacitate the delicate Western stomach for days with something certain to baffle the medical world. Compared to the water in Bombay, Mexico's water is like Evian. But if you are brave and insist on drinking tap water in Bombay, be sure to first hold a glassful up to the light to see if anything inside returns your stare.

High above the China Sea, I begin to prepare a list of my Hong Kong bargains for U.S. customs when the flight engineer asks us to listen to the high-frequency radio on 6624 kHz. But instead of hearing controllers, we hear Radio Peking's modern-day version of Tokyo Rose spewing her dally dose of anti-American air pollution.

On another frequency, Saigon Control clears us across South Vietnam via Green 67. I carefully check the chart, having been cautioned about anonymous or misleading clearances that might originate in Red China or North Vietnam. An American jetliner with 117 passengers would be a prize fish for the Communists to capture over their territory.

At times, navigation and communication problems occur over Southeast Asia. None are serious, but all are annoying. The Chinese are invariably blamed for these and anything else that goes wrong, even the aft toilet that will not flush.

The 115-mile flight across South Vietnam takes only 13 minutes and begins over the coastal town of Qui Nhon, south of Danang, north of Saigon. Broad, spotless and inviting beaches characterize the scalloped coast. From our vantage point, Vietnam appears peaceful. But looking carefully, we can still see numerous bomb craters, pockmarks on the face of the Earth and on the face of man.

We streak across the muddy, swollen Mekong River and then the rice-rich fields of Cambodia and Thailand as we prepare for an en route stop. But while on final for one of Bangkok's two parallel runways, I gape at what lies between them: a golf course. Can you imagine teeing off while being assaulted by the thunder of F-4 Phantoms taking off in formation? Like the rabbits that dwell between the runways at Los Angeles, the duffers at Don Muang Airport must be stone deaf.

A feminist would have difficulty adjusting to life in Bangkok. The entire crew orders breakfast at a small restaurant near the airport from a petite Eurasian waitress with extraordinarily delicate, flowerlike features. In typical Thai tradition, the men are served first, and our flight attendants are not served until we are finished.

We are over the narrow, southern extremity of Burma, a devoutly Buddhist land with pagodas so large they are visible from 7 miles above.

Ahead is the 1,000-mile-wide Bay of Bengal and on the other side, India. I turn off the transponder, giving it and us a rest from the rigors of positive control. Secondary radar is non-existent on the "backside" of the world, and primary radar coverage is spotty.

We estimate landing in Bombay at 2000 GMT, which is 0130 local time. Because Bombay is 5-1/2 hours ahead of Greenwich, we conclude that Indian leaders could not decide whether their country should be Zulu plus 5 or 6 hours, so they compromised. We wonder, though, what logic was used by the Liberians who decided that their country should be 44 minutes and 30 seconds behind Greenwich. On the other hand, Saudi Arabia has no zone time at all. Saudis observed Arabic or solar time. Watches are set to midnight at sundown every day.

Please forgive this preoccupation with time, but when constantly crossing time zones, it becomes a vital issue. We are in constant psycho-physiological turmoil, trying to synchronize our body clocks with the sun. After flying halfway around the world, we frequently go to bed hungry and fall asleep at the lunch table. Perhaps the Mongolians have the right idea. Their People's Republic has no legal time whatsoever.

Our radar confirms that we are passing south of the mouths of the Irrawaddy and 2 hours later, the ADF needles flip over Vishakhapatnam, a fishing village on India's east coast.

Fortunately we are not required to pronounce these tongue-twisting names or we would be unintelligible to traffic controllers. We simply report passing the Victor Zulu Beacon. Even more difficult to pronounce is Inoucdjouac, a beacon on the east coast of Hudson Bay.

The lights of innumerable small towns passing below are like jewels scattered on ebony, giving India an unblemished appearance. But those who have been here before are not deceived. India, a country where people are its major commodity, its most pressing problem, its hope for the future.

We are cleared for an ILS approach to Bombay's Santa Cruz Airport, and after executing the required procedure turn, begin sliding down from the sky. The landing lights spike the blackness, and we pray that there are no holy cows on the runway.

After passing through customs, we are confronted by a group of consummate beggars, pathetic, destitute children ranging in age from 2 to 5. But we are prepared and pass out candy to these undernourished, scantily clad urchins.

The crew bus rattles and chugs through unlit streets, weaving once to miss a toddler straying in the night. Numerous people are asleep in the gutters, on the sidewalks, and in doorways. An airline crew is normally a jovial group, but during this ride, we are silent. Once at the hotel, we meet at one of the flight attendant's rooms for needed refreshments and a "debriefing."

Progress around the world can be measured in minutes and miles, but for pilots it is easier to compare the stack of unused charts with the stack of used ones. In Bombay, the two stacks are equally tall.

The unrelenting monsoon rains have begun their seasonal assault on India, dampening my spirit and adding fuel to my desire to leave. Bombay may not be the wettest spot in the world, but it is not far from it. Cherrapunji, northwest of here on the southern slopes of the Himalayas, boasts an average annual rainfall of 482 inches and an all-time record of 905 inches.

It is raining so heavily that it would almost be easier to swim from the terminal to the aircraft. Any three raindrops would fill a coffee cup. It is so hot and humid that unfolding the wilted charts in the cockpit requires the same care you would use to unravel cooked spaghetti.

We taxi cautiously between two rows of blue lights that look like indigo lanterns floating on a black lake. The runway lights, however, have not survived the deluge; sheltered flare pots line the runway. As the aircraft gathers speed, the flickering candle lights become indistinguishable blurs. Visibility through the wall of rain is less than half a mile, and we curse the windshield wipers, which are more noisy than effective. The wings soon flex their muscles, and we are airborne in a flying Noah's Ark.

Having risen above the wet, lumpy cumulus, we are sailing on velvet air beneath a canopy dotted with distant diamonds. We are strangers flying over foreign lands, but these celestial compatriots of the night sky accompany us wherever in the world we wander and provide comforting familiarity. Polaris winks from starboard, the Southern Cross watches from port and the constellation, Leo, motionless at our zenith, stalks prey in his heavenly hunting ground.

The flight to Tel Aviv takes 6 hours 25 minutes, 90 minutes longer than would be necessary if Middle East nations could live in peace.

Because we are headed for Tel Aviv, Israel, it is neither kosher nor allowable to take the direct route via Iraq, Saudi Arabia, and Jordan. Instead, we must fly 850 miles out of the way via Iran and Turkey, giving the Arab kingdoms a wide berth.

In this region, flight planning is determined as much by political climate as by winds and weather.

Once, on an Athens-to-Bombay nonstop, we were cleared across Arab countries. Approaching the Mediterranean coast of Lebanon, Beirut Control asked for our aircraft registration number presumably to verify that our airplane was neither of Israeli registry nor had been a recent visitor to the Holy Land. No one seems to know how the latter is determined.

After passing Beirut, the one-time Riviera of the Middle East, we gazed upon Damascus, the world's oldest, continuously inhabited city. Moments later, we pointed the nose toward the expansive bleakness of Saudi Arabia. There were only a few electronic navaids in the Arabian Desert, but they were widely spaced and no more reliable than a politician's promise. Pilotage is impossible unless you can tell one dune from another in this uncharted ocean of sand. One must either have an experienced camel driver or, like us, have a pair of Doppler radar units to do the work. Instrument flying below 10,000 feet is risky because the minimum terrain-clearance altitudes had yet to be determined in this high-rise desert at that time.

The navigation chart was a mass of "unsurveyed" notations. It seemed paradoxical that we are so intent on mapping the moon's surface when so many areas of our planet required similar attention.

The safest way to cross the Arabian Peninsula was to follow the 1,000-mile-long pipeline from the Mediterranean to the oil-rich Sheikdom of Bahrain. At night, burning natural gasses from nearby oil wells are like airway beacons that illuminate the route from one horizon to the other.

Communications, on the other hand, were difficult or impossible over large areas of the desert. While side-stepping some electrifying thunderstorms southwest of Baghdad, we tried repeatedly to obtain a routing change from Basra Control, but our calls went unanswered. Nor were any aircraft within radio range to relay our request. We felt more alone over Saudi Arabia than over any of the world's oceans.

Our shadow streaks across the tiny Sheikdom of Oman, and soon we are over the barren, mountainous spine of Iran. The right wing tip points toward sunlight reflected across the Soviet border from the Caspian Sea, the world's largest lake, 5 times larger than Lake Superior. As we stare upon a world seemingly uninhabited, it becomes difficult to appreciate the reality of global overpopulation. From our perch, it seems that most of the Earth is undiscovered, untapped, untouched.

The flight engineer calculates the amount of fuel remaining while monitoring a special HF frequency and listening for news of disturbances in the Middle East. Should another Arab-Israeli conflict develop while en route to Tel Aviv, we would divert to Nicosia, Cyprus. On the VHF receiver, we overhear an Air France pilot relaying a clearance in English from Tehran Center to a Soviet flight en route from Moscow to Karachi. It underscores the cooperation and camaraderie that exists between the pilots of all nations. If only those on the ground could get along as well.

During a lull in cockpit activity over Iran, I daydream about the fabled past of this land, where Scheherazade held King Shahriar spellbound for a thousand and one nights with tales of Sinbad, Ali Baba, and other mythical Arabian heroes. Iran, known as Persia in ancient times, tickles the imagination with visions of flying carpets, Aladdin's lamp, and harems of exotic women who danced behind diaphanous veils and knew how to hold a man's attention by never revealing too much.

The passengers are awakened by our announcement on the public-address system that we are over Cyprus. Staring through wispy cirrus that seems to disappear as we approach it, the passengers gaze upon the one-time "prison" where the British detained thousands of Jews to prevent their immigration to Israel.

In the cockpit, the landing at Tel Aviv's Lod International Airport is routine, but to some Jewish passengers it is like seeing their newborn child for the first time. The touchdown on Israeli soil triggers cheers and applause that echo throughout the cabin, a spontaneous flood of emotion from people who have struggled for centuries to make this moment possible. An elderly couple bolts from the aircraft and weep uninhibitedly as they fall to their knees to kiss the cold tarmac apron. Israel, the Promised Land.

It is miraculous that general aviation can survive, much less thrive, in a country where such stringent security measures must be enforced. But thrive it does, as if to illustrate the Israeli adage that anyone who does not believe in miracles is simply unrealistic.

Flying a lightplane in Israel is not without frustration. Flights may be conducted only within narrow corridors and at specific altitudes. An ATC clearance is required regardless of the weather. The busy general aviation airport at Herzliya has a control tower but is closed on Saturdays when it is needed most because controllers are home enjoying the Sabbath.

There is an adage saying that the most dangerous phase of flight is the drive to and from the airport. Nowhere is this truer than in Israel. The Israeli driver is a breed unto himself and drives as if he were on his way to Damascus in a Sherman tank. We survive another taxi ride from Tel Aviv to the airport and scan the en route weather across Europe to London.

We pull our contrails over the jagged coast of Greece. It lies fragmented at the base of the Balkan Peninsula like the ruins of an Athenian temple. Soon we are over the Ionian Sea, passing south of Albania, and are amused by Albania's charted warning that aircraft trespassing through its airspace may be fired upon without warning. What will they fire? Spitballs? Albania is a barren, primitive land without military capability.

It can be challenging to fly across Europe. The rules change every time we cross a border, which is frequently. Just when you become accustomed to the heavily accented English of one nationality, we switch to another. (The French controllers seem most difficult to understand.)

A flight across Europe, though, is more than conforming to regulation and chasing needles in the sky. It is sailing above a fairyland of castles, cultures, and contrasts. A glance in any direction finds a scene lifted from the pages of history. From our vantage point, we also see signs of man's race to extinction. The sparkling blue of the Danube River may have inspired Johann Strauss to write a classic waltz, but were he alive today, he would have to call it *The Dirty Danube*. Stretches of the river are so polluted that they are fire hazards.

London's Heathrow Airport is the busiest and often the foggiest in Europe. A "pea souper" at Heathrow can be so thick that a pilot could get lost for hours trying to taxi to his gate. To make things easier, the British cleverly installed a unique guidance system. Working like the track switcher at a railroad yard, the Heathrow ground controller leads a pilot to his gate or wherever else he needs to go by turning on only the appropriate taxiway lights.

The wings sag under the load of 80 tons of fuel, flexing resiliently as the aircraft is taxied onto the runway for the last and longest leg of our global odyssey, a 6,000-mile shortcut across the roof of the world, an aerial Northwest Passage to Los Angeles.

Takeoff thrust is applied and 4 flaming Niagaras strain to overcome more than a third of a million pounds of inertia. The Boeing 707 yields grudgingly and accelerates slowly. The nosewheel tires bump and thump, betraying surface imperfections on the 12,800-foot-long runway. The aircraft seems to demonstrate little will to fly.

In the cabin, an attentive flight attendant sits in her jump seat facing her passengers. Having been on many polar flights, she is accustomed to this necessarily long takeoff, but the concern written on the passengers' faces reveal that they are not. She reaches for the public-address microphone and announces with a smile, "Ladies and gentlemen, you can help by lifting your feet." Obediently, hundreds of feet rise, and the Boeing pushes the ground away at nearly 200 mph.

We are over Scotland heading north-northwest along the great-circle route to Los Angeles. Behind us are the spider web of European airways and the incessant chatter of VHF communications. Ahead is peace and quiet, the serenity of watching ice floes, brilliant white drifting on black, frigid water. The High Arctic, where visibility can be so good that it hurts your eyes to look that far.

Thirteen miles south of Iceland, a plume of sulphuric smoke rises from Surtsey, a volcanic island that recently emerged from the icy waters. After crossing the Denmark Strait, we interrupt the cabin movies so that our passengers can gaze at the spectacle passing below. Greenland is the world's largest island and has the most inappropriate name. Jagged peaks cast ragged shadows across the 2-mile-thick icecap. Fingers of glacial ice probe for the sea, grinding down mountains that stand in their way, the same awesome, slow-motion process that carved the continents.

We cross the Davis Strait, aiming for Frobisher on Baffin Island in extreme northeastern Canada. As our distance from the Magnetic North Pole shrinks, the compasses become unreliable and fluctuate wildly or point east when they should point west. For the next 2 hours, directional guidance will be provided by a pair of polar-path gyros with very low precession rates.

From above, the Arctic has a fearsome, almost inviting beauty, yet to survive on the ice would test the limit of human endurance. A pilot forced to land on an ice shelf would have to be familiar with several bizarre rules of Arctic survival. There is, for example, the danger of touching extremely cold metal with a bare, moist hand. The skin can freeze instantly to the super-cold metal, and the only way to remove it without leaving behind several layers of skin is to warm the contact area with urine. If both hands are stuck, it would be handy to have a companion nearby.

Abandoning the aircraft in search of assistance is always risky but especially in the Arctic. Scientists believe that someone attempting to walk across the white wastes without an aiming point will invariably travel in a large circle in the direction of his shorter leg.

There is an incongruity about the treacherous Arctic that makes flying there most pleasant. The north polar region is a vast desert, characterized by light winds, low humidity, infrequent and thin stratoform clouds, and little rain or snow. By contrast, a flight across the United States presents far greater problems: fronts, thunderstorms (which are unknown in the Arctic), tornados, strong winds, and all sorts of precipitation. When clouds do form in the Arctic, they seldom are higher than 10,000 feet. Winds aloft seldom exceed 30 mph at any altitude.

Our track angles southwest and leaves behind the white wilderness. We cross the griddle-flat tundra, a treeless expanse covered with flowerless plants, a marshy wasteland frozen rock-hard much of the year.

We then cross the tree line, the northernmost limit of the coniferous forests that girdle the globe in these latitudes. Mt. Rainier soon pokes its lofty head above the clouds, welcoming us home.

We now have 19 days to recover from this journey and prepare for our next 11-day global odyssey, but our Boeing 707 is given no such relief. Within a few hours and with a fresh crew, it will begin another 23,423-mile flight around the world.

## Boeing 757-200

| | |
|---|---|
| Engines | 2 Pratt & Whitney 2037 |
| Power | 36,600 lb thrust each |
| Length | 155 ft 3 in |
| Height | 44 ft 6 in |
| Wingspan | 124 ft 10 in |
| Wing Loading | 127.9 lb/sq ft |
| Power Loading | 3.5 lb/lb of thrust |
| Maximum Takeoff Weight | 255,000 lb |
| Maximum Landing Weight | 198,000 lb |
| Fuel Capacity | 76,976 lb |
| Range | 3,900 nm |
| Cruise Speed | Mach 0.80 |
| Stall Speed (flaps down, 198,000 lb) | 102 knots |
| Maximum operating altitude | 42,000 feet |

# Sentimental Journey

## I advanced the thrust levers of the Boeing 757-200

and a pair of flaming Niagaras propelled TWA Flight 347 along Runway 30L at St. Louis with 76,400 pounds of enthusiastic thrust. This was not the beginning of an ordinary flight; it was the beginning of the end of my career with TWA. In two days, I would be 60 years old. By federal mandate, I would be an ancient pelican, an airman too old to continue life on the flight deck of an airliner.

Irrespective of being forced out of the left seat, good fortune smiled at me during my last flight. It was Father's Day, June 21, 1998, and no father could have received a finer gift. My son, Brian, was seated to my right. He had begun his career with TWA in 1989. Having him follow in my footsteps and being my first officer during this final flight was so much more meaningful than ribbon-wrapped ties that somehow never got worn. It was an affirmation that he approves of who I am and what I have done with my life. No father could ask for more.

In the passenger cabin was another son, Paul, who works for Jeppesen and recently earned his commercial pilot certificate. Seated nearby was eight-week-old Brett, Brian's son and my first grandchild, who was making his first flight as I was making my last. He was nattily dressed in a miniaturized pilot's uniform complete with shoulder boards, wings, a tie, and a photo I.D badge, which were artfully handcrafted by Brian's wife, Lynn. Such lineage suggests that there will always be a Schiff on a seniority list somewhere.

*Barry, Brian and Brett Schiff (aka BS1, BS2 and BS3, respectively).*

Also in the cabin were my friends Glen Beattie, Erik Bernstein, Mick and Mary Ann Jennings, Bruce Kaufman, and Doug and Sue Ritter, who had purchased tickets to share in the celebration.

We reached our assigned cruising altitude of 35,000 feet 21 minutes after liftoff. I relinquished control of the airplane to Brian, took a deep breath, and gazed out the left cockpit window. Not much below seems to have changed during the past 34 years. The small towns and farms of central Missouri still dot the rolling terrain as far as the eye can see.

Aviation, however, has changed since I was hired by TWA in 1964 to fly the right seat of a Lockheed Constellation:

- In those days, the captain was an absolute dictator; there was no crew-resource management, and what he said was law even if it led to carnage.

- During my first checkout in a jet (the Boeing 707), there was no 250-knot speed limit below 10,000 feet, which made the experience all the more thrilling at low altitude (especially when maneuvering to avoid general aviation traffic).

- Kerosene cost only ten cents per gallon. Fuel burn was of little or no consequence, so we flew across continents and oceans at high speed with three or four engines. Airline survival today depends on efficiency, which is why twin-engine airplanes cruising more slowly are the rule rather than the exception.

- Economics and advanced technology did away with the flight engineer, although I remain convinced that removing the third crewmember from the cockpit was not in the best interest of safety.

- During the early years of my career, stewardesses passed out chewing gum and small packets of cigarettes with every meal.

- There was no sterile-cockpit rule, and pilots were allowed to talk to one another when below 10,000 feet. Not only is this now banned, but airliners are also equipped with cockpit voice recorders that can snitch on a violator. (When the CVR was introduced, we were convinced that the chief pilot had a receiver in his office with which to monitor cockpit conversations as they occurred.)

- Pilots used to walk through the cabin during flight to socialize with their passengers or assuage their fear of flight. Current regulations forbid a pilot to leave the flight deck except in response to a "physiological necessity."

- We were allowed to invite passengers to the cockpit during flight. (My favorite visitor was John Wayne.) Today, the FAA bans this courtesy on U.S. air carriers. Foreign airlines are not so restricted.

- There used to be good-natured kidding between pilots and "stewardesses." The same thing today can result in a sexual harassment suit.

- The cockpit used to be a club for white men only although not by design. Thankfully, the flight deck door is now open to increasingly more women and minorities.

Although I concede that most of these changes are beneficial, I cannot allow this opportunity to pass without commenting on the intrusive security screening to which crewmembers are now subjected when reporting for duty. Although such humiliation while in uniform might pacify the public and the FAA, there isn't a pilot I know who couldn't smuggle arms aboard his aircraft if he were so inclined.

Another significant change involves passenger attitude. When I first walked in public while in uniform, I could see heads turning in my direction and sense respect for my profession. It made me feel proud. That is when taking an airline flight was an adventure. But as the magic carpet began to evolve into an airborne conveyer belt, passengers began to view airline pilots more like bus drivers.

My reverie was interrupted when Brian advised that ATC had approved our request for Flight Level 180, the lowest we could fly without encountering uncontrolled traffic. The sun was low on this, the longest day of the year, and I wanted to use this last opportunity to share some of my favorite sights with our passengers.

We passed Shiprock (near Four Corners, the only place where four states come together at a common point). We then made S-turns over Monument Valley where giant monoliths cast shadows as long as our contrails. Finally we arrived over the Grand Canyon, the grandest sight of all. The floor of the canyon was already dark, but the west-facing walls were ablaze with shades of red, orange, and yellow as they basked in the last remnants of a spectacular sunset. It was my sunset, too, the last time that I would be allowed to fly a Canyon Tour in command of a TWA airplane.

We returned to FL350 for the short remainder of our journey to Los Angeles, which provided more time for reflection.

People always ask about emergencies. I have been fortunate and never had so much as an engine failure, although I did shut down a few engines for precautionary reasons (each time in VFR conditions and near a suitable airport). Messrs. Pratt, Whitney, Rolls, and Royce have been kind to me. I also have had a variety of mechanical difficulties, but none were threatening.

Most of my problems have been the same as those experienced by others who ply the airways for a living: weather. I have had my share of confrontations with blizzards, thunderstorms, wind shear, icy runways, and the like. My most effective weapon in combating such powerful adversaries was the encouragement provided by TWA for its pilots to exercise command authority and divert to an alternate when this appeared to be the wisest course of action. Every pilot-in-command—whether flying a Boeing or a Beech—has the same weapon of discretion in his arsenal, but some fail to use it.

I have been blessed with a remarkably fine career and have enough wonderful memories to fill a book. Many of these are from when I was in TWA's International Division and flew around the world once a month: 10 days of adventure and excitement followed by 20 days at home. Such highlights included flying an on-pylon around the Sphinx while on base leg to Cairo, being cleared (via HF radio) for an approach to Bombay while more than a 1,000 miles away (because the tower would be closed upon our arrival), and making approaches to Hong Kong's Kai Tak Airport. This required aiming for an illuminated checkerboard on a hill and getting as close to it as one dared before turning sharply onto short final. Nor will I ever forget my first Cat IIIb landing at Paris where the ceiling was zero and the visibility was less than the length of our fuselage. The best memories, however, involve the people of TWA, and I will miss them the most.

Airline life also has sour notes. For 34 years, my family never knew for which holidays I would be home and for which I would not; making plans more than a month ahead of time was always a gamble. When on reserve, I never knew whether that phone waking me in the middle of the night was a wrong number or Operations calling to tell me that TWA needed my presence more than my children did at a birthday party or graduation ceremony.

Nor will I ever forget the three days enveloping Christmas of 1971 during which I spent the holidays staring at the walls of a cold motel near O'Hare in Chicago. A winter storm had disrupted my schedule and intermittently knocked out electrical service. My Christmas meals were lonely and served by Denny's, the only open restaurant within walking distance.

My final flight was highlighted by the comments of well-wishing controllers, faceless friends who helped to keep me out of harm's way for more than 34 years. Eavesdropping pilots also added notes of levity and poignancy to the occasion.

While approaching Los Angeles, I reminded myself that this flight probably would be judged by its landing. Such is the way passengers grade pilots.

Unfortunately, every pilot makes an occasional landing that registers on the Richter Scale, and I am no exception. I learned long ago, however, that one must maintain a sense of humor about such things. After a bad landing, I would apologize to my passengers for the abrupt arrival and add "that this was one of my better landings." If that didn't relieve anxiety in the cabin, than perhaps the comment of one flight attendant did: "Ladies and gentlemen, Captain Schiff has requested that you keep your seat belts fastened until the airplane—or what's left of it—comes to a stop at the gate."

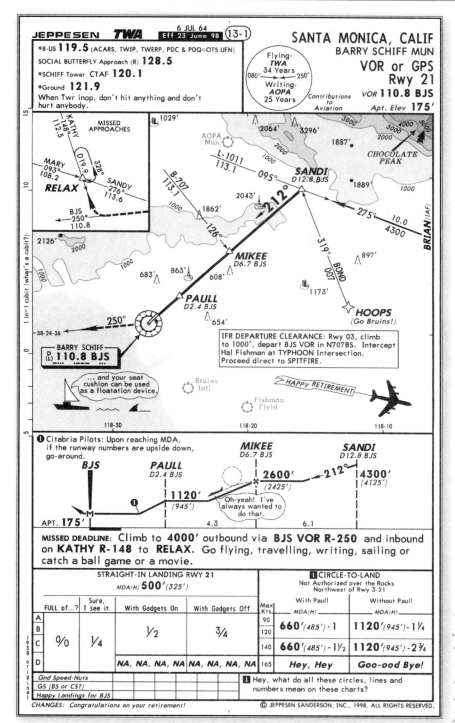

*The author's son, Paul Schiff, worked for Jeppesen-Sanderson and arranged to have this custom approach chart prepared as a memento of his father's retirement.*

There was an outbreak of applause following touchdown, not so much because of my landing. Our passengers probably were releasing nervous energy after realizing that they had survived a flight commanded by a 60-year-old captain.

While taxiing toward the gate, I found myself riding the brakes and moving progressively more slowly, as if wanting to prolong my career even if by only a minute. Brian looked in my direction; he knew what I was doing; he knew what I was thinking.

I could not help thinking about how it was of no consequence that I had never scratched a TWA airplane or passenger; it did not matter how much experience I had accrued during 26,000 hours in the

air. I was being set aside only because I was about to celebrate a birthday that had been arbitrarily chosen by the FAA to be an airline pilot's last. Someday, I hope, there will be a more equitable way to determine when an airline pilot's career should end. The FAA's age-60 rule is one of the few remaining bastions of legalized age discrimination.

Earlier that day, when departing Los Angeles for St. Louis, ground control had cleared us to Runway 25R, which is a considerable distance from our gate. Brian noted my dismay at having to taxi so far and tried to obtain a clearance for nearby Runway 24L, our usual departure runway. No luck; we were to taxi for miles to the distant runway or not taxi at all.

While grumbling and responding to the Taxi Checklist, I did not notice the fire trucks pulling alongside our wingtips. But I did notice the torrents of water arcing above and from each side of the airplane, a form of salute sometimes accorded retiring airline captains. I then understood why we had been told that "flow control" necessitated such circuitous taxi routing. I was grateful and honored. But I could only wonder what my passengers had thought as fire trucks began to spray the airplane. I quickly explained over the P.A. what had happened before anyone might think that our airplane was on fire.

That had been almost 12 hours earlier.

After coming to a stop at the gate, I set the parking brake, shut down the engines, and responded to the Secure-Cockpit Checklist for the last time.

A gate agent entered the cockpit with a wheelchair that had been requested for me by one of my "friends." It was tempting.

Where, I wondered, had those 34 years gone?

# About the Author

**Barry Schiff** was born on June 23, 1938 and began flying in 1952 at the age of 14. Since then he has developed a number of simultaneous aviation careers during which he has made numerous lasting and significant contributions to aviation safety.

As an aviation writer, Captain Schiff is known well by aviation readers for his more than 1,400 articles published in 98 aviation magazines, notably AOPA *Pilot*, for which he is a contributing editor and has been writing for 45 years. Many of his articles discuss personally developed concepts, procedures, and techniques that have received international acclaim. (Many of his articles have been translated into other languages and published by various foreign air forces, airlines, and governing aviation authorities.) He also has written 12 aviation books of which his award-winning, 3-volume series, *The Proficient Pilot*, is an ongoing bestseller (published by Aviation Supplies and Academics).

He was a technical advisor, writer, and on-camera performer for ABC's *Wide World of Flying*, for which he received international accolades. From this, he evolved into an aviation safety consultant for the print and electronic media as well as the motion picture industry.

Schiff began his career as an aviation writer at the age of 21 (1959) when he founded Aero Progress, Inc. This is when he conceived, developed, wrote, and published a series of unique and innovative aviation education products that were marketed commercially and received international acclaim. His product line was purchased by the Times-Mirror Corporation in 1963 on behalf of its subsidiary, Jeppesen Sanderson.

For his significant and lifetime contributions to aviation safety, Captain Schiff has received numerous awards and honors. These include an honorary doctorate by Embry-Riddle Aeronautical University, induction into the National Flight Instructors

Hall of Fame, and induction into the Aviation Hall of Fame of New Jersey. He also was chosen as the General Aviation Journalist of the Year (2003) by the Aéro-Club de France, selected by the National Aeronautic Association as an Elder Statesman of Aviation, was presented with AOPA's prestigious Lawrence F. Sharples Perpetual Award (1990). He also received the Alfred and Constance Wolfe Aviation Fund Award (1992) as well as a U.S. Congressional Commendation, to name only a few.

**An aviation activist**, Captain Schiff sought and received direct and personal approval from Jordan's King Hussein and Israeli Prime Minister Itzhak Rabin in 1995 to organize a "fly-in" from Jerusalem to Amman, Jordan. He led a formation of 35 general aviation airplanes carrying 135 Americans, Israelis, and Jordanians on what was called "Operation Peace Flight." Schiff's historic flight was heralded by the international press as a "significant contribution to the Middle East peace process." Schiff became the first pilot ever allowed to conduct any kind of flight — civil, airline, or military — between those previously warring nations. He also became the only pilot in the world to earn pilot certificates by the governments of both Israel and Jordan.

Several years ago, Schiff innovated and developed a charting concept that provided guidance for VFR pilots through complex, high-density airspace. These unique and creative charts were published by Jeppesen Sanderson, and a legislative bill, H.R. 3243 was written by then-Oklahoma representative, now Senator, James M. Inhofe, that mandated the adoption of Schiff's concept by the Federal Aviation Administration.

Schiff has been active in numerous other general aviation causes. He was very influential, for example, in preventing the closure of Santa Monica Municipal Airport (a major reliever airport in the Los Angeles Basin). He also worked with the FAA to provide airspace access to general aviation aircraft subsequent to FAA's emergency closure of the Los Angeles Terminal Control Area (Class B airspace) Corridor.

In addition, Schiff has conducted numerous flight-safety seminars all over the world and has served as chair and participant on numerous FAA-advisory committees.

**As a pilot**, Captain Schiff has accumulated more than 27,000 hours of logged flight time and is one of few who has flown more than 300 different types of aircraft (including the Lockheed U-2 and the *Spirit of St. Louis* replica). He obtained a waiver to become an Airline Transport Pilot at the age of 21 and has every category and class rating issued by the FAA (except for airship). He also has every flight instructor rating (with gold seal) and a fistful of type ratings ranging from the Ford Trimotor and the Douglas DC-3 to the Lockheed L-1011 and the Boeing 747. Captain Schiff retired from TWA in 1998 (because of FAA's age-60 rule) after an unblemished 34-

year career during which he flew in both domestic and international operations. He also was a check captain on the Boeing 757 and 767.

As a general aviation pilot he held several world aviation records including a 500-km, closed-circuit course speed record captured from the Soviet Union (Class C1-d, January 21, 1975), a 100-km, closed-circuit course speed record captured from France (Class C1-b, March 29, 1969), and a time-to-climb record to 6,000 meters (Class C1-d, August 2, 1978). He also holds a few airline records and was awarded the Louis Blériot Medal by the *Fédération Aéronautique Internationale* in 1969.

Schiff has a Ground Instructor Certificate, a lifetime teaching credential (in aerospace science) issued by the California State Department of Education, was an FAA-Designated Pilot Examiner from 1977 to 1990, and was the first of only a few to be awarded a lifetime designation as an Aviation Safety Counselor by the FAA.

Schiff has substantial experience in experimental flight testing and is the only American to be awarded the Gold Proficiency Award by the Federal Aero Club of Switzerland.

These wide-ranging aeronautical activities have been conducted concurrently. He continues to investigate and report to the aviation community various aspects of proficiency and safety, and remains a vigorous and outspoken advocate for general aviation both at home and abroad.

Schiff is a member of the Society of Experimental Test Pilots, the American Institute of Aeronautics and Astronautics, the International Society of Air Safety Investigators, and is a Fellow of the Royal Aeronautic Society (FRAeS).